Praise for

THE LAST DROPOUT:

A Model for Creating Educational Equity

"At the Ford Foundation, we believe in the inherent dignity of all people. Yet around the world, billions of people are excluded from full participation in the political, economic, and cultural systems that shape their lives. We view this fundamental inequality as the defining challenge of our time, one that limits the potential of all people, everywhere. Addressing inequality is at the center of everything we do. Communities In Schools has been a standard-bearer for social justice, beginning with its roots in Harlem during the 1960s. The CIS model is proven and effective and their mission going forward is not just to help low-income children and families and people of color to navigate the barriers but to take down the barriers to equality altogether. Bill Milliken's book reveals so much about the roots—and the heart—of the CIS movement."

— **Darren Walker**, president, Ford Foundation

"I've supported Bill Milliken and Communities In Schools for many years. More than ever, their work is vitally necessary as we strive to become one nation. The catastrophic division between the rich and those left behind disproportionately affects children. The Last Dropout explains what schools and communities can do in plain and compelling language."

— **Arianna Huffington**, founder and CEO, Thrive Global

"I'm consistently amazed by the excellent work Communities In Schools does every year. They continue to set the standard for helping kids, and it all starts with Bill Milliken's and Rey Saldaña's leadership. As a CIS National Board member, I am proud to be a part of their efforts to remove barriers and empower students."

— **Shaquille O'Neal**

"Bill's uplifting story of his life's work shows us that every child has something to contribute, and that to achieve that potential, we must create the right environment for our children. Through better access to community services, rich connections with others, and a sense of ownership for their own success, our children can thrive in both academics and in life. In his comprehensive book, Bill engages us to envision the CIS model scaled to reach every schoolchild across the country, and he challenges all of us to work together to help our children achieve the success they deserve."

— **Pam and Pierre Omidyar**, co-founders, The Omidyar Group

"Bill Milliken has distilled 40 years of experience—with kids on the streets, with teachers and staff in schools, with laypeople and clergy in churches and temples, with corporate leaders in boardrooms, and with public leaders in halls of government—to legions of key teachers and principals—with a single, compelling purpose: helping troubled students do well in school and reclaim their futures. The support for Bill's founding work in cities and schools just continues to grow. The title of Part I summarizes not only the book but also the theme of Bill Milliken's own life and work: 'It all starts with relationships.' This is both a powerfully practical and spiritually moving book. Now there's a combination!"

— **Jim Wallis**, Inaugural Chair of Faith and Justice at the McCourt School of Public Policy and Founding Director of the Center on Faith and Justice at Georgetown University; author of *God's Politics: Why the Right Gets It Wrong and the Left Doesn't Get It* and *America's Original Sin: Racism, White Privilege, and the Bridge to a New America*

"Bill Milliken's book is essential reading for any donor who cares about the future of education in America and the importance of an educated workforce. He vividly illustrates the power of collaboration and innovation to combat the dropout epidemic that plagues our local school systems. The Last Dropout *describes a leveraged alternative to throwing money at seemingly intractable problems; it describes a robust strategy that delivers breakthrough results—and offers a significant multiplier on charitable dollars. America's children deserve to benefit from these insights."

— **Thomas J. Tierney**, co-chairman and co-founder, the Bridgespan Group

THE
LAST
DROPOUT

THE
LAST
DROPOUT

A Model for Creating
Educational Equity

BILL MILLIKEN

HAY HOUSE, INC.
Carlsbad, California • New York City
London • Sydney • New Delhi

Copyright ©2007, 2022 by Communities in Schools, Inc.

Published in the United States by: Hay House, Inc.: www.hayhouse.com®
Published in Australia by: Hay House Australia Pty. Ltd.: www.hayhouse.com
.au • *Published in the United Kingdom by:* Hay House UK, Ltd.: www.hayhouse
.co.uk • *Published in India by:* Hay House Publishers India: www.hayhouse.co.in

Cover design: Howie Severson, Arina Stopa
Interior design: Nick C. Welch
Interior photos/illustrations: Communities In Schools National

This book was previously published in a modified form as *The Last Dropout* (Hay House, 2007, ISBN: 978-1-4019-1906-1).

Cataloging-in-Publication Data is on file at the Library of Congress

Tradepaper ISBN: 978-1-4019-7140-3
E-book ISBN: 978-1-4019-7141-0
Audiobook ISBN: 978-1-4019-7142-7

10 9 8 7 6 5 4 3 2 1
1st edition, September 2007
2nd revised edition, November 2022

Printed in the United States of America

To my wife and best friend, Jean;
our son and daughter, Sean and Lani;
our daughter-in-law, Jill; our grandchildren, Alex and Jack;
and the wonderful extended family of Millikens, Marquises,
Kondases, and Curtises—the family I always wanted,
the reason I keep going.

CONTENTS

WHAT IS COMMUNITIES IN SCHOOLS?

This book contains information and descriptions drawn from the history of the Communities In Schools (CIS) organization. For readers not familiar with CIS, a brief description follows; more information is available at www.communitiesinschools.org.

Communities In Schools® (CIS®) is a national organization that ensures every student, regardless of race, zip code, or socio-economic background, has what they need to realize their potential in school and beyond.

Working directly inside 2,860 schools across the country, our network of 117 organizations connects students to caring adults and community resources that help them see, confront, and overcome the barriers that stand between them and a brighter future. Together, we build a powerful change movement made up of peers, students, and alumni committed to building an equitable path to education for future generations.

CIS creates comprehensive, locally controlled nonprofit support systems around schools. Coordination of effort and accountability for results are essential aspects of the service that the organization provides. CIS ensures that the work of outside agencies and volunteers is interconnected and integrated to provide the support schools need most.

Each year, more than 1.6 million young people and their families in 26 states and the District of Columbia receive services through Communities In Schools.

A NOTE FROM ELAINE WYNN

Chair, Board of Directors, Communities In Schools National

At this particularly perilous time in our history, our children are not only dropping out of school—they are dropping out of life. Along with their families, they feel disconnected, demoralized, and confused about their present and their future.

Bill Milliken's philosophy and prophecy about developing human potential are as valid today as when he first began his journey as "a caring adult in a child's life." His holistic approach to human interaction and connectivity has been the recipe for uplifting hundreds of thousands of students and their loved ones. Although many years of data prove that his model is successful, it is his personal example of selflessness and commitment that has guided his followers for decades. He consistently shows us how to retain hope, while always reaching for the light.

No single event epitomizes Bill's success more than the ascendance of Rey Saldaña from a CIS case-managed youngster in San Antonio, Texas, to president and CEO of Communities In Schools. Through Rey, Bill's example and leadership will extend to the next generation and beyond.

It has been the privilege of a lifetime to work alongside Bill and learn from his wisdom. And it is gratifying to know the baton is in Rey's capable hands to carry forward the promise of "a caring adult in *every* child's life."

Onward!

FOREWORD

by President and Mrs. Jimmy Carter

We first met Bill Milliken and Neil Shorthouse more than 40 years ago when they came to us in Georgia with an innovative response to the loss of so many young people from the public school system. We supported the fledgling program, then called EXODUS, from the governor's office. Upon entering the White House in 1977, we helped Bill take his work to a national level and have continued our interest in the years since.

Having helped get Communities In Schools off to a good start, it has been a joy to watch it become an important force for change. Our affection for and commitment to Bill Milliken and Neil Shorthouse have never wavered—they are truly life companions for both of us. Bill's faithful insistence that "programs don't change people—*relationships* do" has been a constant reminder and inspiration for us in all of our endeavors.

This extraordinary account tells how Bill and Neil and their colleagues developed the insights that have meant so much to communities across the country. The publication of *The Last Dropout* couldn't be more timely. Americans are waking up to the truth about how we do—or don't—serve our children through the public school system. Dropping out of school is economically disastrous for the dropout, who is crying out for social justice, not more discrimination. That poor people bear the burden of our failure to create an equitable public education system is one of the major themes of this work. Anyone who hopes to reverse the economic injustices of our society must confront this reality.

The epidemic is costing America too many children, too many tears, too many futures. *The Last Dropout* is a declaration of hope and a call to action, showing how we can change schools and communities, one student and one family at a time. It is also a book of wonderful human stories from a deeply caring and spiritual individual.

FOREWORD

by Rey Saldaña
President and CEO,
Communities In Schools National

For me, San Antonio was always the place. That's where I get my identity. As long as I have air in my lungs, people will know I'm from San Antonio, and it's where I find so much of who I am today.

Growing up in the '90s, I had a strong, warm sense of belonging to a community. But there was also a feeling about my city that I picked up from how other people would talk about where I was from: this is a place to *escape*.

I grew up on the south side of San Antonio, a majority Latino community. Very blue collar, very working class. Growing up, I sat in church pews with families who were "mixed status." That is, some were immigrants to the U.S., some were first generation, some second generation, and some were undocumented.

My household reflected that. My father, Reynold Saldaña, was an immigrant, undocumented for about half of his life in this country. When I was born in 1986, he'd been in the U.S. for six years. He was from a small town called Sabinas Hidalgo, about an hour from the Texas–Mexico border, in the state of Nuevo León. He came across the border in 1980; he was 18. My mother's family was from Mexico, but she was born in San Antonio. So I had a mother who was an American citizen, a father who was undocumented when I was growing up, and they both landed on the south side of San Antonio.

It was not odd for somebody who grew up in Sabinas Hidalgo to aspire to come to the U.S. In my father's community, there wasn't much work outside of selling recycled bottles and making a meager living. He told me the stories of what it was like to watch others come to the U.S. And he also told me stories of my grandfather, who had come to the U.S. himself.

My grandfather was part of the Bracero program, which was in place from 1942 to 1964, when there was a shortage of labor for the Texas workforce, mostly males. The U.S. government tried to fill that need, especially during World War II, and brought folks over to work. My grandfather was *invited* to come to the U.S., and once he was here, and working and making a living, he didn't want to leave. He would stay in the U.S. to work as long as he could, or as long as his tourist or work visa allowed, in order to make enough to send back home. My father, as the oldest in the family, had to play the role of father figure to his four siblings while my grandfather planted roots in the U.S. and worked toward a pathway for the rest of his family. My grandfather would return for a few weeks at a time, then head back north to work.

It did not escape me, growing up, that my father was undocumented. And it certainly instilled an uneasiness in me as I navigated the various social systems. Going to doctor appointments, or going to school and having folks ask questions about who my parents were and what they did, I always felt a sense of insecurity and inferiority. I had many things about my family that I didn't like to talk about because, frankly, I was ashamed. That wasn't uncommon in our community. People tended to keep their feelings in a lockbox. My father worked at a slaughterhouse, killing the cows and cutting out their innards and preparing them to go out in the refrigerated truck to the rest of the world. I remember how tired he would be, coming home from work, and the way he smelled, because the smell of a slaughterhouse comes with you.

So I return to this sense of San Antonio as divided into "the nice side of town" and "my side of town," and I just knew that ours was not the side where opportunity was overflowing. I needed to figure out a way to get out of there—to the place where success was.

I come from a family of five children. I have an older sister and three younger brothers. All the families around us when I was growing up seemed to be making it on the same level of income as we were, which was not much. I didn't think about being poor. It wasn't until high school, when I had to fill out financial aid forms for college, that I realized my parents collectively made $26,000 a year for a family of seven. And even then I didn't really reflect on that—I thought that was probably what everybody made. Now, of course, looking back, I realize it's a tough way for a family to get through life.

At the time in San Antonio, there was lots of gang activity. Much depended on what neighborhood you were in and what colors you were wearing. But I got along well with the folks who wore red or wore blue, and they didn't mess with me much. I was just a young kid with a heavy backpack who walked to school, not looking for any trouble. Primarily, I didn't want to upset my parents or call any unwanted attention to them.

In middle school I began to understand that the reason the gang members had nice cars, clothes, shoes, the whole deal, was because they were part of an underground economy that paid much better than anything else I knew. And because they were our neighbors, our friends, we tended to look up to them as role models. There was one particular drug dealer who also happened to be pretty nice to most folks. He kept his lawn clean; he waved to his neighbors. To my mind, these people were not villains; they'd just found a way to "make it" in our neighborhood. But I knew that if *I* wanted to make it, I would need to get out.

I was in sixth grade when I was offered my first joint. I turned it down; I was too afraid. That had a lot to do with a strict Christian church that felt to me—as a young and impressionable kid—like it was more about command and control than deep spiritual love. But it had its intended effect. I was afraid to do anything to get in trouble. And anyway, I didn't want to disappoint my parents.

For young people in my community, there was a certain expectation of what we might be able to do. When I'd gone to the guidance counselor my freshman year and told her I was interested in college, I had to wait a month even to get the appointment with her. And even then I was so disheartened by that conversation. The counselor told me, "Well, there are a lot of students who *want* to go to college. Take a look at some of these applications. Let me know what you think."

I got the sense she was not going to be there to hold my hand in navigating this process, particularly when she said, "There are other opportunities for you to think about locally, right after high school.

You want to have a backup plan in case college doesn't work out." For someone whose parents never made it past the eighth grade, it felt like there were not many places or people for me to turn to.

The signals were clear from that experience: there was a certain ceiling on my expectations, on my ambitions. And I'm sure I wasn't singled out—the student before me and the student after me were probably told the same thing in the 5 or 10 minutes each of us had for the appointment. Drugs, teen pregnancies, low expectations, and poverty had a grip on my community. It was constantly reinforced to me by both educators and the media: nobody who looked like me was going to college. Nobody in my community was even doing much about graduating from school, and I remember how much of a huge deal it was to see one of my younger aunts graduate from high school—the first on my father's side of the family to do so. I knew more people who had gone to prison than to college.

It made it so hard to really imagine what a future would be, what "success" would look like for me. I knew I wanted nice things my family couldn't afford. I wanted a nice house, a nice car. And I knew the people in my neighborhood who had those things weren't my father or my family members. It was the guys wearing red and blue. So was that success? Getting these material possessions? I remember thinking, *Whatever it takes, that's what I will do.* I could have gone down so many different forks in the road. But I had a family who really cared about education. My father would say to me and my siblings, "There's not a lot of help I can give you with your math or your English. But I can help you succeed in school by keeping food in the fridge and a roof over your head, because if there's anything that's true about this country, it's that you have access to something I never had, which is the American dream. And the place where you find that is in your books."

I've often been asked how I got interested in government or elected office. It began when I was a fifth grader and helping my dad study for his citizenship exam. Part of that is basically a U.S. government history lesson. We test new Americans who can barely speak English, barely read the English language: "Can you name the 13 original colonies? How many members of the House of Representatives are there? How many branches of government?" I remember continually reminding my dad that it was Patrick Henry who said, "Give me liberty, or give me death!" He had a mental block on that one. We prepped for the test for close to a year to make sure he passed it, which he did in 1999.

My father spoke again about the importance of the American dream when he raised his hand and made his pledge of allegiance in downtown San Antonio at a place called the Institute of Texan Cultures, where most folks went through their citizenship ceremony. He held his citizenship paper in his hand, and he told the rest of his family, "Now that I've got this, it gives you the opportunity to run past any place I could ever dream of getting to." It's one of my most vivid memories; I can picture the room and hear him speaking.

I never wanted to let him down. There was a razor-thin margin for error. *One* mistake was one too many. Let's say I got caught with marijuana in my pocket. My family didn't have the money to bail me out or access to a lawyer. Or if any serious health issue came up, the expenses would set us completely back. Or if I failed a class, I would get held back, and my father, who hardly speaks the language, was not going to go to the principal and be an advocate for me. Instead my father would say to me, "What did you do wrong?!"

But even this tightrope that seemed impossible to walk could be navigated—*if* I had the support I needed to get to the other side. These resources were available to me, even from a young age. Free full-day pre-K was introduced to my elementary school. There were free classes at the community college through a middle-school program called Prep. And then, in my third week as a high school sophomore, I met my Communities In Schools site coordinators.

A friend of mine was enthusing about a program he was involved in. He said something like, "Hey, I don't know exactly what role these people play here. I *think* they're part of the school, I'm not sure. But they're going to be helping me out with a summer program. It's free, and we get to go to a college campus and take some classes, and then they help you apply to college, or so I've been told. Maybe you should check it out, too." So I met Miss Gladys Reyes and Miss Daphne Bell. These CIS site coordinators provided the opposite experience from my guidance counselor. They said, "We have high expectations for everybody we're working with. We're going to be here for you, even when you slip and fall, to pick you up and push you to run even faster."

The thing about potential is that you don't really know you have it until someone tells you. I grabbed on to this message like it was a lifeboat, and that was the beginning of my relationship with CIS.

The summer before my junior year, the CIS program connected me with a local college access program. That was the first time I ever spent a night anywhere but my house. My parents dropped me off on Monday and picked me up on Friday. I was just down the street, 10 minutes from home, at a local university called Our Lady of the Lake. For me, though, it really felt like "going off to college." More importantly, it gave my parents practice in letting me go, which continues to be a barrier in many first-generation households when it comes to college and career.

Then, in my junior year, Miss Reyes told me that my grades were strong, that I'd done really well, and that I would probably test well on college entrance exams. I told her I wanted to go to the local community college, or maybe the University of Texas at San Antonio. She said, "No, we need to be thinking bigger. What's your highest goal, your 'reach school'?"

"Maybe UT–Austin up the road?" I said.

"No, that's not good enough for you. Have you heard of a school in California called Stanford? The reason I bring it up is there's a couple of young twins, Julián and Joaquin Castro, one of whom is a city councilman right now and running for mayor, and the other is a state representative. They're from the west side of San Antonio, from a community just like yours, and they went to Stanford. We could look them up and you could talk to them." Today Joaquin is a U.S. congressman, and Julián is the former U.S. secretary of housing and urban development and mayor of San Antonio. Seeing Julián and Joaquin's journey kindled a real spark of possibility for me, along with Miss Reyes's encouragement.

I didn't have any idea how hard it was to get into Stanford. I just said to Miss Reyes, "Okay, I'll do everything you tell me to. I can write essays!" And I would write some required essay for Stanford and show it to her, and my English teacher would proofread. It came back just bloody red with corrections.

The college essay prompt asked that I include a photo that was meaningful and tell them why. I submitted a photo of my father standing outside his work, posing with six of his co-workers. I wrote about my father's journey to the U.S. and his time working at the slaughterhouse. I recounted all my memories of him coming home each evening, smelling like chemicals and dead animals. I would hear the rumble of his truck, because he had one of those old Chevy Silverados with big engines and you could hear it coming two blocks away. I would always rush to the door and make sure to greet him with a big hug, and then I liked to take his hard hat and put it on.

One time, when I was seven or eight, he stopped me. He said, "I know you like wearing my hard hat. I know it's fun. But you are not allowed to wear this hard hat again. And I'm going to tell you why: It's because *I* wear this hard hat. *I* do this work. That's for me, but it is *not* for you. You won't have to wear one where you're going to work." The photo I included in my essay shows my father hiding his hard hat behind his back.

I'd done well in school, but so does everybody else who goes to a place like Stanford. When I talked to one of the admissions counselors, they said, "What we really loved in your application was the way you talked about your father—his work, his sacrifice, and what you could do to pay it back."

When we got the letter of acceptance, I knew my life had changed. I was running around the house shouting, "I'm gonna go to Stanford!" My mother said, "Stanford? Is that a good school?" I did my best job to explain that it was a *great* school, but she wasn't thrilled about me leaving for California. However, both my parents were convinced when Stanford offered a really generous financial aid package, and it didn't hurt that Miss Reyes and a high school counselor, Mr. Ruby Rocha, helped me fill out scholarship applications, one of which was the Bill and Melinda Gates Millennium Scholarship. The CIS folks were with me every step of the way, helping me identify what I had to do and making sure I did a quality job.

When my mother and father dropped me off at the airport for the first time, my dad said, "I know you're worried about taking this plane. But you've got everything you need. *No mas, échale ganas.* Give it everything you got." He then went on to say, "You know, when I was eighteen, I also took a big trip that had me worried. I didn't have as many bags as you do. I just had a backpack with a little food and water when I crossed the U.S.–Mexico border. Compared to border patrol agents, I think you'll be fine with those TSA agents." I have to say, that humbled me.

I went off to Stanford, and boy, was I homesick, and boy, was I scared, and boy, was I shocked by the culture! Even before I got there, I called my CIS coordinator from the airport because I didn't know how to walk through an airport and get on a plane. I was deathly afraid of the whole college experience, even though I'd been saying for years that I wanted to go. Now I realized that I didn't know what it would mean for me, and I just didn't know how to handle myself.

In my first year, I failed a class for the first time ever, and the fear that joined me on the flight to Stanford was made real, as I felt the weight of being an imposter. I called Miss Reyes, because she said it was very important that we keep our relationship going. She helped me pick myself up and try again. And it paid off.

Not really knowing what I wanted to do, I followed the only model I had seen and majored in the same areas as Julián and Joaquin Castro, political science and communication. When I came home during the summers, I interned with Joaquin, then a Texas state representative. Then I went on to the Graduate School of Education at Stanford and got my master's degree in education policy. For a kid who grew up in a 98 percent Latino community, the cultural diversity was amazing and often hard to navigate.

I guess in order to come home, you have to leave home at some point. I always thought of San Antonio as the place to escape, but after college I realized I wanted to return there and show the world who I was becoming.

I played baseball at Stanford and had a chance to visit a lot of cities. I saw things I had never seen growing up in San Antonio— in San Francisco, there was a rail system and expansive parks and museums! That was just not built into San Antonio, or at least not the part of town I was from. I started to have the feeling of wanting to give something back to my community, to help it grow and prosper. My definition of "success" was changing. It wasn't just a nice house or a nice car or a good income. I came back home and announced that I wanted to run for city council. I was 23.

I knew the city council position didn't pay—or rather, it paid $1,000 a year, a token stipend. In the 1950s, they'd written the city charter law so that only individuals who could afford to take no salary would run for local office. This had a very practical effect of keeping out poor people, and specifically the majority of residents who were people of color. But it meant a lot to me to be part of something that included improving my home community.

I moved back in with my parents, recycled two suits, and kept driving the car that I drove in high school. My dad and my mom were confused, to put it mildly. "Wait, you went to Stanford, which costs $65,000 a year, times four, then you needed another expensive degree called a master's, so add another $65K. Your brain is worth $300,000 or $400,000 by now. And you're going to come back here and take a job that pays you $1,000 a year? Great."

"Yep, that's what I want to do. You got it. So can I stay with you all to save on rent?"

My opponent was the wife of the incumbent, so I was the underdog. But I practiced my door-knocking pitch and went around the neighborhood. My first door was Ms. Rodriguez's home. It was a Saturday morning. When Ms. Rodriguez came to the door, I said, "I'm sorry to bother you. I wanted to come and introduce myself and make sure that you knew that I'm running for city council. I was born and raised in the community here. I went to the local high school, South San, and then I went off to college at Stanford, came back, and now I want to be your city councilman. Can I count on your vote?"

She looked at me and said, "Are you talking about the city council or the *student* council? You're not old enough to be a city councilman."

I had 3,000 more doors on my list.

That was the hottest Texas summer I can remember, and there were no days off. In the end, I was elected as the youngest city councilman in our city's history and seated at the table as 1 of 10, with the mayor in the middle, who was Julián Castro.

The other big thing that happened during this period was that I met my future wife, Jessica Flynn. She's half Irish and half El Salvadorean. Jessica and I actually met back in 2007, when I was still at Stanford and she was at UT–Austin. But a couple of years into my tenure on the city council, we decided we wanted to get married. I remember going to ask her father for his daughter's hand. I was still making $1,000 a year as a councilman. Naturally, Jessica's father was very curious about how I was going to make a living. I don't know what I said or how I said it, but he gave us his blessing.

While serving on the San Antonio City Council, which was a full-time role overseeing a district of 130,000 residents, I also worked as an adjunct professor at the local community college, teaching a class on education policy, and as grant writer for the University of Texas at San Antonio, in their office of community engagement. A few years later, I served as an administrator with KIPP Texas–San Antonio, a network of K–12 public charter schools that was growing on the west side of the city.

I ended up serving the full eight years as a city councilman—that's the term limit. We had just elected a new mayor. I decided to take a break from politics for about a year and just take a look around, and inside myself. This was 2019. I joined a local Texas foundation called Raise Your Hand Texas started by Charles Butt—the owner of the largest grocery company in Texas, H-E-B—that works on education issues and advocacy for Texas public schools.

Midway through my city council service, I'd been contacted by Dale Erquiaga, then president and CEO of CIS National. He said the national board was looking to have a CIS alumnus as a board member, and that I might be a good choice. I was honored to be asked, and in due course, I did join the board. I didn't even really know CIS existed as a separate entity, because at my high school it just melted into the school—which is how it's supposed to work! I definitely did not know about this larger network all across the country called Communities In Schools. But I got to know their work pretty intimately after serving on the board for a few years.

Then in 2019, while I was taking my break from public office and working at Raise Your Hand Texas, I got a call from the CIS National Board chair, Elaine Wynn. She said, "I want to let you know that Dale Erquiaga is going to be announcing his retirement soon. There's going to be an opening for the president/CEO position, and I think you would be a strong candidate. Just think on that, sleep on it. And if you think it's a good idea, you should apply for the job."

The idea had never crossed my mind beforehand. I was perfectly happy working at the foundation. I had just come off eight years of city council work. So the concept of leading an organization like CIS evoked all of my imposter syndrome—who am I to do a job like this? I had to do a lot of soul-searching before I even agreed to apply. By now I'd met Bill Milliken, of course, and I talked it over with him. Bill told me he was just blown away by the concept of it—an alumnus standing up to lead the organization that had made such a difference in his life as a kid. It fit right into his "hundred-year plan"!

At the January 2020 board meeting, they made the decision to hire me.

How lucky was I to have CIS in my high school? Very lucky. And realizing that, it's a big part of my motivation now as president of the national office.

I'm still living on the south side of San Antonio, three blocks from where my parents lived when I was growing up. They're still with us, doing fine. My family isn't always good at using words to show how emotionally invested and supportive they are. But they do let me know they're proud of me.

I still see Miss Reyes—she's Mrs. Gladys Gradilla now. She is still with CIS, and we recently walked through my middle school with her and the superintendent. My wife, Jessica, and I have two lovely children, Eli and Olivia. I have a great opportunity with CIS to affect how we educate *all* our children. But it's by the grace of God, the lottery of life, that I feel like I get to sit where I do and have the chance to leave a mark.

We have no control over some things, of course, and we never will. But we're also living in a society that doesn't give everybody a fair shake. Growing up in challenging communities, you kind of know it—those are the odds, and there is nothing you can really do to control it. You feel powerless to an extent, but you don't think about it too much. It's just how it is; that's how the rules were set up.

That's what I want to see change. The game should *not* be played that way, and I think millions of Americans know this and are ready to help. We need to create a more equitable system where students don't have to be lucky. We don't need to create a separate new school structure or find a different place to support students. If you want to improve student outcomes and help students write their success stories, the center of gravity is inside public schools.

As we look out into the future, our goal is clear: we want to see a CIS site coordinator in every Title I school in the country. It's simple, it's strong. It's not an easy goal, but it's an understandable one. It took us 45 years to get into 2,800 schools, and we obviously can't take another 45 years to get to the next 2,800. There are about 70,000 Title I schools in total. So we need to find new ways to grow and teach, and that's what we're doing.

The pandemic created an opportunity to stop and think, to notice the role that schools play. We've seen what it's like to remove school completely. Fifty million students departed from their schools. The doors were shut, and they were told, "Go home and do the work from there." It let us recognize how schools have been such an important safety net for many of our communities, and in some cases, the safest place for students.

I worry that when the pandemic subsides, we'll revert to just continuing to do things the way we used to. We'll evaluate students, teachers, and school leaders based exclusively on their test scores or academic results. And yet we've been learning new ways to measure how students are growing. We have social and emotional measures that can show if students are connecting positively with more people at the end of the year than they were at the beginning of the year. That's an important measure for us as we consider whether we're meeting the needs of all students.

And this has to continue beyond high school. My CIS coordinator, Miss Reyes, helped walk me down from the ledge when I was talking about quitting college in the first semester. But how many high school graduates have that kind of relationship with a caring adult? Who will help you handle the discouragement of that job interview where you're turned down and you think, *If they're not going to hire me here, they're not going to hire me anywhere. I'll settle for what I can get?* Many of our students need this continuing support.

At this moment, Communities In Schools is by far the largest provider of evidence-based integrated student supports (ISS) in the U.S. We're in 2,860 schools. Foundations and policy makers have responded because they know how committed we are to evaluation, to an accreditation system, and to standards about how our model is deployed based on what the research tells us. Thanks to MacKenzie Scott's philanthropy—an unrestricted gift of $133.5 million to our national and local programs—we're poised to have the kind of impact that's necessary if we're going to reach thousands more communities that want our help in the future.

But I think it's equally important to look back and understand where we've come from. We have gotten to this point because of an incredibly strong foundation of public and private support and a vision that has remained evergreen: it's not programs that are changing students' lives; it's relationships.

I'm so excited to be lending my voice to this new edition of Bill Milliken's classic book about the roots and early history of CIS. I'll just conclude by saying: Bill, we still haven't seen the last dropout, but we're getting closer, and a lot of that is due to your inspiration and effort. I am honored to continue your work.

INTRODUCTION

Dropout Nation

This book was first published in 2007. As a result of several high-profile studies and media reports, including a *Time* magazine cover story called "Dropout Nation," many Americans were hearing for the first time that the United States has a "dropout epidemic"—millions of young people failing to graduate from high school. And they were learning about the grim real-life consequences in a new century, demanding workplace skills that most often require at least post-high-school study.

In the past 15 years, much has been done to address this crisis. The fact remains, though, that dropping out of school is still one of the most visible and tragic results of a situation that grows worse, not better. Economic inequality, on the rise in this country, exacts its harshest penalties on children. The U.S. poverty measure finds 11.6 million children living in poverty in 2020. This represents *an increase of more than one million children* in a single year, and comprises 16 percent of all youth nationwide.[1]

Poverty rates are also disproportionately high for children of color. According to the Census Bureau, Black (28 percent), American Indian (25 percent), and Latino (23 percent) kids are more likely to grow up poor.[2]

In this book, I tell the story of Communities In Schools, which has worked for more than 40 years to end the dropout epidemic. One of the things you'll learn is that dropping out of school is a symptom of a host of dysfunctions that plague children, families, and schools. CIS is known, and rightly so, as a very successful dropout-prevention program—but we can never forget that "the dropout epidemic" is ultimately an epidemic of poverty, inequity, and lack of resolve and resources. As I say many times in what you're about to read, this is a *justice* issue.

America's two million dropouts ages 16 to 24 are truly have-nots: they don't have a high school diploma, and as a result are far more likely than their peers to earn less, experience poor health outcomes, need government assistance, and get involved in criminal activity.[3]

The U.S. Department of Education's 2019 publication, "Trends in High School Dropout and Completion Rates," notes that "dropouts also make up a higher percentage of the nation's institutionalized population, including persons living in adult and juvenile correctional facilities, nursing facilities, and other health-care facilities. Among 25- to 34-year-olds in the labor force, the unemployment rate for dropouts is nearly twice as high as the rate for those who graduated, even if those graduates didn't go on to college."[4]

The dire consequences for these young people are mirrored in the costs to American society—to you, your children, and the future of our country. Dropouts are costing us *billions* of dollars in lost wages and increased social support, including medical care and welfare benefits.

The average high school dropout costs the economy approximately $272,000 over their lifetime, calculated in terms of lower tax contributions, higher reliance on Medicaid and Medicare, higher rates of criminal activity, and higher reliance on government assistance.[5]

Just imagine what we could accomplish if this same amount were spent on education instead.

Business leaders, economists, and chambers of commerce across the country agree: in a time of intense international competition, America is unable to recruit an adequate workforce if this failure to educate *all* our children continues. The opportunities that you and your children take for granted are being eroded day by day as the country is transformed into a society of haves and have-nots. All too soon, the impact of fiscal failure and social division will be felt keenly by the haves, as U.S. global economic leadership dwindles and the nation is unable to pay its huge "bill" generated by the have-nots.

This divided society will reap consequences that are devastating for all Americans, not just the young people themselves. It is at once a practical disaster for our economy, a human tragedy for the children and families directly concerned, and a justice issue that confronts every citizen.

IN SEARCH OF THE LAST DROPOUT

Although the challenge is enormous, we can stop the dropout epidemic. A growing consensus of educators and social-service providers is rallying behind a solution that works. The purpose of this book is to describe that solution and show how Americans at every level of society—local leaders desperate to stop the hemorrhaging of youth from their school systems, foundation heads and corporate CEOs equally determined to put their money and influence to work for this vital cause, and of course the parents and teachers of these students—can come together and *stop the epidemic*.

A million dropouts, or two million, or three, is an outrageous tragedy. But even *one* young person abandoned to a life with no future is equally tragic, equally unacceptable. Our collective goal must be a 21st-century America in which, at long last, we've seen the last dropout.

Who will be the last dropout? The last American youth who doesn't make it through our public school system?

Will it be Marcy? She lives with her mother, her grandmother, and her three siblings in the Anacostia neighborhood of Washington, D.C. Anacostia has had its ups and downs over the years and was hit especially hard by the crack epidemic and crime waves of the 1980s and '90s. Still, it's an area with a long, proud history, and Marcy's mother believes there are a lot of worse places to raise your children. She has a full-time job at the local grocery store, but it pays only minimum wage and the family income is well below the poverty level. And lately, Marcy hasn't been well—the usual childhood ailments, but also some worrisome concerns about potential asthma.

Will Marcy be the last dropout? She's only two years old now, so it's hard to say.

Will it be Jaime? His family lives in Las Vegas, but their life is a different kind of gamble. Like a surprising number of youth in the city and in Clark County, Jaime is homeless. With his parents and five siblings, he moves from shelter to shelter, relative to friend—and spends a lot of time sleeping rough under the Nevada stars. Jaime is five and ready to enroll in the public school system. I wonder where he'll be doing his homework.

Or perhaps the last dropout will be Linda, whose family has lived in the same rural North Carolina county for generations. None of them has ever graduated from high school—there's always been work on the farm and in the nearby mills as soon as a child is old enough to hold a job. Education is all very well, but every dollar is needed just to get by. In the 2020s, though, work opportunities for nongraduates are drying up as the county's economy changes. Seven-year-old Linda is going to need a new vision for her future—and some very practical help achieving it.

When will we see the last dropout? No one knows, of course, other than to say, "Not in this generation." But we *can* say this: young people will stop dropping out when they receive the community support and resources they need to learn, stay in school, and graduate prepared for life.

They'll stop dropping out when we admit that our country doesn't have a "youth problem"; we have an *adult* problem. We—the grown-ups, including parents, who have a stake in the community's children—haven't succeeded in weaving a safety net of support that will keep kids safe, healthy, and motivated. The business community in particular hasn't yet committed its full energy and expertise to champion the connection of resources with schools. Nor has America modeled the kind of caring society that can serve as an inspiration and a source of hope for young people. All the "school reform" in the world won't accomplish this. It isn't only about better teachers, better schools, or more money. It is about *hope*.

My colleagues and I have spent the past 40 years developing an antidote to the dropout epidemic. **This is the good news I want to share with you in this book: There is a cure for the dropout epidemic. It's at work in hundreds of communities, and it will work in yours, too.**

The Last Dropout is about a journey that began in Harlem in the 1960s and took us to Wall Street, to Atlanta, and ultimately to the White House. We were "street workers," trying to help young people who had already dropped out to return to school and get their diplomas. Over time, we realized it was useless to keep bailing out the basement unless we also turned off the tap, and that meant working inside the public school system. The Communities In Schools organization, originally founded in 1977 as Cities In Schools, was the result. CIS now reaches more than 1.6 million young people and their families annually, in 2,860 schools. The majority of these students are often underserved and at risk of falling below the national averages for measuring student success.[6] **Yet CIS-tracked students are staying in school and graduating prepared for life.** Why? What makes the difference?

The key principles in *The Last Dropout* weren't developed in a think tank or a graduate school. Our work with kids and families has benefited enormously from the research and documentation of the academic community, but I do want to make clear that most of the lessons in this book were learned through firsthand experience, from the ground up, by sitting down and breaking bread with families, students, teachers, and community members, as well as business and government leaders.

Similarly, my hat is off to our dedicated American educators, and this book in no way means to disparage their efforts. The school-reform movement has generated important gains for kids: Teachers have revised curricula to emphasize strategies for student success based on carefully researched models and set high standards for student achievement. Policy makers have created legislation—most recently the Every Student Succeeds Act (ESSA)—which endorses these high standards for all children, recognizing that every kid can learn, regardless of class, ethnicity, or place of origin. And we've invested a great deal of innovation and creativity into the governance of schools, holding them accountable for their students' progress.

So both the *content* of education—the curricula, the pedagogical strategies—and the *form* of education—school management and governance—are the subject of intense reform efforts. **What's** too often missing, though, is what I call the "third side of the triangle": the community component that will meet the non-academic needs of children. To put it simply, it's pretty hard to concentrate on your third-grade reading achievement test if your bedroom has no heat and you need glasses, you go to school every day scared and hungry, or you're distracted by family problems.

I've said that the dropout epidemic is also a justice issue, and I want to emphasize that again. How we respond to it will determine whether the United States becomes a permanently divided nation of those who make it and those who don't. Is that the kind of world we want our children to inherit? A place divided between gated communities and prisons, between winners and losers? I promise you, the prospect will be bleak, *no matter which side of the fence you're on.* We simply can't continue on a path that produces such drastic economic and human inequity.

ABOUT THIS BOOK

The Last Dropout offers the key principles that the Communities In Schools movement has tested over four decades, principles that lead to better schools and successful kids. Chapters 1 through 3 focus on principles for positive relationships among adults and between adults and students; Chapters 4 through 6 detail practical, organizational precepts; and Chapters 7 through 9 focus on sustainability for the long term.

You may find some of the language familiar from other contexts, but I hope that this book will help you see the words in a new light. Most certainly, I hope that you'll be inspired to apply these concepts in your own communities and to further the missions of your own organizations.

Here are the essential principles that will keep young people in school and prepare them for successful lives:

- Programs don't change kids—*relationships* do.
- The dropout crisis isn't just an education issue.

- Young people need the five *real* basics, not just the three *R*'s: a one-on-one relationship with a caring adult, a safe place to learn and grow, a healthy start and a healthy future, a marketable skill to use upon graduation, and a chance to give back to peers and community.

- The community must weave a safety net around its children in a manner that's personal, accountable, and coordinated.

- Every community needs a "Champion for Children": a neutral third party with "magic eyes" to see things—and people—differently, and coordinate and broker the diverse community resources into the schools on behalf of young people and families.

- Educators and policy makers can't do it alone . . . and they'll welcome your help.

- Curing the dropout epidemic will demand *change*, not just charity.

- *Scalability, sustainability,* and *evidence-based strategies* are essential to creating permanent change in the way our education system combats the dropout epidemic.

- Our children need three things from you: your *awareness*, your *advocacy*, and your *action*.

I'll clarify and expand upon each of these in the chapters that follow. However, I want first to caution you to avoid the "silver bullet syndrome"—that is, the temptation to adopt and implement only one or two of these key principles and disregard the rest. In fact, it's precisely this fragmented approach that has doomed other community-development and school-reform efforts in the past, including some state and local Communities In Schools efforts. If there's one thing we've learned over 40 years of doing this work, it's that it takes a total commitment to *all* of these principles to yield any meaningful and lasting effect on the dropout problem.

Finally, I want to address a few words to the business and philanthropic leaders who I believe will find in *The Last Dropout* a cause for optimism and a blueprint for change. Our view is that you have a special, critical role to play in ending the dropout epidemic. Your community needs you to use the power of the private and nonprofit sectors—your connections, your knowledge, your organizational skills, your practical experience—to leverage resources for schools, children, and families and to influence how private-, public-, and nonprofit-sector institutions at all levels distribute funds for education and family services. Moreover, your *nation* needs you to champion and help spread these effective strategies for student success widely enough to meet the immense need, in a way that will change, permanently and effectively, how America's schools educate their students.

We don't need you to create more charities. We need you to think and work differently. I hope this book will help. Most important, we need you to *lead*. A lot of lives are depending on you.

PART I

IT ALL STARTS WITH RELATIONSHIPS

CHAPTER 1

PROGRAMS DON'T CHANGE KIDS— CHANGE KIDS— RELATIONSHIPS DO

BEING DUMB

I wasn't a high school dropout. I'm sure I would have been, but I didn't get the chance—the school kicked me out before I could quit.

It was 1957, I was 17, and by most people's standards, I had it made. I was a white Anglo-Saxon Protestant. I grew up in a middle-class suburb of Pittsburgh on a quiet, shady street in a nice neighborhood. My father and his brothers had a good business, and the country club was at our disposal.

But that was just on the surface. Underneath, my home was a mess. My mother was chronically ill with emotional and physical problems, and my father was distant. I had two brothers, but they were much older and had already moved out of the house by the time I entered my teens. I'm sure my parents loved me, but they couldn't be there for me, emotionally or in any other way.

I started to rebel against all the 1950s conformist values around me as a way of hiding the loneliness and hurt I felt. And I *hated* school. I felt inferior to most of the students, and my D average reflected it. I couldn't read well and bluffed my way through most classes. Many years later, I found out that I "learned differently," but back in my day, they called it "being dumb." And so I told myself none of it mattered to me anyway—school was just a bunch of facts that I didn't need or care about.

I started getting in trouble, getting sent to detention, and hanging around with the "bad crowd" at Nobbie's Pool Hall. They called us the "Green Street Animals." Finally, the principal brought my mom into school and told her that she ought to take me out. The reason I was in so much trouble, he said, was that I "couldn't handle the work." Once again, that meant only one thing: I was dumb. No surprise, really—for three years I'd been in a special class for "slow learners." We were all labeled, and the other guys who weren't making it were my only friends.

The closest I came to feeling anything like acceptance was at that pool hall. There, hanging out with a couple dozen guys my age and older, I talked the way I liked to talk and didn't feel rejected for it. In that scruffy room with its six pool tables and dim lights, there was a sense of community that I felt nowhere else. It was real, it was honest—but also violent and purposeless. What I remember most is how the time dragged and stretched. We had all the time in the world to go . . . nowhere. I used to lie in bed at night in tears, wondering what I was doing, where I was headed, and what my life was about.

One day at Nobbie's, an older guy came in, a guy in his 30s whom I'd never seen before. He just sat there and watched us. I turned to my friend Lefty and asked, "Who is that guy?" Lefty had no idea. The man showed up each day, but we never spoke. Finally he offered to shoot a game of pool with us—"I'll pay," he said, which sounded good—and we kidded him about his lousy cue technique, and he took it and kidded us back, and eventually I got around to asking him his name and what he was doing there. "My name is Bob, and I'm trying to start a club for kids from your high school."

"Good luck, man," I told him.

Bob was part of Young Life, a nondenominational Christian organization committed to making a positive impact on kids' lives and preparing them for the future. It was founded in 1941, and it's still going strong today across the United States and in more than 100 foreign countries. You can be sure I wasn't too interested in the Christian stuff at first. The group sponsored a camp at a ranch in Colorado, and that was more to my liking. "And we'll give you a scholarship," Bob said when he told me about it. No one had ever offered me a scholarship for anything before. Even better, he told me it was a co-ed camp. I took a look at the photos of the girls riding horses. "Okay," I said, "I think I can make time for this."

So, along with five of my friends, I rode a bus out west, and on the bus I met Jerry Kirk, the man with whom I went on to form the most important relationship of my life so far. Jerry was the head of Young Life in Pittsburgh. The first thing I remember noticing about him was that he could fall asleep on the road in the midst of all the ruckus we were making. He even had a smile on his face while he slept!

He was a slight, wiry guy—he'd done a lot of long-distance running back in school and still had the look of an athlete. At this time he was perhaps 30 or so. I liked him right away, but he puzzled me just as much as Bob had. What was his angle? Why did this guy seem to care about me?

At the camp there was plenty of stuff to do: horseback riding, basketball, hiking. But most of all, there was time to hang out. In addition to Jerry, there were two other counselors assigned to my friends and me, and once again . . . what *was* it with those guys? I could see immediately that they wanted to know me as a person; they cared about who I was, no matter whether I "believed in God" or was willing to accept what Young Life was all about. I didn't know what to call it, but I perceived that Jerry Kirk loved me unconditionally. He believed in me as a human being, whatever I did—there were no strings attached.

It was the first time I'd ever experienced anything like this. Shouldn't I have received unconditional love from my parents? Sure—but like millions of young people, I didn't. I was desperate for a caring adult in my life.

I didn't open up to Jerry or the others right away. I was extremely distrustful, and I had to do a lot of testing to find out if their caring was real. We had work crews at the camp, doing things like filling holes in the roads. One morning I was slacking off, and Bob, who was the crew boss, said, "Milliken, you're lazy!" (Did I mention he was an ex-Marine?) *Wham!* My next shovelful of dirt just happened to catch him right in the face.

The staff had a big meeting over this incident. I knew they were going to send me home. But instead, they told me that they were going to stick it out with me. I realized that Bob wasn't being a jerk; on the contrary, he was consistent and fair, because when I did my job well, he was there to tell me so. When I didn't, he told me that, too. I was inconsistent, but he was not. And he had a sense of humor. So I apologized to him and found that I respected him even more.

The real turning point in my feelings of trust for Jerry came when I went back to Pittsburgh. Somehow I was afraid I'd never see him again. He'd gotten me to the camp and had helped me learn about God—so his job was over and he'd move on to someone else. That didn't happen. Jerry stayed with me and continued to be my friend. The unconditional love didn't disappear, and neither did he. (The trip to the Colorado camp became an annual event, too—many years later I was still going out there each summer, taking kids from the streets of New York to experience what I had as a teen.)

Something started to change within me. I was realizing that no matter how tough I thought I was, no matter how screwed up I felt my life had been, I wanted to be connected. It was the basic driving force for me, and—I understand now—for every single human being on the planet. A few years ago, I was deeply moved while watching the Tom Hanks film *Castaway*. Here's this guy all alone on a deserted island for years and he winds up establishing a personal, one-on-one relationship with a volleyball! The ball had "Wilson" written on it, so that's what the Hanks character called it. This was the best he could do, the only friend he had. He just had to be connected.

I firmly believe that I'm alive today because of a caring adult. Jerry, Bob, and the other Young Life counselors didn't think my friends and I were worthless. They believed we had a future, something we could give. They didn't offer us an "answer" or a "program"—they offered *themselves;* they offered the time, love, and energy it takes to form a relationship with another human being. And there's no human being harder to relate to than an alienated teenager. Jerry walked with me through "the valley of the shadow of adolescence," and, as I've learned dozens of times since, that's no easy walk. Without someone to believe in them, a teenager gets angry, and they start to take it out on other people and themselves.

Programs don't change kids—relationships do. This principle is the cornerstone for everything you'll ever do for children in your communities. They'll probably put it on my tombstone because I've said it so often, in so many ways. But in this increasingly high-tech "virtual" century, I believe you can't say it too often: it all starts with relationships. A good program creates an environment in which healthy relationships can occur.

"THEY USED TO CALL ME LOSER"

"Don't *ever* do that to me again!" General Colin Powell was frowning at me—and believe me, the man can frown. Of course, he was only kidding . . . at least, I think he was.

We were backstage at a hotel just outside of Washington, D.C., in 1997, and the general had just finished his keynote address to more than a thousand Communities In Schools network members from around the nation. It was the organization's 20th anniversary—20 years of loving kids into change, of learning how to "walk our talk" in some of the toughest neighborhoods in America.

General Powell kept glaring. I'd thought his speech was terrific. As head of the newly formed nonprofit America's Promise, he had a strong and essential message to deliver about bringing community resources to children and families. The CIS crowd loved him. Then I thought I saw the hint of a smile.

"You brought in a ringer, Milliken," he said. "Reggie Beaty gave one of the greatest talks I've ever heard."

He was referring to Lieutenant Colonel Reginald Beaty, an alumnus of the CIS affiliate in Atlanta, whom we'd asked to introduce the general and tell a little of his own story. Atlanta was where my colleagues and I started the first prototypes of what later became known as Communities In Schools. Reggie was one of the first graduates of our "Street Academy" initiative there, and he'd received a lot of honors since. Now he had a new one: the man who almost upstaged Colin Powell.

What Reggie told that audience was a story about a personal relationship. He talked about what he used to be like, what happened to him, and what he's like today. "They used to call me Loser," he said. "Now they call me Lieutenant Colonel!" It was all about how a positive bond with a caring adult made the difference.

LIFE OF CRIME

Reggie grew up in Atlanta during the 1960s, and for his first 10 years, he and school got along fine. He and his four siblings were raised by his mother, who had only made it through the 10th grade herself but understood the importance of education. Then, in 1969, the Beaty family had to move to a new neighborhood: Bankhead Courts, which had the dubious distinction of being featured on *60 Minutes* as one of the worst communities in the United States. Violent crimes, murders, drugs, burglaries— Bankhead Courts had it all.

For two more years, Reggie held his ground. He was making the honor roll, studying hard, and trying to ignore the devastating poverty and insecurity that surrounded him. "We weren't short on love," he told me once, "but there was a lot of competition for a young boy's attention: drugs, sex, crime, you name it." By the eighth grade, Reggie was into it all. You didn't hear the term "gangs" too much back then, but gang activity is what it was. Reggie carried a .22 and a .38 when he was 14 years old; robbery and drug addiction were an accepted part of his world.

School was the next thing to go. In the ninth grade, he was expelled. "I started a life of crime," he'll tell you bluntly. For two years he was in and out of juvenile detention, usually for breaking and entering, sometimes for drug dealing. People in the community who knew him kept saying: "Reggie, you're too smart for this. What happened to all that potential you had?" But as far as Reggie was concerned, the normal world—especially school—had given up on him, and he had no interest in trying to find a way back in.

Then one day while he was hanging with his friends and playing basketball when he should have been at school, two older guys started hanging around, too. Like Reggie, they were African American, but he'd never seen them before. They definitely weren't from Bankhead Courts. These two guys kept showing up, and after a while they explained why: They said that they were "street workers" and they were starting something called a Street Academy for kids who had left school. It was a way to get back inside the system and get that diploma—but in a very different environment. The academy was small (never more than 100 students at any one time), and the learning was intensive and geared to the personal pace of each young person.

At first Reggie took a pass on it, but then a couple of young women he'd grown up with—both of them now teenage mothers—said they were going to enroll in Academy T, as it was called. The *T* stood for *Transition*. After a bit, they told Reggie: "You really should consider this. It's making a difference. These guys are okay." And the two street workers, Bobby Garrett and Dave Lewis, kept coming back to that basketball court. Basically, they wouldn't leave Reggie alone. They kept bugging him about giving Academy T a try.

Reggie has told me that he probably would have gone over to the storefront building that housed the academy and checked it out, just out of curiosity, even if he hadn't started to feel a connection with the men who kept encouraging him. He might even have enrolled on his own. But he never would have made it to graduation without Bobby Garrett, who became his mentor. Academy T was a great program. But, more important, Bobby gave Reggie a great *relationship*, and that was what made the difference.

Millions of American youth don't have a positive, one-on-one relationship with a caring adult. How did this happen?

In the years following World War II, millions of troops returning to the U.S. moved to small towns and cities instead of back to their farms. The economy picked up and the G.I. Bill got people through college, leading to suburbs springing up all across the country. At the same time, there was a huge migration from south to north as Black people from poor rural areas went looking for hope and work but ended up in ghettos. (Claude Brown's book *Manchild in the Promised Land* tells this story in the most vivid, personal terms.)

The result pulled apart what had been a fairly effective community structure, both in the agrarian states and even in some industrial sections of the country: Where I grew up in Pittsburgh, people were involved with each other around the steel mills. But over the years, the safety net—woven largely by the extended family and the faith community—slowly unraveled.

I once heard General Powell speak about the "Aunt-net"; that was what they had in his neighborhood growing up instead of the Internet. The aunts all leaned out of their windows on his street in the Bronx. If young Colin got in trouble at school, his parents knew about it before he got home. The word went out, neighbor to neighbor, relative to relative, right down the grapevine. That was true community, the extended family at its best. There are many neighborhoods where kids can still count on such a safety net . . . but many, many more where they can't.

Realizing that young Reggie was going to need something useful to do when he wasn't going to classes (and was no longer living the street life), Bobby helped him find a job. He introduced him to life skills—the "hidden rules" of how to get along and get ahead in society—that nobody had ever shown him before. And Bobby began acting as the male role model that the boy had never had. Reggie calls it "hard love."

Bobby Garrett decided to make Reggie his personal project, and he invested blood, sweat, and tears in the young man. Perhaps most important of all, he never judged Reggie for all the mistakes he'd made up till then. He insisted on looking at the good and helped Reggie rediscover the talents and abilities he'd enjoyed as a small child.

And something changed. "New ways of thinking and feeling" is how Reggie puts it. I know exactly what he means. I was a white, middle-class screwup from Pittsburgh; he was a young criminal from Atlanta's worst ghetto, but we both needed the same thing—a personal relationship with a caring adult. Thank God we both found it.

Much to his surprise, Reggie discovered that going back to school wasn't hard at all. His last school, the one that expelled him, had felt unsafe, full of fights and threats. Academy T wasn't like that. There, he was secure, people cared about him, and he was shown respect. The atmosphere was serious. Even though all the students were dropouts or "pushouts" who (to use Reggie's wry phrase) had "done a lot of foolishness" before showing up at the academy, there was no trouble in class. Everyone was there to work, which was a good thing because expectations were high, and excellence was both encouraged and expected.

"I made some stupid mistakes," Reggie says. "But I wasn't penalized with a life sentence."

When it came time for Reggie to graduate from Academy T, Bobby had another surprise for him: "You're going to college," he told the boy. The two of them sat down with Reggie's mother and a college counselor, who helped the young man navigate college admission and scholarship forms. No one in his family had ever tried this before. In the end, he applied to just one college and hit the bull's-eye: Stillman College accepted him for the class of 1980.

From here on, Reggie's story sounds like something I'm making up, but every word is true. He became president of the United Negro College Fund at Stillman, vice president of his fraternity, and president of his dormitory. He served on the mayor's advisory council and commanded the ROTC drill team. He received a full scholarship for the next three years as a result of his outstanding abilities in ROTC. By the end of his career at Stillman, Reggie was commander of the entire ROTC program. And he entered the army as a commissioned officer, a second lieutenant.

Reggie's love of teaching flourished while he was in the military with superb results: He was named the nation's best ROTC instructor in any college or university, and his work with youth in Oklahoma earned him "Man of the Year" honors. He chaired fundraising committees for charity groups, started a mentoring program for young minority officers, and commanded a battalion of 2,000 soldiers. When he retired from the army as a lieutenant colonel in 2000, I know he must have been asking himself: *What next? What more?*

I'll return to Reggie's story and answer that question later in this book. Right now, I just want to reemphasize what this chapter has been all about. When Reggie spoke to our Communities In Schools conference, he made it very clear how high the stakes had been for him. "The guys in my neighborhood who were getting their heads blown off, going to jail for the rest of their lives, getting strung out on drugs—these were my *friends*," he said. "These were the people I was hanging with. My relationship with a caring adult saved my life."

HANGING OUT—AND HITTING THE WALL

Reggie Beaty and I have a lot in common, and a lot of differences, too. His road was harder than mine, for one thing. But once he rediscovered his gifts and abilities, the sky was the limit. I wish I'd had that drive and confidence when I was his age, but I didn't.

As a result of my relationship with Jerry Kirk, I was aware that I really did have something to give. But I didn't know what. I was worth something—but what? Back in Pittsburgh, I got my high school diploma after all and tried college. After my third time through freshman year, I gave that up. I still couldn't seem to learn, and the frustration of being labeled dumb stuck with me.

Then, in the midst of all the renewed questioning about who I was and what I might do, I ran into Harv Oostdyk, a Young Life leader I'd met at the Colorado ranch on my second trip out there. He was three or four years older than I was; I'd formed a strong bond with him and with Vinnie Pasquale from Newark, who formerly struggled with drug addiction. Harv had the vision of starting Young Life in New York City, and he got me excited about working with him among street kids. Something finally made sense for me.

If I had a degree, it would be in "hanging out"—I'd perfected the art in all kinds of situations. And by watching Jerry Kirk and the other Young Life counselors, I'd picked up a few tricks about how to do so in a positive way—especially on the basketball court—in order to start a conversation with younger kids. I wasn't sure what gifts I had, but I knew how to go and connect with people. That's where I felt most comfortable.

A couple of months after renewing our friendship, I got a call from Harv telling me to come to New York. It was that simple. I packed a few things, and on June 17, 1960, I headed east. I met Vinnie at the Newark YMCA, where he worked part-time. We spent the night on Harv's living room floor, and the next morning we grabbed a basketball and started across the George Washington Bridge to look for some kids who wanted to shoot baskets.

We had no idea what we were getting into.

When Vinnie and I moved to the city, we had one gift between us: like me, Vinnie could have earned a degree in hanging out. But that was exactly what was missing in the lives of those young people. Nobody was out on the streets with them, walking with them, talking with them, shooting hoops.

I wasn't very good at basketball, but I could dribble more or less and at least attempt to put the ball through the hoop; you could maybe fit a piece of paper underneath my feet when I went for my jump shot. But I wasn't afraid to get out there and mix it up and try. *Being here* was what it was all about. Sometimes we were in the midst of some frightening situations, but Vinnie had spent a lot of his time in prison, sleeping on rooftops, and addicted to heroin. He'd seen it all, so he knew how to handle himself. He didn't look much like a kid.

We hung out in Harlem and on the Lower East Side, and needless to say, we were pretty much the only white guys around. But that didn't turn out to be important. There was so much need, and people could tell we cared—no matter what color our skin was.

They knew we'd been there, too; we weren't outsiders with clean, safe offices downtown. A few of the kids thought we might be undercover cops. But the police wouldn't move in to the neighborhood and live there day and night. So they wound up deciding we were just nuts—but we had to go where the kids were.

Harv continued to run Young Life in New Jersey, but he came into the city almost every day to give Vinnie and me a hand. His support was critical. He was somewhere between a boss and a mentor, helping us raise funds when we needed them and also doing his share of one-on-one street work with the kids. Together, Vinnie, Harv, and I—in our own stumbling fashion—were discovering the first principle of any transformational action with young people. We just knew that positive relationships were going to get these kids off drugs, off the streets, and back to school. It had worked for us; it would work for them.

And it did work . . . sort of. We were able to convince quite a few young people to get out of gangs, get off the streets, get "clean," and start doing something with their lives. But immediately we ran into a big problem. Vinnie said it best: "How can we say we love our neighbors but let them live on rooftops? We go out there and tell them how much we care and then go back to our nice warm beds."

At this point we were living in a little $32-a-month cold-water flat in Harlem. The bathtub was right in the middle of the kitchen—but at least we *had* a bathtub, and a roof over our heads and a door with multiple locks. That was more than a lot of the street kids had. No one started talking about homelessness until the 1980s, when it became such a big "issue," but it was always a reality for the economically disenfranchised.

We were starting to realize that the first great key we'd discovered—building relationships with young people—wasn't going to unlock the door of success all by itself. We'd hit a wall. We had a lot more to learn.

. . . AND BEYOND

In his Foreword, CIS President Rey Saldaña talked about the "razor-thin margins" that so many young people face as they try to navigate school and life. One mistake can be one too many if you lack resources, knowledge, and support when trouble strikes. Not everyone is as fortunate as Reggie Beaty, who managed not to be "penalized with a life sentence" for his mistakes.

As CIS moves into the next decade, our focus will increasingly broaden to encompass "changing the rules" so that young people no longer face such overwhelming odds. Of course we'll continue to provide the support we always have, within the schoolhouse, but we're also going to advocate for policy change that will make young lives safer and their chances more equitable.

We're not only about helping kids overcome obstacles—we want to take the obstacles down.

CHAPTER 2

WHY THE DROPOUT CRISIS ISN'T JUST AN EDUCATION ISSUE

THE ADULT PROBLEM

On April 30, 1997, along with then president Bill Clinton, three former presidents, and former first lady Nancy Reagan, I was in Philadelphia for an extraordinary three-day event called The Presidents' Summit for America's Future. I'd greeted what felt like a thousand other dignitaries. I was so tired that I didn't think I could shake another hand.

Notable speakers—including Presidents Ford, Carter, Bush, and Clinton—presented their pictures of what America's youth needed and how the nation could meet those needs. General Colin Powell presided, and out of this forum was to come his America's Promise movement: a heartfelt initiative to connect youth across the land with vital resources.

I'd had the privilege of joining the general and others to help organize the April event, and the Summit team offered me the chance to be one of the speakers on the final day. I said yes, of course, although I was full of nerves and uncertainty. Day after day the speakers just got better and better. I realized that this was by far the most illustrious platform I'd ever been given. I wanted to make the most of it, but after weeks of intense effort in doing my small part to help pull the Summit together, I was several steps past exhausted. Not only that, but I'd had no time—not even 15 minutes—to sit down alone and decide what to say to this audience of national leaders.

When my turn came, I walked to the podium and realized that I still didn't know what to talk about. I've done a lot of public speaking and was just praying the words would come, but they didn't. I just stood there. I thought about the goodwill, the commitment, and the wealth of ideas represented in the audience. The past three days had been incredibly moving. In many ways, it was the convention I'd dreamed of attending for 30 years—and when I'm moved, I have trouble hiding it.

So I got choked up and tears began to flow. *Oh, great start, Milliken*, I thought, but then I found some words. I'm sure they were coming from a part of my brain I have no conscious control over. I said something like this: "All my life I've tried to do everything I could to be an advocate for young people and their needs. If you want to know what I've learned, here it is: we don't have a youth problem in America—we have an *adult* problem."

Even through my fatigue, I could see I'd hit a nerve. The room was silent. "I've never been trained as a teacher. I don't know how to give a course on male/female relations or Black/white/brown relations or anything like that. But I can tell you, I've seen kids start to eat together in a school cafeteria where whites and Blacks weren't sitting at the same table because they saw *adults* coming together who happened to be Black and white and brown, male and female, eating together and caring about one another. Kids learn from what they see, not just what they're taught. We can talk about values, but if we're not living them out, it won't matter. You can't give away what you don't have. If *we* don't care about each other—if *we* don't have community—how can we expect young people to do any better?"

I went on to talk about some of the basic principles of Communities In Schools, and it was wonderful to see how receptive the audience was. Then, after the Summit was over and I'd rested up, I thought more about this "adult problem" idea. I decided it was another way of explaining how Communities In Schools has viewed dropouts ever since its inception.

The dropout crisis is not just an education issue. It isn't just about schools, academics, curricula, and learning. There's a crisis because we adults have failed to provide and model a community that acts as a safety net for young people, ensuring that their needs are met. We can blame it on the educational system, but that's simplistic and, in fact, irresponsible. The schools have fallen into the vacuum that was created when everything else unraveled. We expect teachers and school administrators to be mother, father, sister, brother, counselor, social worker, good cop, bad cop—and also be great teachers.

This is impossible. The needs of millions of students are simply too large and too complicated for educators to handle alone. And it isn't their responsibility to do so anyway. They need a community of concerned adults to step forward and be their partners. We have to free teachers to do their jobs again. And that means creating safe, responsive learning environments for them, for school administrators, and ultimately for the students and their families.

In his July 26, 2006, column, *Washington Post* writer Courtland Milloy quoted Johnny W. Allem, a longtime advocate for addiction treatment in Washington: "Our failure to engage and prepare our young to cope and prosper as adults is a chain of many broken promises. Most visible is our broken school system. Less visible is our health, social service, and criminal justice systems. Our businesses and churches offer little hope for these citizens of tomorrow.

Allem's remark gets to the heart of the issue. It is indeed our failure—not just the kids', not just the parents', and not just the schools'. Many school systems are obviously in trouble, but it's the "less visible" structures that are broken as well.

I have to disagree with Allem's last point, though. It is precisely our businesses and faith communities, joining with social-service providers and volunteers, that can take the lead in offering not only hope but real accomplishments that can help our young people become prosperous citizens of tomorrow."[1]

School-community partnership is at the core of the Communities In Schools idea, as its name would suggest. The many helping services that young people and their families need are concentrated—or better, perhaps, to say diffused—in a wide array of social agencies, nonprofits, and volunteer groups throughout a typical community. The critical step is to get these services to students and families by using the school as the delivery point. Thus, the community we're building comprises partners and volunteers who can truly help; these are adults with the expertise and the mission to meet kids' needs.

Partnership begins in one-on-one relationships. You'd be amazed by what a difference it makes to simply get adults into the school building. I remember taking a couple of businesspeople on a tour of a school with a CIS presence, located in a very fragmented, violent community. We always invite students to meet visitors and give their input. One young man—on the surface, a really tough type—was with us when the guests asked the principal, "Why does this place feel so calm, so safe, in the midst of this troubled community?"

The kid spoke up: "There's so many damn adults in here, we *can't* get into trouble."

And it was true: In addition to the teachers and administrators, a dozen carefully screened volunteers came each day to meet with the kids during their free periods to help with homework or just to hang out. Social workers and health-care providers had office space they shared among themselves, and the students knew where to find them.

When the final bell sounded, the school didn't empty out. It got *more* crowded, as recreation specialists, tutors, and other caring adults arrived to supervise the various after-school programs available to students. And keeping watch over this beehive of activity was the CIS coordinator, whose unique role you'll learn more about in the pages ahead. Suffice it to say, he was the one who knew where everyone—kids and adults alike—fit into the big picture. And he was also the one who cared enough to stand outside the front door every morning and greet students by name.

The CIS coordinator at that school also brought life to a senior-citizen facility down the street. Not long ago, many of these elders would have been part of an extended family, still connected to the younger generations and playing a vital role in weaving the safety net for kids. But the trend in our society is toward fragmentation. Just as children are placed into "social institutions" such as day care and preschool at younger and younger ages, so too are older citizens often placed in isolated settings, removed from their neighborhoods and loved ones.

The elders in this particular facility were poor people, and the building they lived in and the care they received was also poor. They sat there, day after day, watching their soap operas and talking to each other with no purpose to their lives. They were literally dying because they had nothing to give themselves to. (This isn't always the case in senior-citizen homes, fortunately. The vibrant, effective ones offer many opportunities for volunteering and connection to the community.)

The CIS coordinator had the idea of asking the seniors to come down to the school and eat lunch with the students. These kids needed more "grandparenting," since their own extended families were broken down by the same forces that had placed the elders in such isolation. This program immediately made the lunchroom so much calmer. The seniors *were* like grandparents, and kids, as we all know, often respect grandparents more than their parents. They also knew that "Grandma" was going to be tougher than anyone. She very well might say, "I'm gonna tell your momma!" The students needed guidance, and the seniors needed a reason to live and something to give to. And, like all grandparents, they could get up after lunch and leave!

This is an example of doing more than delivering services, although that is, of course, a vital part of what CIS does. The coordinator brought *life* into that school. He took two fragmented institutions and, by bringing them together, helped make them whole. He created an opportunity for adults and children to love and care for one another, not just "give things." That's the most powerful attraction in the world—whether it occurs at home with parents, with an extended family, or with an even broader community of caring adults.

BACKING INTO EDUCATION

The dropout crisis isn't just an education issue—but our education system is the arena where the battle will be won or lost. So almost from the start, my street work has taken me into the world of education.

When I told the Presidents' Summit that I wasn't an educator, that was an understatement. A number of years ago, a CIS site was launched at my old high school, and I was invited back to cut the ribbon. The mayor was there, and he said, "I was in Bill's class. I know God has a great sense of humor—Bill's here to talk about education!"

The truth is that my colleagues and I got into the field because the kids needed it, not because we had any calling to be teachers. Helping young people get their diplomas was simply part of helping them learn how to live; a decent foundation in learning was one component among many that they were lacking. So we backed into education, just as we improvised so much else in our early days in New York City.

You couldn't have started a street worker program with two less experienced people than Vinnie Pasquale and me. I was immature and in many ways emotionally unstable, and the only work Vinnie had ever done before his part-time job at the Y was to push drugs.

But it's clear to me that a higher power—the source of the spiritual journey we were both on—took a hand in what happened, and somehow we kept finding the strength to take the next step. I had to learn to deal with rejection. For every kid who was willing to listen to me, two more would give me a very cold shoulder. I'd walk up to a guy on a park bench and he'd move away to avoid me. If I stuck out my hand to shake hands, he'd look away, pretending he didn't see. If I tried to join a group for basketball, everyone else would be chosen instead of me.

It was a lesson in humility, and in a funny way it also helped teach me even more about the power of personal relationships. It was these kids' refusal to relate or acknowledge I was even there that really hurt. At least if somebody yelled at me or gave me a hard time, there was interaction, dialogue—I could get something going, start *some* kind of relationship, look each other in the eye.

During our second summer in New York City, Vinnie decided to go back to school, which he'd left in the eighth grade. I needed a new apartment mate, and I joined forces with a great guy from Young Life named Dean Borgman, an ex-paratrooper from Connecticut. Like me, he'd hung around with a bunch of suburban kids in trouble with the law both before and after his tour of duty. After hooking up with Young Life and getting a new perspective on his life, he came to New York to work toward a doctorate on the G.I. Bill, and he began teaching high school while doing graduate work at Columbia.

Dean and I found a new home, an apartment at 215 Madison Street on the Lower East Side, thanks to Dr. Eugene Callender, senior pastor of Church of the Master in Harlem. Dr. Callender had given us one of our first footholds in Harlem by "blessing" us through his church, and he also had connections at Trinity Parish, a big Episcopal community on Wall Street. One of their missions was called St. Christopher's Chapel, and through the chapel's generosity, Dean and I received free rent on Madison Street. We also got free meals at the church each evening for ourselves and the young people we took in. Our little kitchen wouldn't have been able to handle a real supper, but the church gave us a place to come for sustenance and a sense of community.

It was there, at 215 Madison, that we began to create relationships, safe places, and healthy—or at least healthier—starts for young people in 1960s New York. But the question continued to haunt us: How can we say that we care about these kids when they've got an eighth-grade education at 18 years old? Like it or not, we were going to have to become "educators." And if we couldn't do that, we'd have to find some real teachers to work with us.

Our partner Harv Oostdyk had become friendly with a retired public school principal who asked us straight out, "Why don't you start your own school? You could hold classes to prepare the students to pass the high school equivalency exams and get their GED (General Educational Development) certification." Harv liked the idea, and with his typical passion and brilliance, he found a way to make it happen.

As best I can remember, no one was using the term "storefront school" back then. Harv's inspiration was to rent a commercial space right on the street and hold classes there to tutor the kids. When you're young, you don't know what "won't work," so we didn't see the difficulties, just the excitement and possibilities. And it was such a natural extension of the logic that had motivated us ever since we began working in New York: If you care about kids and they're sleeping on rooftops, get them a place to live. If they're 18 years old and can't read or write . . .

So Harv started a storefront school up in Harlem, and others of us stayed on the Lower East Side, renting an old warehouse building under a bridge. It was a "white elephant," but we painted it blue, so it was called the Blue Elephant. Julian Robertson, one of our earliest and most loyal business supporters, and some others on the Young Life committee raised money so that we could rent it in the fall of 1965. It was two floors of decrepitude, but we fixed it up as best we could. The neighborhood was terrible; a few years later, Senator Richard Lugar, then mayor of Indianapolis, came as a guest of the Lilly Endowment to check out our work, and the cab driver didn't want to take him there. The senator managed to talk him into it, liked what he saw, and was later instrumental in helping start Communities In Schools.

The Blue Elephant needed teachers, and fortunately for us, the times were right for a whole cadre of college students from Columbia, Princeton, and New York University to volunteer their time. We welcomed them, but none of us were under any illusion that it would be easy. Our student body was exclusively composed of dropouts and street kids.

We held classes on the second floor of the Blue Elephant, but before a young person was allowed to go upstairs, they had to spend time with us on the ground floor, learning basic life skills and disciplines. Part of that involved a hard look at their spiritual lives, too. These kids needed to be *turned on to living* before we could *turn them on to learning.*

We had a concept called the Steps of Life: The first step was to take responsibility for yourself, no matter how rough your situation. Then we urged the kids to look around and realize that they weren't alone—they had a community of peers and adults who were in this with them, and together they could make it happen.

We adapted a practice from our home at 215 Madison and took it to the Blue Elephant: "family meetings" to talk about our differences; discuss how to help each other rather than hurt each other; and find out who was in trouble, who was facing up to problems, and who was skirting the truth. These kids knew they were in deep trouble, that they'd taken the wrong direction. We organized the potential students into small discussion groups where the first order of business was to help them talk about the often poisonous emotions that nearly two decades of rejection and pain had created.

The most frequent question we asked was: "Why are you angry?" We confronted them about drugs: "I know you're still sneaking off and using smack. The only thing that will get you kicked out of here is lying about it. Tell us if you screwed up and we'll try to help you." Lying is the number one thing that will break down community, and all of us—teachers and students alike—had to learn this the hard way.

The next step was to replace these negative mindsets with *hope*. We coined a slogan: "Hope is the antidote to dope," and slowly these kids came to believe it. Equally important was an emphasis on *dignity* and *respect*. We insisted that everyone who came through the door of the Blue Elephant—students, teachers, family, and street workers—be treated with respect. Those who couldn't do this (and that included some of the adults, too) were asked to come back when they were ready. These kids needed to believe in their hearts that they were accepted and afforded dignity for who they were, no matter what grade level they read at or what their home life was like. There was nothing to be ashamed of, and everyone could learn.

But we discovered that our students had almost no conception of why they ought to be back in school. "*Why* do you want to learn?" we kept asking them. We knew that we had to give them a clear grasp of the outcomes—jobs, security, a sense of self-worth, and a basis on which to raise a family—before they'd be willing to stick it out and pay the price of discipline and perseverance. We had to expose the myths of easy money on the streets: "Sure, you can make a lot dealing drugs for a year or two, but open your eyes and look at reality. The dealers you thought were so cool when you were younger are all dead or in jail. There's no hope and no future in that."

Another important tactic to help these kids answer the question "Why learn?" was to make the Blue Elephant truly *their* school. We tried to involve them in everything from painting the building and routine maintenance to decision-making about schedules and the pace of learning. Sure enough, a sense of community started to form. We called them "a gang for good," and they found they could rely on each other for encouragement. Their pride was apparent, and they began to enjoy spreading the word among their friends on the street. To our amazement, learning became the "in thing," and the storefront school became the place to go if you wanted to be hip. One of our students on the way to school would pass an idling friend, point a finger at him, and say, "Smart up!" Soon enough, our entire enrollment was word of mouth. Kids were coming to the Blue Elephant, asking to be part of it.

I don't mean to imply that we had a 100 percent success rate. It wasn't even close to that, and a lot of kids simply couldn't make it, but our successes grew as we learned to get tougher and shake off the temptation to be paternalistic. Excuses were unacceptable. Hard as it was, we had to look young people in the eye and say, "I don't care how bad you had it. A lot of people have it bad. You still have a responsibility to yourselves and to your younger brothers and sisters to succeed."

CALL THEM ACADEMIES

Over the next five years, Harv and his colleagues in Harlem opened more and more storefront schools there. By the end of the '60s, we had schools in Harlem and Bedford–Stuyvesant and on the Lower East Side. It was a time of amazing changes for us—and for me personally. I married my longtime Pittsburgh sweetheart, Jean. As she soon discovered, our wedding meant "marrying" all the young folks at 215 Madison, too.

But we got a place of our own, and in 1968 our son, Sean, was born. Two years later, Jean had a miscarriage, which led us both to wonder if God was pointing the way toward adoption. Almost at once, we had the great fortune to adopt a lovely six-week-old girl whom we named Lani.

Meanwhile, the storefront schools continued to evolve. At some point Harv and I realized that we probably shouldn't give our schools unorthodox names like "the Blue Elephant" or "Liberation School" (another popular choice). We asked around: What do wealthy, successful people call their schools? The answer was *academies,* so that was what we called ours.

We also needed a base in the community, since we couldn't run schools under the auspices of Young Life. Dr. Callender from Church of the Master in Harlem was now the head of the New York City Urban League. Harv approached him and he agreed to sponsor our new work as educators, so all of a sudden we could boast of Urban League Street Academies.

At the same time, Harv and I began to get to know more of the Wall Street business leaders who'd occasionally shown interest in our work. This was facilitated, sadly, by the riots that hit New York City in the mid-'60s. These events were a wake-up call to many business leaders. They realized that the larger world out there beyond Wall Street was in big trouble, and—sometimes out of enlightened self-interest but more often out of genuine concern and desire to contribute—they were very open to finding ways to partner with street workers like us.

Young Life supporters such as Julian Robertson, who'd helped us get financing for the Blue Elephant, were willing to build bridges for us. At the time, Julian was working at Kidder, Peabody (the securities and investment-banking firm), and he and several of his colleagues were involved at Trinity Parish, which supported us at 215 Madison . . . so gradually the connections were made. This was a big realization for me: relationships are the key *everywhere.* Wall Street is a street like any other, and what I'd learned on the streets of the Lower East Side worked here as well. Our hanging-out skills remained our biggest asset.

Once we were established with the Urban League, thanks to Harv and Dr. Callender, there was an additional incentive for the business community to take part. It was one of those moments of synchronicity—you had major corporations looking for ways to help the community, and here we were with a program that was in place and achieving success.

By 1968, 16 corporations—including American Express, Time, Morgan Guaranty, Chase Manhattan, Union Carbide, and Burlington Mills—were convinced that business needed to build bridges to its neighbors, and each funded one of the academies.

We also developed four "prep schools": Lower East Side Prep, Harambee Prep, Newark Prep, and Harlem Prep, which became known as places where everyone was expected to go on to college. The whole prep-school idea was again borrowed from our sense of what wealthy people called their elite institutions. Well, these were for *our* elite—students who'd shown exceptional promise in the academies and could clearly do well in a college environment if they had a regular high school diploma. So the prep schools were accredited by the school system, and our graduates, armed with a "normal" diploma, found acceptance at colleges around the country. It was a wonderful evolution for the Street Academies, which had no accreditation and worked to prepare students to take the GED exam.

I continued to stay in touch with Vinnie Pasquale, by the way. He'd gotten his degree, married, and gone on to work with kids through the YMCA. Tragically, he died just a few years later, suffering a heart attack on a basketball court while doing what he loved best: hanging out with, and giving hope to, young people.

The "Street Academy movement," as it came to be known, has since been called "the most imitated social program of the 1960s" by the Ford Foundation. And it's true that outside-the-system academies (started both by us and by others) sprang up in many cities during the period from the mid-'60s to the early '70s. In fact, the small- or alternative-school movement has never really stopped. Today the country has thousands of such initiatives.

Proud as we were of our successes back then, we saw two things with increasing clarity:

- Dropouts had already been scarred by the failures of the system; their road back was tough.

- For all our accomplishments, more and more kids kept quitting school. Our storefront academies couldn't begin to handle the flood of young people who needed a second chance.

So the answer was obvious, although incredibly difficult to implement: we had to find a way to move our operation *inside* the public schools and reach potential dropouts *before* they quit.

There was another benefit to this approach. When you get right down to it, school is where most of the kids are. It's a lot easier to reach them there than on the streets—although it took us more than a decade to admit this. Being "anti-establishment" had a high value in the '60s. We were reluctant to become part of a system we perceived as negligent and unjust. But we had to acknowledge that it was crucial to find a way to stop the wave of dropouts before they overwhelmed our—or anyone else's—ability to respond. We wanted to inoculate kids against the dropout epidemic rather than try to cure them after they'd fallen victim to the disease.

> This is a lot of ground to cover. Let me pause to repeat three key points here.
>
> 1. The dropout crisis isn't just an education issue. It reflects the failure of the adult community.
>
> 2. Students at risk of dropping out have needs that are too pressing and too complicated for educators to handle alone. Again, a group of concerned adults must join forces with schools to meet these needs.
>
> 3. Delivering services *at the school* is the critical step that adults can take, forming a community that can provide the resources kids and families need.

I've tried to make it clear that my colleagues and I didn't sit down and think up these insights. We learned them through experience, slowly and painfully. So, rather than offer more theory, I want to tell you about a living example of the principles I'm discussing. The setting is Los Angeles, and no movie studio could have dreamed up such a story. It begins in tragedy and grows into an odyssey of redemption and hope for thousands of the most despised young people in America: the violent gangs of the San Fernando Valley.

PEACE IN THE VALLEY?

The news came to Blinky Rodriguez and his wife, Lilly, at 12:15 A.M. on a Saturday morning in 1990. The phone rang, and when Blinky answered, a young man said, "I'm at the hospital. Something happened to Sonny."

The Rodriguezes found themselves in a car driving down to a hospital in Mission Hills. When they arrived, a priest came to meet them. "Mr. and Mrs. Rodriguez," he said, "we have a body in Room 2, and we need you to identify it."

Their 16-year-old son was dead, murdered in a drive-by shooting by Pacoima gangbangers.

"It dug a deep, deep trench in our lives," Blinky says. Community violence, which the Rodriguezes had tried so hard to channel in productive ways through their commitment to sports in the San Fernando Valley, had shattered their family.

Blinky is a man of faith, and he knew that he had to make a response that would honor his son and—somehow—bring good out of evil. He resolved to do the impossible: bring peace to the Valley's 75 gangs.

The San Fernando Valley had three million inhabitants. Were it an independent city (an initiative rejected by voters a few years before), it would be the sixth largest in the U.S. It was, and is, an astonishingly diverse and complex world.

It was also a very different place from the Valley that William "Blinky" Rodriguez grew up in during the 1960s. ("Blinky," by the way, is an Anglicization of an affectionate name given to him as a toddler by his grandmother.) Back then there were clubs, not gangs—car clubs, mostly, with guys competing to see whose ride could outpace the rest. Guns on the street were almost unheard of, and school was a smaller and more personal place.

One day when he was 16, Blinky was sent to the vice principal's office for refusing to strip down for gym class. "I'd heard that this guy, Jack Jacobson, swung a mean paddle, so when I walked into his office, I immediately assumed the position. 'What are you doing?' he asked. I looked back over my shoulder at him and replied, 'Aren't you going to give me a swat?' 'No, sit down,' he told me."

It turned out that the dean of discipline was more interested in finding out *why* Blinky was in trouble than administering punishment. He finally got the youngster to admit that he was ashamed to take off his shoes and socks because he had a raging case of athlete's foot. Jacobson immediately took him off campus to the nearest drugstore and bought him a new pair of sneakers, a pair of white socks, and his first can of Desenex.

After this demonstration of concern, it was no wonder that Blinky bonded with Jacobson. He learned that the vice principal's extracurricular passion was martial arts, so the teen began taking classes.

He was a natural. Focusing on kickboxing as his sport of choice, in a matter of years he became one of the great U.S. champions and the foremost pioneer to introduce the pastime to millions of new fans. He met his wife, Lilly (also a world-champion boxer and kickboxer), and they became the first husband and wife ever to perform on a professional boxing show. Their son, Sonny, was born in 1974, the first of five children.

Blinky's kickboxing gym was state of the art, and a stone's throw from the neighborhood of his youth. He made sure to offer scholarships to neighborhood kids and preach the message that the discipline of sports was a priceless way to learn values such as integrity, perseverance, and fairness.

"I had a heartbeat for working with this population," he says. "You can't just incarcerate them when they do wrong."

Then Sonny was shot dead.

The story, as Blinky eventually pieced it together, was both ridiculous and tragic. Sonny and his girlfriend were riding in her car; she was teaching him how to drive. Busy with the lesson, neither noticed that they'd driven into an off-limits neighborhood. It was the wrong turf, "belonging" to a Pacoima gang. This sign of disrespect ignited tempers, and a young life ended.

Blinky made his vow to end the violence in a community that saw a gang-on-gang killing nearly every day. But there was a step that needed to come first. "Lilly and I had to forgive the three men who murdered our son," he says matter-of-factly. His faith gave him the strength to do this publicly, at their trial. "Father Offers Forgiveness," the headlines read, and it triggered a reaction in the community that further strengthened Blinky's new mission.

He began helping gang members leave their violent lifestyles behind, walking the streets and preaching "to anyone who would listen, trying to speak some sense to all the nonsense." Aided by Donald "Big D" Garcia, a friend who'd spent 31 years behind bars and understood the culture, Blinky made his kickboxing gym a safe place for youths to come for counseling and support. He opened his home to Bible study groups and soon had more than 100 young people from six gangs.

He also began acting as a moderator between rival gangs. The Pacoima ones knew Blinky had publicly forgiven their "homies" for gunning down his son, and it added immeasurably to his credibility as a spokesperson for peace. Others, of course, knew him as a legendary figure in the martial arts. Eventually, gang members formed a peace treaty council and, with Blinky's help, began their peacemaking efforts. On October 31, 1993, representatives of all 75 gangs—with a population of more than 1,000—signed the treaty at a huge gathering at a local church. Celebrities such as Jane Goodall and Stevie Wonder were there, and community members covered the stage with roses.

The treaty called for leaders to bring any divisive issues to a weekly facilitation meeting before resorting to violence. Gang representatives also exchanged phone numbers and pledged to call each other to inquire about perceived insults or signs of disrespect before assuming the worst.

The truce was inaugurated with a football game in February 1994 between rival gangs, attended by city officials and hosted by Blinky and Donald Garcia. Big D was dubious at first: "Come on, Blinky, these guys are gangbangers. They don't want to play football!" Just watch, Blinky told him—and he was right. Everyone wanted in. YMCA officials were recruited to wear the "zebra" shirts, a business supporter sprang for jerseys for the players, and a city councilman presided at the kickoff. All told, more than 600 people participated.

During the year that followed, the number of Latino gang-on-gang killings dropped from 52 to 2. Members turned to football to release aggression and attended intense group meetings to air grievances. As Blinky put it, "A game is more than a one-time event—it creates a forum for relationships and dialogue."

Blinky came up with a phrase to celebrate the treaty. It touches my heart every time I hear it, and it became a rallying cry for hundreds of other anti-gang-violence efforts across the country: "No mothers crying and no babies dying."

You may be thinking, *This guy is amazing, but what exactly does his story have to do with schools?* In fact, Blinky wondered the same thing. He was having an experience very similar to mine back in New York. It was all well and good to work solo, trying to stop gang members from killing each other, but wasn't there a way to reach more kids earlier—to stop gang membership before it started, before lives were lost?

Blinky knew a guy named Robert "Bobby" Arias, who happened to be the Southwest regional director for Communities In Schools. Bobby was based in LA, and his daughter was a cheerleader for the Pop Warner football league one of Blinky's children played in. One day when both fathers were attending a game, Blinky challenged Bobby Arias: "You're doing this great work for kids in California— what about your own backyard? What about the Valley?" And Bobby threw back the challenge: "Your mission is great, too, but you need to get organized, become a registered nonprofit, and get some funding. You and Big D can't keep doing this all by yourselves."

It was a true meeting of the minds. Before he knew it, Blinky found himself the executive director of the newly formed CIS of the San Fernando Valley. It was his first exposure to the principles of CIS, but in a sense he already knew them. Pull together a caring community of adults (just as he'd done at that first football game and dozens of times since), show them working together for something they care about, and young people would want to be part of it.

Gang members weren't monsters; they weren't evil, no matter how much harm they did and however much the community reviled them. So many times I've heard Blinky tell an audience: "They're *kids*, man! Do you realize the bullcrap they have to navigate growing up? The violence in movies, music, video games? The disrespect and immorality of society? It's not 'the way it used to be' anymore—it's not even close. Think about that before you demonize these kids."

Blinky's karate and kickboxing students were a good place to start building the community of adults he needed. Many were judges, attorneys, and businesspeople, and their respect for Blinky was high. They were willing to listen to this new thing called Communities In Schools. Two influential churches—one affluent, the other a street ministry—also lent critical support.

"It's not just one punch that's going to do it," Blinky says. "It's the setup, the combination of punches." Perhaps the most important pieces of the fledgling CIS community were the Los Angeles Police Department and the county's gang-prevention and probation agencies, which recognized a natural ally in Blinky and lent their wholehearted support to CIS's work in schools.

Today, the CIS effort in Los Angeles is under the leadership of Executive Director Elmer G. Roldan. This affiliate now works in 13 schools, serving over 5,000 students. Community partners are in place to provide youth the resources they'll need to get out and stay out of gangs, remain in school, and find their place as productive citizens. Site coordinators within these schools "collaborate with community partners and businesses to recruit volunteers for tutoring programs, build up clothing closets with support from local businesses, or connect struggling families with much-needed medical attention—just to name a few."[2]

Community building through sports remained a centerpiece of Blinky's work with CIS. In 2003, he sponsored a softball tournament featuring six gang teams, a team of LAPD officers, and a team fielded from the Los Angeles County Gang Probation Unit. That tournament became an annual event. And Blinky kicked off 170 gang-versus-gang football games since the first one in 1994.

The heart of his work remained his commitment to stop the plague of gang violence, keep kids in school, and prepare them for life. The state of California named CIS of Greater Los Angeles a model gang-prevention program. In 1999, Blinky and Lilly flew to Geneva, Switzerland, to receive the Medaille d'Excellence at the 50th anniversary of the United Nations' Universal Declaration of Human Rights.

I can't improve on Blinky's eloquent description of how he connects with the kids society has demonized: "Speak the truth, speak to their hearts and minds, and breathe hope and vision. We're a community for youth."

BEFORE THE THREE *R*'S

Blinky Rodriguez is one of the most extraordinary people I know, and his story moves me every time I hear it. But there's another reason I wanted to introduce you to him and his work.

I've said that the dropout crisis isn't just an education issue. I can't think of a clearer illustration of this than the story you've just read. Can anyone really believe that the thousands of Los Angeles gang-involved or gang-threatened youth who leave school every year are quitting because they "don't like school" or are "challenged academically"? **They are dropping out because of gangs.** The gangs got there first, offering a community (however flawed) that many young people deeply crave. And for many others, it is simply unsafe to go to school while such groups own the streets. Getting from home to school may involve crossing hostile turf, and as Sonny Rodriguez found out, that's a mortal danger. To keep these kids in school, you're going to have to provide a viable alternative to the terrible dilemma they face. *Then* you can work on academic success. Blinky began by intervening on the streets, then moved his efforts into the school through CIS, but it's all part of the same big picture.

Not every community is victimized by gang violence, but this basic model is true for virtually any other roadblock to graduation you can name. We learned it back at the Blue Elephant: *Kids need to be turned on to living before you can turn them on to learning.* Whether it's drug addiction, family dysfunction, lack of health care, homelessness, joblessness, or plain poverty, the strategy must be the same: meet these pressing needs *first*, and then young people can concentrate on the three *R*'s.

Communities In Schools has a name for the nonacademic needs of students. We call them the Five Basics, and they're the subject of the next chapter.

///

. . . AND BEYOND

At CIS's January 2020 board meeting, the members were asked to envision the single "headline" we want to see written about CIS in the next five years. Rey Saldaña offered this: "Communities In Schools is working within the system to change the way schools are built." And I came up with "Rebuilding public education from the bottom up."

Rey and I are singing variations on the same theme here. CIS practitioners have known for 40 years that the dropout crisis (and all the other negative outcomes that students face) is not just an education issue. Now we're willing to commit resources and energy to change, to rebuilding the very nature of a public school. Rey and I talk a lot more about this in the Afterword. It's an exciting, challenging, and absolutely necessary expansion of the CIS mission.

\\

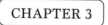
BEFORE THE THREE *R*'S . . . THE REAL BASICS

WHAT EVERY CHILD NEEDS

If you're a parent, you're probably far too busy ever to sit down with a pencil and paper and make a list of what your children need. It isn't really necessary anyway. You address your kids' needs as they come, day by day. Parenting is complicated and demanding enough without trying to write it all down.

But imagine what such a list might look like: nutritious food, regular checkups, recreation, affirmation of your children's gifts and abilities, clear rules to keep them safe ("Don't cross the street in the middle of the block"), strong ethical guidance ("Be kind to people and animals"), constant reassurance that they're secure and cared about ("I love you and you can always trust me to have your best interests at heart").

These are the sorts of things our children need; they're what *all* children need. If you combined the dozens of daily needs into a few key groups, you might come up with this:

Every young person needs and deserves:

1. A one-on-one relationship with a caring adult

2. A safe place to learn and grow

3. A healthy start and a healthy future

4. A marketable skill to use upon graduation

5. A chance to give back to peers and community

Communities In Schools calls these the Five Basics. Our experience has shown us that if these things aren't addressed, kids are going to have a hard time succeeding in school. The first three in particular need attention *early*—the seeds of dropping out are sown long before students reach their teen years. Children can't begin to learn if they're convinced that nobody cares about them, that they're worthless and unsafe physically and emotionally. Nor can they concentrate on schoolwork if their most basic needs— nutrition, shelter, health care, and the like—aren't being met.

It's certainly true that most of the kids we reach through CIS are from poor families, often victimized by multigenerational poverty. And low-income families equal "bad" neighborhoods and underfunded schools, so they're also frequently bearing the burden of decrepit, dangerous school buildings, outdated textbooks, and, sometimes, unqualified teachers.

But when we say that every child needs the Five Basics, we really mean *every* child. Suburban kids from middle-class homes are also at risk of quitting school if they don't get the essentials. My own example shows that clearly enough. I grew up in a nice house, but it wasn't a home. My parents didn't or couldn't discover what I needed; alcoholism and emotional dysfunction wrecked my home. I seldom had an evening meal with my family—they were too busy. That's true for many families who are running around so much that they don't have time to create a genuine sense of home.

Pain-filled, dysfunctional households send kids to school in bad shape. It doesn't matter how much money a family has. Poverty can create dreadful childhoods, but so can abusive, uncaring parenting in $500,000 "starter castles."

So I strongly believe that the Five Basics are what *every* child needs and deserves. At the same time, I'm not trying to say that poor families and those who are well-off are starting at "Go" with the same chance for success. That's not so, and the well-being of children is perhaps the number one justice issue in America today.

You can argue back and forth, depending on your politics, about what kind of assistance, if any, poor adults may need. The debate usually hinges on questions of personal responsibility. But children are a different story. A five-year-old girl who goes to school hungry isn't going to learn anything about "personal responsibility" (let alone anything about the three *R*'s) if she continues to go unfed. It won't be good for her character; it won't do anything except hurt her. Denying her what she needs is, quite simply, unjust. She has done nothing wrong—other than to be born in a ghetto, on a failing farm, or in a former mining community with no more work to offer adults. And blaming her parents won't help either.

I applaud the school-reform movement for insisting that "no child should be left behind" and "every student must succeed." But to believe that every child comes to school with the same resources and support is wishful thinking. It flies in the face of the grim reality: millions of American children are uninsured, underfed, and unprepared to take that walk to school.

THE FIRST BASIC

As I've said, I wouldn't be here today without a positive relationship with a caring adult. The First Basic, "a one-on-one relationship with a caring adult," remains the cornerstone and the most directly experiential of all Five Basics. Think about your own life. There was someone—a parent, an uncle, a teacher, a coach, or perhaps a faith community leader—who cared enough about you to hang in with you and be real.

Today, mentors are the most common and successful means for providing the First Basic to students. Programs in schools in particular have repeatedly shown their effectiveness. Dr. Jean Rhodes's article "School-Based Mentoring" (written for MENTOR, formerly the National Mentoring Partnership, an organization CIS is proud to partner with) reviews the literature and provides clear evidence to supplement the intuitive sense we all have that positive relationships with adults make a big difference:

- School-based mentoring programs sponsored by Big Brothers Big Sisters show "substantial improvements in students' school performance, attendance, confidence, attitudes, expression, trust, respect, and relationships with adults. Because they correlated with report card data, these impressions appeared to be grounded in actual progress. Youth in longer-lasting relationships enjoyed additional academic benefits."

- A research study by Public/Private Ventures found that school-based mentoring produced "improvements in the students' behavior (particularly academic), attitudes, and self-confidence. About half of the parents interviewed reported that their children had made significant academic improvements subsequent to being involved in the program. Teachers noted that children improved in a range of subjects, including math, reading, social studies, and citizenship. Three of the four teachers also mentioned increased confidence as a common area of improvement."[1]

We know that "young people do best when they experience strong, positive relationships in all parts of their lives."[2] As a Search Institute publication states:

A great deal of research from numerous scholars in many different settings offer evidence that support this claim. Research to date shows that young people who experience strong developmental relationships across different parts of their lives are more likely to show signs of positive development in many areas, including:

- Increased academic motivation;
- Increased social-emotional growth and learning;
- Increased sense of personal responsibility; and
- Reduced engagement in a variety of high-risk behaviors.[3]

THE SECOND BASIC

The Second Basic, "a safe place to learn and grow," also developed out of personal experience. The kids we worked with in New York City lacked that most basic of needs: a roof over their heads. And that's often true of young people today, too. The National Center for Homeless Education reports that "during the 2019–20 school year, public schools identified about 1,281,000 students who experienced homelessness. That's 2.5 percent of all students enrolled in public schools."[4]

Even more children, however, need safe places in addition to their homes. While the issue of violence inside schools has been, in my opinion, exaggerated and sensationalized, it's true that too many of them pose physical and emotional dangers to students, and a climate of hostility and threat must be faced directly. The best solution, as I noted earlier, is to bring so many caring adults into the building that kids *can't* get into trouble. It's also extremely important not to let schools grow so large that individual students get lost and become potential victims of cliques and bullies.

Equally important, though, is the question of safe neighborhoods and communities. When children are afraid to walk to school and have nowhere to go and nothing to do after school hours, the Second Basic isn't being met.

There are many positive and successful responses to this situation. One of the best is the new enthusiasm for using schools as true community centers and creating before- and after-school programs that give kids—and their families—a safe and productive place to spend time. The Afterschool Alliance has concluded from its research that such programs have strongly positive outcomes, including:

- Improved school attendance and engagement in learning
- Improved test scores and grades
- Greatest gains for the students at greatest risk
- Best results correlated with frequency and duration of after-school participation

The behavioral outcomes are equally conclusive; these programs succeed in:

- Keeping children safe
- Having a positive impact on children's self-concept and decision-making
- Helping working families and encouraging parental participation
- Reducing truancy and improving behavior in school[5]

One of the themes we'll look at in the next chapter is the critical importance of coordinating and interweaving all of the Five Basics rather than regarding them as isolated "fixes" for students' issues. With that in mind, consider this reminder from MENTOR:

Although not fully appreciated, after-school settings provide wonderful opportunities for the formation of informal mentoring relationships. Faced with fewer curricular demands than teachers, the staff who work in after-school programs have unique opportunities to engage in the sorts of informal conversations and activities that give rise to close bonds with youth. Similarly, working parents, who are often stretched to their limits by job and family, rarely have the luxury of spending hours of quality "downtime" with their children each afternoon. In fact, there is growing consensus that caring youth-staff relationships may be a key determinant of both retention and success in after-school programming.[6]

THE THIRD BASIC

Children need to be healthy—physically, emotionally, spiritually. My understanding of the Third Basic, "a healthy start and a healthy future," was born out of the catastrophe of drug addiction among the young people of Harlem and the Lower East Side. Vinnie, Dean, and I could often get kids out of the street gangs. But, ironically, at that time those very groups offered a kind of community that had kept the members clean. Drugs and gangs didn't mix back then. You couldn't be a reliable member if you were getting high. So the downside of breaking up gangs was that the kids, now isolated, turned to heroin to relieve their pain.

Drugs were everywhere, starting with pot and alcohol for the little kids—eight-, nine-, and ten-year-old addicts were commonplace. The ruined lives are almost impossible to comprehend unless you've seen them yourself. If you want to destroy a community, a nation, this is the way. There were few treatment options back then, no fancy rehab clinics and no Narcotics Anonymous. Sometimes I could persuade a kid to check into a hospital, where the medical staff might or might not know how to help him or care whether he got help.

More often it was "cold turkey." I never want to sit through that again, watching helplessly for hours while a young person shivered and screamed and wept in our apartment at 215 Madison. You can't insulate yourself from that kind of pain—it changes you forever. And the worst of it was, a kid might come out of the hospital or leave the apartment, hit the street, and a few hours later be high again. The pressure of reality, of the life he or she was faced with, was too much.

Over the years I saw a lot of young people die. I spoke at a lot of funerals. Kids would do their best but then start lying about it and get back on drugs. This is when the whole concept of "tough love" began emerging, and *Tough Love* was the title of my first book, published in 1968. I knew it was the only kind of caring that would work under those conditions. Dean and I had to find the courage to say what a good father would tell his children: "I don't care how this makes you feel toward me. You may hate my guts, but I love you, and I'm doing this because I love you. I don't expect you to understand right now, but I have to do it anyway. Either tell the truth about whether you're getting high or move out."

When we were too afraid to be tough, we usually lost the kid. At the same time, we had to learn when to take on the traditional "mothering" roles as well, doing our best to provide emotional nurturing and hot meals.

Drugs and alcohol are still a huge challenge to growing up healthy, but so are the less dramatic dangers: poor eyesight, asthma, lack of proper nutrition, and teeth that hurt so much that a kid bangs his head against the wall. (I saw this happen.) As we launched the first Communities In Schools sites, we knew we'd have to take this on in a very direct way. It was another major impetus for us to create *partnerships*: If we weren't educators, we certainly weren't doctors either. It was vital that community health centers, along with volunteer nurses, physicians, dentists, ophthalmologists, and therapists, be linked through the school site with their young patients.

One eight-year-old girl's statement says more about the value of the Third Basic than any words of mine. She was asked why her grades had improved so much in the second semester of the school year. Touching her new eyeglasses, she said happily, "I can see the blackboard!"

THE FOURTH BASIC

The Fourth Basic, "a marketable skill to use upon graduation," sprang directly from our early experiences as "educators." We knew that young people needed a high school diploma to become part of mainstream American society. We also discovered that kids needed a *reason* to get that certification—they had to be given reasons to hope, to believe in themselves. It isn't enough to say, "Well, reading, writing, and math are good things, and people expect you to know them, so please spend the next five years studying." We had to help create concrete goals for our students, and usually that involved helping them think about career paths. If we could get them to see that education led to skills that would earn them money and give them a way out of poverty, it was a big motivational step.

I've known some people who are skeptical about this. They believe that poor kids, especially those from urban environments, are all about the easy allure of drug money and crime-based lifestyles. While it's true that those role models need to be explicitly debunked, the idea that "inner-city youth would rather deal drugs than work" is a middle-class myth. Most of these kids are just like you and me: They don't want to feel their heart going 50 miles an hour, desperately afraid that they might be shot down in a drug deal. They want to live. They'd much rather learn the skills that qualify them for legitimate work and a path to a future, even if the jobs pay less money than illegal activity.

Fifty years ago, graduating from high school with a marketable skill represented an excellent start. Even dropouts could find work, with luck. Today, the world is different. Our Fourth Basic is about careers, and that means it has to be about higher education, too. Fewer and fewer options are available without a college degree; dropouts are two to three times more likely to be unemployed than are college graduates.[7]

Another way of stating this principle might be: "Every child needs and deserves a clear career path to follow upon graduation from high school." Naturally enough, the majority of our CIS sites around the country are concentrating on helping kids get into college as part of providing this Basic. They're also connecting students with high-quality career-preparation programs to train them for future employment markets.

THE FIFTH BASIC

Of all the Five Basics, it's the last one, "a chance to give back to peers and community," that surprises many people. Once you accept the idea that kids need some nonacademic bedrock on which to stand before they can succeed in school, the first four ideas are pretty intuitive. As I said, it's no different from what you'd want for your own children. But the Fifth Basic, while equally critical, isn't always so obvious. Yet receiving young people's gifts is the key to helping them find their own identity, meaning, and self-worth.

Many years ago I was part of a panel invited to testify at a government hearing about the plight of the education system. Sometimes I feel that these gatherings are totally irrelevant; they call them "hearings" because nobody's listening. This one was the usual scene: people making speeches, talking past each other, and looking good for the cameras. Finally, in the last minute or so, I was asked: "What's the difference between the kids you've seen make it and those who haven't?"

I spent the first 30 of the 60 seconds I'd been allotted dealing with my anger and pain. Somehow it just seemed outrageous that a politician wanted me to sum up decades of one-on-one successes and failures in a tidy sound bite. Then I said, "The ones who made it did so because we *allowed* them to make it."

"What do you mean?"

"I mean that **the greatest gift you can give someone is to allow them to give something to *you*.**"

That's what the Fifth Basic is.

One-on-one, there's an incredible, precious thing that happens to young people when they find out they have a gift that somebody else values. They may be feeling all this hatred, hostility, and anger, and then suddenly they see that a grown-up wants to *receive* something from them. An adult *values* an ability or talent or gift of theirs. This, by the way, is one of the reasons why it's such a mistake to cut funding for arts programs in schools. You're eliminating so many opportunities for students to discover a talent they'd never dreamed of.

If you don't think kids have anything to give you—if you think you're better off than they are in this area, with all *your* gifts— then you'd better stay away from young people, because you'll do them more harm than good. You do have things to contribute, but children have plenty to share with you, too. It's a two-way street.

One-way help isn't always beneficial. You can destroy people and keep them in poverty by "helping" them, especially if your attitude screams out: *Here I am sharing my abilities with you, who have none!* And consider the effect of this kind of belief on communities that, for generations, have been on the receiving end of impersonal, paternalistic "help" from various governmental sources. By emphasizing the *value* of giving back, we also emphasize the *responsibility* to do so.

We have to learn how to receive as well as give. I'm still working on it. I like the image of myself as "someone who helps others." It's a lot harder to identify and accept my own vulnerabilities and limitations and admit that I need to receive something from you. But to help, to give, is a profound spiritual need, and an eight-year-old boy in Appalachia feels it just as strongly as any of the rest of us do.

It's not always easy. You have to start by believing in that young person and finding the patience and love to get beyond his hostility, pain, or shame—whatever may be keeping him from embracing his gifts. When a kid discovers that he or she has something valuable to give, it can open so many doors.

Kodak once donated some cameras to the young people in our Los Angeles affiliate, and a number of students found out they were naturals at photography. Their pictures were published in *Los Angeles Times Magazine*, and they were encouraged to consider turning their talents into careers. But to do so, they had to "smart up" and find out more about how photography worked. They had to learn math, English, and some practical science. Suddenly school was no longer remote from life; it was a clear path to doing what they loved. The experience of having their gift valued made them appreciate, in turn, the value of education. They'd found their passion, and they couldn't wait to learn more.

Every child wants to give—even those who literally have nothing to give you. I no longer remember where I first heard this story, but I've never forgotten it: A young boy from an extremely poor family formed a close relationship with his fourth-grade teacher. At the end of the school year, he handed her something wrapped in newspaper. She opened it; inside was an old Sears Roebuck catalog. "I wanted to give you a present, but I don't have money to buy you anything," the boy told her. "So I found this old book in our closet. Look through it and pick whatever you want most. Then pretend that's what I gave you."

SPREADING THE WORD

The Five Basics were all born out of personal experience—my own, my colleagues', and the thousands of kids we've known—coupled with a collective discussion within the CIS network that occurred over many years.

I don't think the ideas themselves are startling or revolutionary. We didn't invent each one of them, and in a sense every parent already knows them. But we were able to frame and articulate them in a way that struck a chord with many people. This, too, occurred over time—I wouldn't want to give the impression that we always thought of them as "the Five Basics," or indeed that we even considered them as discrete principles at all. That came later, as we tried to create a replicable process that communities across the country could use to fight their own dropout problem. By the mid-1990s, though, I'd come to refer to Four Basics—minus the "healthy start" one—and most of the Communities In Schools network had adopted them as a cornerstone of their strategies.

As I mentioned in Chapter 2, I was asked to help organize the Presidents' Summit for America's Future in 1997. General Powell wanted to harness the energy that came out of that event to launch a new movement called America's Promise, dedicated to providing children with the resources they need to succeed. The organization's symbol would be the "little red wagon" so beloved by children everywhere—an excellent image for an organization pledged to resource delivery. One of our CIS board members, Ray Chambers, was the driving force behind the Summit and in the formation of America's Promise. Not long after the event, he called me to say that General Powell and his advisors felt that CIS's Four Basics would make a perfect framework around which to organize the goals of America's Promise.

I was overjoyed. Here was an incredible opportunity to disseminate our principles to what I hoped would be hundreds of new communities. It felt appropriate and humbling to be able to share the fruits of our many decades of work with this new organization. We were honored that America's Promise embraced our Basics.

A few days later, Ray called again. How would I feel about adding a Fifth Basic? The United Way of America and Marian Wright Edelman, head of the Children's Defense Fund, wanted to include something about a healthy start for kids. Ray had heard me speak about this many times, and he knew that our CIS affiliates put a great deal of stress on it. I told him that was fine—it struck me as an excellent improvement.

So CIS now had Five Basics, and the new group had its Five Promises. These critically important principles were part of the "little red wagon" mission, advocated for by America's Promise affiliates in all 50 states.

GETTING IT TOGETHER

Let's imagine, once again, that you've made a list of all the things your children need. You've grouped them according to the Five Basics. What do you do next?

Here's one thing you *don't* do: You don't draw a map of your house and start dividing it up into little "help stations." You don't say to your spouse, "Okay, you deal with the caring relationship here in the living room. I'll be downstairs in the rec room waiting to assess the kids' health situation. When we're both done with that, you go up to the attic and do some math tutoring and then send everybody down to the porch so that I can talk to them about community service."

This would be insane. A caring home is an integrated, one-stop shop. Parents and extended family members, with help from others in the adult community when appropriate, work together to find out what the children need and figure out how to coordinate the necessary resources in the most efficient way.

But this safety net—woven by parents, extended families, faith communities, and tightly knit neighborhoods—no longer exists in the lives of millions of kids. The public schools have fallen into that vacuum. So schools, we realized, are the ideal place to deliver all those missing components that prevent students from succeeding academically—what we later came to call the

Five Basics. Just as important, we discovered that the *way* these resources are delivered is also critical. To understand why, we'll take a look at the hurdles families face in a typical community.

. . . AND BEYOND

"The well-being of children is perhaps the number one justice issue in America today." That was the case when I wrote *The Last Dropout* in 2007, and it remains true today. What's different is the urgency. Income inequality is worsening at a terrifying pace. More and more children are falling below the poverty line.

To quote Rey Saldaña from the Afterword:

> Advocating for social justice, for equity, for diversity, for inclusion, has been part of our story from the beginning. And it will be part of our continuing evolution. The events of the last several years, the protests around issues of racial equity, put the question front and center for us: Are we only about *educational* equity, or are we willing to say that we stand for social justice across the board? We believe our work in the schools has a role to play in the larger fight for social justice. We're not afraid to own that. In a way, this might be the biggest "and beyond" of all. But in another sense it's nothing new—this is how we started.

PART II

IN SEARCH OF COMMUNITY

BUREAUCRATIC, FRAGMENTED, AND DUPLICATIVE . . . OR PERSONAL, ACCOUNTABLE, AND COORDINATED?

"WHAT SHOULD I DO?"

Tara Larson isn't feeling well. The pretty, shy 11-year-old has begun her first semester at Van Buren Middle School, a large urban facility that's seen better days. Classes are crowded, textbooks are in short supply, and even after eight weeks of classes, Tara's teachers seem to have trouble remembering her name.

Her mother, Ruth, is starting to worry about her. The girl is losing weight, often picking at her food or skipping meals altogether. She's tired and listless. At least once a week, she asks to stay home from school because she has a bad headache.

Ruth Larson is a divorced mother of three, working a full-time job as a veterinary assistant plus an additional 18 hours three nights a week at a local big-box store. It's hard enough to arrange day care for Tara's two little sisters, ages three and four. If Tara is too sick to go to school, her mom doesn't have many options. She can call in sick herself or ask her nice neighbor, a retired public-school teacher named Mrs. Hartshorne, if she'd mind helping out.

Clearly, something must be done. And now she's been called to the school to meet with Tara's guidance counselor. The counselor seems kind enough but harassed and rushed. After quickly reading through the girl's folder (Ruth suspects that the counselor needs to remind herself which parent this is), she informs Ruth that her daughter's grades are plummeting. Tara has been inattentive in class, has failed to turn in homework, and has done poorly on tests. If this keeps up, she'll likely be held back a grade.

"What should I do?" Ruth asks. "What's the matter with her?"

Well, the counselor replies, it could be so many things. A physical checkup is a must, and the doctor might recommend some counseling. Of course, 11 is a very difficult age for girls—there are so many social and maturational changes going on. And speaking of changes, yes, going to middle school is a big shift in and of itself. A lot of new sixth graders have difficulty adjusting. Some of the older students are involved with drugs, sexual activity, and even gangs. The counselor says, sighing, that she knows this isn't good, but what can the school do? The entire community has changed, hasn't it? Or maybe Tara just needs some tutoring, something to snap her out of her academic doldrums. The counselor gives Ruth a recommendation for a private tutoring service.

Ruth Larson leaves the meeting feeling overwhelmed. She's tried talking to her daughter about what's wrong, of course, but Tara doesn't appear to know. "I just don't feel good," she repeats. So it's up to her mother, who loves her children very much, to find the help the girl needs.

Where to begin? Health insurance will pay for a visit to the HMO—which is across town and not particularly near public transportation. But Ruth doesn't have a car.

She calls the HMO, and the only available appointment that isn't weeks off is on a Monday morning at 10 o'clock. To keep it, Ruth will have to take yet another sick day from work. Her boss, Ms. Brown, the vet's office manager, has been understanding about all these days off, but this time Ruth can tell from the expression on her face that she's run out of patience.

Getting to the HMO involves two buses and five blocks on foot in a part of town Ruth would rather not have to take her daughter through. It doesn't feel safe, but they walk quickly and try not to meet the stares of the idling young men on the street corners.

At the HMO, Dr. Edwards gives Tara a thorough exam. Nothing is obviously wrong, she tells Ruth, although the girl is clearly underweight and tired. She recommends several more tests. Will the insurance cover it? She looks away and says, "I think so. Probably. But you need to talk to the folks out front about that." She also recommends that an adolescent mental health counselor evaluate Tara and writes a referral—to a different building in another part of the city. "And be sure to check with the folks out front about that, too," she says. "Mental health coverage varies from policy to policy, you know."

"The folks out front" are polite and helpful, but Ruth gets the feeling they've given up on the health-care system. Their answers to her questions are tentative and full of a resigned, half-humorous tone that seems to say, *This crazy system—who knows how it works? Everything will probably be okay. Just make sure you do the paperwork right! Gotta do that paperwork right.*

Even after three pregnancies, Ruth has never mastered the paperwork of the health-care system. She doesn't know any-one who has. She can feel her stomach tensing as she makes the appointments for Tara's tests and a visit to the mental health coun-selor. All the appointments are—of course—during working hours. What will she say to her boss *this* time?

Back home, Ruth calls the tutoring service recommended by the guidance counselor. It's located near the city line in a rather affluent neighborhood Ruth doesn't often visit. Her phone call is discouraging: Yes, they'd be happy to meet Ruth and Tara—in three weeks, their first opening. No, there are no reductions in the hefty tutoring fees for people of moderate income—and no, it's not something health insurance would cover. Public transportation to the office? "Oh, I think you should take your car, dear," says the woman on the phone.

Ruth says nothing. As the call is concluding, she asks, "Do you know if there are any volunteer tutoring organizations? We just don't have a lot of funds right now." The woman on the phone has no problem answering this question. She provides the names of five different nonprofit tutoring groups. Ruth writes down the names and numbers, wondering how she can possibly manage to contact them all and figure out which one would be best for Tara. The visit to the HMO and the call to the tutoring service have taken, all told, five hours of Ruth's day. At this rate, she realizes despondently, meeting her daughter's needs will be another part-time job, one that she'll somehow have to fit in without losing either of her other jobs.

A NAME ON A FORM

The adolescent mental health specialist is named Gwendolyn Smith. She's warm and funny. Ruth likes her immediately, and she can tell that Tara does, too. Hopefully, it will be worth the half-day leave Ruth took from work. Ms. Brown, the office manager, didn't even try to be nice about it this time. She said that this was the last "sick day" she could authorize—from now on any more leave would be without pay. And, she said firmly, "We need to have a talk about your situation. Dr. Hagen can't keep doing without you like this."

Tara is in Gwendolyn Smith's office (which looks more like a cheerful recreation room) for nearly an hour and a half while her mother leafs through magazines and tries to find a balance between worry and hope. When the appointment is over, the counselor speaks to Ruth alone.

To begin with, Gwendolyn says, we have to rule out some possible physical issues. She then proceeds to recommend the same three tests Dr. Edwards called for. When Ruth says that she has already scheduled them, the other woman looks abashed.

"I'm so sorry," she says. "They didn't put that in the referral." She shakes her head. "With every client, it's like starting over. And if I call over there and ask for more information about the physical workup, they'll either refuse to talk to me or put me through so many holds and loops that it might be weeks before I get anyone who knows who Tara Larson is. I'm sorry to sound so discouraging."

It's all right, Ruth assures her. This mother has already begun to see how the system "works"—or doesn't. Tara, her precious daughter, is just a name on a form, on many forms scattered throughout the agencies of this big city. It's not the *people* who don't care. On the contrary, people like Gwendolyn Smith, Dr. Edwards, and even the "folks out front" at the HMO care very much. They're good and decent.

Rather, it's the *system* that doesn't care, Ruth is realizing. All this separation of people and resources seems designed to ensure that no single individual sees Tara as a whole person. Each specialist is brought to bear on their area of expertise.

She tries to convey some of this to Gwendolyn, who nods sadly. "I know," she says. "It's so hard to find anyone who sees the whole picture—except you, of course."

"And I already *have* a job," Ruth says, trying to laugh.

Anyway, Gwendolyn goes on, Tara could probably use some counseling, no matter what the tests show. As the school guidance counselor had said, sixth grade is a big challenge and so is being an 11-year-old girl. She'd be glad to take Tara on as a client. Will insurance cover the sessions?

Ruth is now pretty sure she has the answer to this. Yes, 85 percent of the first 12 sessions are taken care of, and then 50 percent of the next 12, but in between she has to get her HMO to approve the DSM-5 diagnosis sent to them by Gwendolyn, and then . . .

"I *think* the percentages are right," she ends. "And I *think* I can pay my part of it, although I'll have to dip into my savings."

Gwendolyn talks a bit about what to expect from counseling—and what not to expect. "Part of the problem," she says, "is the school itself, I'm sorry to say. For instance, Tara talked to me for quite some time about what she feels walking the halls between classes. She says the older girls are mean to her and the older boys make her feel 'dirty.' She's always afraid somebody's going to bully her."

"She should tell a teacher about that!" Ruth exclaims indignantly.

"Tara says she doesn't know any of the teachers, and they don't seem to know her. She's afraid she'll 'get in trouble' if she talks about what's bothering her. Then there's the problem of making friends. There are a couple of girls she really likes, but they've already asked her if she wants to get high. When she told them no, they stopped talking to her."

"I didn't know that," Ruth murmurs.

"It would probably be a good idea for Tara to have something to do after school, too," Gwendolyn continues. "She told me that she gets bored and lonely in the apartment by herself, but there's nothing going on at school either. I know of a great program called AfterHours that the city runs, and it's free for kids her age. They have sports, games, and study time. In fact, that might be just the thing to help Tara get her grades up. It's held at the community center on Garver Avenue."

Ruth has been smiling at the description of the program, but the smile fades as she says, "But that's more than a mile from the school. How do they expect the kids to get there?"

"I'm not sure," Gwendolyn admits. "It was started to serve the kids in a different neighborhood from yours. But we can find out."

And a few days later, they do find out: there's no regular transportation for the kids from Van Buren Middle School. AfterHours primarily caters to its own neighborhood.

The same day Ruth Larson learns this, her office manager, Ms. Brown, calls her in for that promised—or threatened—talk about the situation. It's more of a monologue, and the message is clear: Ruth needs to start showing up for work consistently or she can look for another job.

"It's just that . . . well, my daughter is having difficulties right now," Ruth pleads. "She really needs me to be there, to take her places . . ." She trails off, realizing that the story of her daughter's needs is long and complicated.

She looks up and sees that Ms. Brown's eyes are tired and gentle. "I know, Ruth," she says softly. "But everyone still has to do their jobs—you, me, and Dr. Hagen. Isn't there somebody who can help you with your daughter?"

No, Ruth thinks, *there isn't. That doesn't appear to be anyone's job.*

When she arrives home after picking up the younger girls from day care, she finds her oldest daughter on the couch, staring at the TV with the sound turned off. "What's wrong, sweetie?" her mother asks.

"I just don't feel good," Tara says.

WHAT'S WRONG WITH THIS PICTURE?

Ruth Larson is a loving mother. She couldn't be more committed to the well-being of her children.

Tara Larson's school is large, under-resourced, and full of the potential for ugly trouble, but in one important sense, it's doing the right thing. The guidance counselor has become aware that Tara is in danger of academic failure and has taken action. The girl's mother has been notified; suggestions for help have been made. Moreover, the helping resources are available: physical and mental health care, tutoring, and some healthy after-school activities. It's not the impossible dream.

And certainly there are no villains here. The individuals Ruth has encountered in her quest to meet her daughter's needs have been polite, professional, and willing to help.

So what's going wrong? Why, after nearly a month of concentrated effort, is there still no plan for helping Tara Larson? Why is her mother on the verge of giving up?

The resources are in place, but they're in the *wrong* place. They're scattered all over town, difficult to access, and open for business during—what else?—business hours. They don't talk to each other. Each encounter involves a barrage of paperwork that even the professionals are often unclear about. Ruth would need a Ph.D. in systems to figure it all out.

It's as if, in order to write a report, you had 26 keyboards in different parts of the office. To type an *A*, you have to use the "*A* keyboard," because that's the only letter it will type. To type a *B*, you set off on your journey to find the "*B* keyboard" . . . and on and on.

When resources are scattered and isolated like this, an already-faulty system starts to experience even more strains and dysfunctions. The natural tendency, if you work in one particular area, is to concentrate on what you do best—what you get paid for—and pass on the rest of the responsibility. If Tara Larson needs a tutor, that's hardly the problem of the guidance counselor. Her job is demanding enough. Who could expect her to be on the phone on her own time, trying to line up a tutor for one girl out of the dozens she sees every week?

So good people get tunnel vision. They hold themselves accountable only for their particular piece of the problem. It's really self-protection. Teachers face the same dilemma. They're not being paid to be counselors, advocates, and experts in social systems. Just teaching is hard enough.

As for Ruth, how in the world is she supposed to find the time to master the "system"—to get that Ph.D.—while she's already working nearly 60 hours a week?

And remember, Tara Larson isn't some special, unusual case. There are Taras in most schools. If teachers, recreation counselors, tutors, and therapists had to spend the time and effort on each one of these children that would be needed to see them holistically, to really coordinate a response to their issues, no one would ever go home. There aren't enough hours in the week.

So each person does their job. There's nothing wrong with that, but it means that Tara and the thousands like her in schools across the country are falling through the cracks because *no one* has the most crucial job of all. Nobody gets paid to make sure the whole system works.

REVERSING THE ARROWS

The solution to this sad, all-too-common situation is simple . . . but not easy. Look at the following diagram. It shows the typical "flow" of energy when students need assistance. All the arrows point out from the schoolhouse in every direction of the compass.

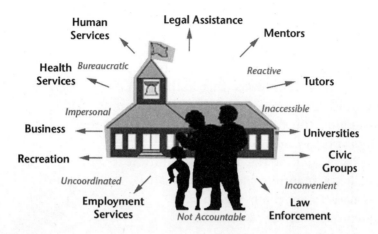

Now imagine the diagram looked like this.

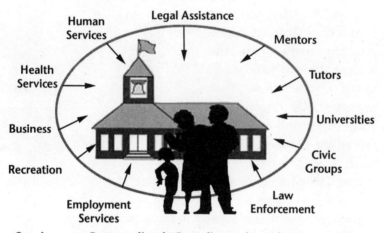

Services are Personalized, Coordinated, and Accountable

All we've done is reverse the direction of the arrows, but what an enormous change that makes! Now the various outside agencies are bringing their services to the school instead of waiting for students and parents to come to them. The school has become the delivery point. Not only are families better able to find the help they need, but the agencies can also find their "customers." We've been looking at the problem from a parent's point of view, but social workers, health-care specialists, and all the other community resource providers are also frustrated by the typically fragmented situation.

With one stroke, we've ended the nerve-racking back-and-forth from office to office that Ruth and Tara experienced. Now the "offices" are down the hall from the girl's homeroom. The after-school program is held at the school, too, instead of at the community center.

Take a look at the following illustration. It's a snapshot showing how all Five Basics can come together at the school. A mentor is meeting one of "his" children and providing the First Basic, a positive, one-on-one relationship with a caring adult. An after-school drug-education program helps with the Second Basic, a safe place to learn and grow. The nurse's office hosts an array of visiting health-care specialists providing the Third Basic, a healthy start and a healthy future. Business volunteers join kids in the computer room for employment training to give them the Fourth Basic, a marketable skill. Community service and service-learning opportunities form a regular part of classroom instruction, thanks to partnerships with neighborhood volunteer groups that are eager to provide the Fifth Basic, a chance to give back to peers and community.

It's a wonderful, vibrant place, and a big improvement over the way it used to be. But all the problems aren't solved yet. The resources are in the schools, but we still need someone whose job it is to ensure that they're delivered to the students who need them in a manner that's personal, accountable, and coordinated.

Such an individual—Communities In Schools calls them the site coordinator—is on-site, in touch with the students and the resources, and an expert at the one job no one else has the time or training to do: connecting the students with the people who care and can back it up with expertise.

As I said, it's simple but not easy. It requires a long-term commitment by the school system and a slow but steady change in the way the community allocates its helping resources.

When it works, it's the best antidote I know to removing obstacles that affect so many students. What's critical is that all these services are delivered in a personal, accountable, and coordinated manner. These three values have been long-standing tenets of the CIS movement and have special meaning in relation to how services are provided at a school site.

Personalism is the keystone of this kind of integrated service delivery. Building and maintaining one-on-one connections among a caring adult, a student, and the student's family brings dignity and respect to the service relationship by acknowledging the worth of all concerned. Resources are tailored to students' and families' unique needs; it can't be "one size fits all."

Accountability means showing up and doing the job with integrity, and it's a direct outgrowth of personalism. When you have ongoing, caring relationships with the people you work with and for, when you look them in the eye each day and ask, "How are you doing?" it's hard to hear the answer and then say, "It's not my problem." Accountability means not passing the buck, and it guarantees that goals are met consistently and responsibly. When parents ask why something has or hasn't happened to their child, "the system" won't be blamed or credited. An individual project team member accepts responsibility. CIS staff are accountable to school personnel, partner agencies and volunteers, students and families, the community at large, and each other.

Coordination ensures that previously fragmented approaches to service delivery are connected into a comprehensive, holistic plan. At the school site, assigned agency staff and volunteers function as an integrated team in providing services to students and families.

The CIS coordinator at each school is the key to making all of this happen. This individual is always available at his or her site to answer questions, provide information, assist teachers and staff, and develop a holistic picture of the needs of children.

A COMMUNITY THAT CARES

It's not hard to picture how a middle school with a CIS presence might respond to Tara Larson's situation.

Her pattern of academic difficulty and absences brings her to the attention of the CIS coordinator. The coordinator makes a home visit—another hallmark of the CIS approach—and Ruth Larson learns about the resources available for her daughter. A CIS volunteer brings Tara to the Healthy Children Center, where she receives a thorough physical exam. The necessary tests are performed, and to everyone's relief, they reveal no serious illnesses. They do indicate, though, that her headaches may result from low blood sugar. Sure enough, once the recommended remedies are in place, that problem disappears.

The coordinator arranges for tutoring at home for Tara. (I like to imagine that her tutor might be the Larsons' nice retired-schoolteacher neighbor, Mrs. Hartshorne, who now has a place to volunteer thanks to CIS.) Tara is enrolled in the CIS/YMCA after-school program, too.

What about a mentor? Ruth Larson is an excellent mother, but she'd be the first to admit that, working so many hours, she doesn't get to spend as much time as she'd like with her children. She welcomes the mentor match that CIS arranges with a young university student. And this person is able to give Tara a ride once a week to meet with Gwendolyn Smith at the adolescent mental health facility.

Of course, all of Tara's problems don't vanish. But a CIS school site is a different place from the one we first described. Yes, there are safety issues around drugs and sex and bullying, but here there are grown-ups whom she can talk to. The entire school climate is different. She doesn't feel as if she's alone, facing the challenges of being a new sixth grader all by herself. And Tara can see that the many adult volunteers at her school are making a difference. Other students are more respectful; there's a general sense of higher standards, higher expectations for the young people. The school is part of a community that cares.

Furthermore, as a "CIS student," Tara isn't viewed as a collection of separate, isolated problems and referrals. The CIS coordinator knows her well, is familiar with her issues, and understands what has been done to deal with them. This person has the knowledge necessary to work with agencies and systems. She gets regular reports from all the volunteers and service providers; she can see the big picture. *Case manager* is the term that social workers use for this role, and many CIS affiliates use it as well. But it's a more successful—you might say "purer"—type of case management because the coordinator truly has access to the necessary resources. She's able to back up her accountability with action.

The coordinator continues to make home visits, and Tara's mother is very much part of the big picture, too. Ruth Larson realizes that she has more friends and resources at her disposal than she'd ever thought possible. She has found an accountable, coordinated team of caring adults—a true "community in school."

HURRICANE

CIS affiliates around the nation were launched to deal with recognizable community issues that affect the well-being and success of students. Poor health, peer pressure, lack of academic assistance, and an unsafe environment—sadly, these are the common or garden-variety problems that plague hundreds of thousands of American students.

Sometimes, though, a challenge that no one could have anticipated will arise, rather like one of those unlucky "Chance" cards in the game of Monopoly. In August and September 2005, the Gulf Coast endured the fury of two devastating hurricanes. In the aftermath of Katrina and Rita, a massive displacement of students and their families occurred during the first week of the school year. Communities In Schools affiliates in nearby areas were among the many groups who rallied to help school systems meet the needs of the displaced students and families: about 30,000 young people, along with 6,000 parents and guardians, received services through 61 CIS affiliates.

Houston, like many other communities in Texas, welcomed the evacuees. By December, Houston-area school districts had absorbed more than 21,000 newly enrolled students. CIS of Houston is one of our oldest and most successful affiliates, and at the time the four districts in which it had programs were serving 12,000 of those children, along with many of their families.

Cynthia Briggs, then executive director of the Houston CIS affiliate, got a call from the mayor in the midst of this crisis, asking her to take on an impossible project. "He said that hundreds of teachers had been displaced by Katrina, too, and he really needed us to be the lead agency to place them in schools in 11 counties. He told me: 'I know you don't have CIS programs in all those counties, but if anyone can do it, you can. This way it won't be an issue in terms of school districts taking the lead. You bring the best of the community.'"

It was an important moment for all of us in CIS—and an enormous challenge. Houston's mayor needed exactly what CIS could provide: a way of responding to an unprecedented disaster that was personal, accountable, and coordinated. I often wonder how differently things might have gone in New Orleans and the rest of the Gulf Coast if the *original* response to the storms had displayed even a little bit of those three qualities. What the entire nation saw instead was a round-robin of finger-pointing and endless explanations of why such a thing was so difficult to achieve.

Cynthia Briggs had spent more than 20 years building confidence and success in Houston's schools, and that experience paid off. In an incredibly short period of time, Houston CIS placed 145 teachers.

"It was really a work of the heart," Cynthia told me. "Those folks had been on the phone with FEMA, trying to understand what was going on. It was awful for them. And suddenly they had a number to call to reach us. Our phones were ringing off the hook with people trying to find jobs. We responded to everyone personally. I answered the phone myself one day and said, 'Hold on, we'll get to you, just hold on,' and the woman on the phone said, 'Ma'am, if you'll just promise me you'll come back to the phone, I'll hold as long as I need to. Just promise me you'll come back.'"

With financial assistance from the Gulf Coast Workforce Board, CIS of Houston launched Operation School Work, placing the teachers as tutors and mentors in Houston-area schools that had received a large number of evacuees. Not only did the educators receive regular paychecks and full benefits, but they also provided invaluable guidance and mentoring to students who, like them, were suddenly uprooted and forced into unfamiliar and often stressful situations.

Although the official project ended at the close of the 2005–06 school year, Operation School Work laid the foundation for continuing success among adults and kids alike. Many tutors have gone on to find permanent, long-term teaching positions in the districts they served.

And what about the displaced students themselves? With the generosity typical of this country following such a tragedy, monetary and in-kind donations poured into CIS of Houston and many other helping agencies. When the Michael & Susan Dell Foundation asked how it could help, the CIS of Texas state office, under the leadership of Nellie Reyes, responded by coordinating the efforts of the dozens of local CIS affiliates throughout the state that were absorbing large numbers of evacuees from the Gulf Coast. They created a program that addressed not only the unique set of needs facing the students and their families, but also the need for community building between these new arrivals and local residents.

CIS was able to place social-service coordinators at the school campuses that had absorbed large concentrations of evacuee students and didn't already have a CIS presence. The coordinators provided direct support to hurricane evacuees at the school sites, including individual and group counseling sessions to assist students with transition issues, grief, and peer relationships.

"We wanted to make sure to address not only the individual needs of the evacuees, but the stress on the school as a whole as students adjusted to the new circumstances," said Sylvia Teague, CIS of Houston's former director of field operations. Again, this kind of coordinated, farsighted response is possible if you're fortunate enough to have a *system* already in place that rewards such efforts.

"THE GLUE THAT HELD THEM TOGETHER"

Our CIS affiliate in Houston's Bay Area (at the time comprising Clear Creek and Dickinson school districts) received a visit from Pulitzer Prize–winning author Jed Horne, who subsequently wrote about his experience in his book *Breach of Faith: Hurricane Katrina and the Near Death of a Great American City*.

Horne went to McWhirter Elementary School in Webster, Texas, to see how displaced New Orleans students were being assimilated into the school's activities. He then wrote:

About two-thirds of McWhirter kids were low-income, and most of them were Latino. Mostly African Americans, the New Orleans kids were immediately identifiable and somewhat exotic. Outside the classroom, a woman named Glenda Rice was the glue that held many of them together. She was the program coordinator for an outfit called Communities In Schools (CIS), a national nonprofit that had set up shop at nine schools within the Clear Creek district, McWhirter being one of them. (CIS had also been a presence in New Orleans.) In essence, Rice hooked up newly arrived low-income families with the services they needed. Someone had a toothache? Rice would scrounge for a dentist willing to pull the tooth for free. Blankets? She'd track down a donor. She leaned a lot on a women's group called ALBA that was good for a pair of quality tennis shoes and two or three outfits per needy child. At the sight of a likely prospect, Rice would whip out a tape and measure the child.

"I walk around the school and look," Rice said. "I'll casually ask a new kid, 'You got a coat?'" She got a school in a rich Clear Creek neighborhood to do a coat drive and came up with 60. Book bags? Rice got Home Depot to kick in 400. She was also known for her signature "birthday boxes," soup-to-nuts party kits that contained candles, cake mix, party favors, and the like.

Rice was also good at thinking well outside the birthday box. One afternoon she was visited in her office by a New Orleanian named Yavana Johnson. Johnson had dropped off her kids at school, except for the baby in her arms. As much as anything, she just needed to reminisce. She needed to talk about what it was like growing up in a city that seemed no longer to exist. . . .

Rice [learned] that Johnson, a woman of fashion, had dreamed of becoming a beautician. Rice urged her to pursue her dream and found a beauty school not only prepared to admit Johnson but to offer her a $4,000 scholarship. Johnson held back. She would need day care. Rice hit the phone again and lined up day care. Johnson began to realize she might have a future in Webster.[1]

Systemic change, once begun, is hard to stop. Epidemics spread, but so do the forces for good. When a community carries out its commitment to help children succeed, it also builds the relationships and trust that can take on any challenge.

///

. . . AND BEYOND

Systemic change, once begun, is hard to stop . . . That remains as true today, thankfully, as it's ever been. CIS is about changes for kids, but we're also trying to change the delivery system.

There are a couple of ways of doing that. You can work on the connections between the community and the school, making them stronger and more all-encompassing and better coordinated, just as this chapter describes. And you can also affect policy, arguing the case for rewarding people to work together rather than in their own silos of expertise.

In the federal education legislation, the Elementary and Secondary Education Act, there's language written into the law that allows school districts with poverty-challenged students to use federal money to pay for a CIS, or CIS-like, site coordinator. Finally, the U.S. Department of Education is saying to school systems, "You have to get everyone working together. It's not optional anymore—we expect you to do this and we will provide support."

An integrated system needs an integrator, just as an orchestra needs a conductor. This is a major breakthrough in validating and spreading the CIS model.

CHAPTER 5

THE "MAGIC EYES" OF A CHAMPION FOR CHILDREN

LEADING THE ORCHESTRA

Let's consider the picture we've painted so far of the situation facing a typical school system as it tries to stop the dropout epidemic. We have talented and committed educators who are stretched far beyond their resources. They'd like to help every student succeed, but the needs of so many children are simply beyond what a teacher, principal, or guidance counselor can handle.

Parents, too, however much they love their children, are overwhelmed by the confusion of "helping agencies" scattered throughout the community.

These organizations, their staff, and their volunteers are by no means unhelpful. In fact, altogether they may well have the solutions to most of the problems children face—but they *aren't* all together. They work in a way that's often fragmented, impersonal, and hard to access.

Now we imagine that concerned community leaders—perhaps from the business community or leaders of the volunteer, faith-based, or philanthropic sectors—have a new idea: bring this important work *to* the schools in a manner that's personal, accountable, and coordinated so that each child can be viewed holistically and matched with the services that they need to succeed in school and in life.

The superintendent of schools listens and likes the idea. What's the next step? What's the effective way to get the resources where they belong?

Every community needs a "Champion for Children," a neutral third party to coordinate and broker the diverse community resources into the schools on behalf of young people and their families. Like the router for a computer network, this person is an expert "relational router" who can get individuals working *together* instead of on separate paths. Or we can borrow an image suggested to me by Quincy Jones, a longtime supporter of CIS: "It's like an orchestra," he said when I first described our work. "CIS is the conductor who makes sure all the individual musicians are playing from the same score and coming in when they're needed."

In practice, a successful local CIS affiliate has Champions on at least two levels. The executive director's job is to identify the most pressing needs of students and families and then create partnerships among helping agencies to bring their resources, talents, and volunteers into the public schools to address those needs. Then, at the various school sites, we've seen how the coordinators implement the executive director's vision for their schools, translating system-wide assets and needs into a one-on-one, student- and family-centered approach.

I've described the Champion for Children as a neutral third party. What does this mean in practice? One of the best and most effective ways to put this person to work is to make him or her responsible to the board of directors of an independent nonprofit corporation.

The Champion's board should be composed of a wide cross section of local leaders. I hope that many readers of this book will be excellent candidates to lead such a board. The active support of the private sector is absolutely critical to effective management and advocacy. So is the participation of the superintendent of schools—ideally, as a board member. Beyond this, different places will have different leaders, but the same overall framework applies: The dropout epidemic is a *community-wide* crisis that affects everyone, so all the key sectors of the community must join together to combat it. After all, an orchestra with nothing but, say, percussion and woodwinds would be awfully limited in what it could play.

The Champion's neutrality is critical. They mustn't be perceived as having a competitive bias toward one of the partnering agencies. Instead, the Champion's task is to ensure that *all* stakeholders are fairly represented so that their ideas and concerns are made part of the new community/school partnership. It's hard enough to convince potential partners that this collaborative approach will be worth the effort and that giving up a certain degree of independence and recognition will further their mission in the long run. We don't want to make it even harder by creating the suspicion that the Champion harbors a hidden agenda, whether political or structural. Again, think of the orchestra: if the conductor keeps favoring loud passages for the horn section, people are going to figure out that this guy used to be a horn player. Rather, the Champion's sole job should be to create the best outcomes, the best music, for children and families.

Another important aspect of neutrality reflects the grassroots, homegrown nature of the initiative. Positive change can't be led or managed from the outside. Without the support of local leaders who know everyone's interests, any process of collaboration is doomed. Groups that just show up to do something "for the community" are often rightly perceived as disempowering, paternalistic, and arrogant. This was a lesson I had to learn in the early days of my street work in New York. Until my colleagues and I were perceived as being *part* of the neighborhood, we couldn't be part of the solution.

These considerations hold true for the entire collaborative board, and most particularly for the Champion. They need to be—and to be perceived as—a homegrown advocate for families and schools.

If you're a businessperson, you've already realized that our Champion must be a fine manager. It's no easy task to wield a small budget against the big problems faced by overburdened school systems and families. The challenges of hands-on, day-to-day coordination of resources are considerable. Management skills are essential to the job, and if you want to start a CIS-like initiative in your community, your Champion had better come equipped with an excellent management résumé.

People skills are obviously critical as well. The Champion has to be comfortable and effective with a wide assortment of individuals and cultures. She's the kind of person who can meet for breakfast with the mayor, have lunch with the school superintendent, talk with union representatives in the afternoon, join the Junior League for dinner, and hang out with the kids in the evening.

But (as this demanding schedule suggests) there's even more to it than administrative ability and a knack for getting along with people. In taking on the dropout epidemic, we're taking on a world of trouble. The challenges that schools, families, and students face didn't arise overnight, and they won't be turned around in a semester or a year. Moreover, we're not talking about manufacturing widgets. Our "customers," if you will, are children. We care about them. We *have* to care, or we wouldn't be taking on this challenge, and every failure hurts. It's like the old metaphor about how much time it takes to turn around an ocean liner— except that in this case children and families are inevitably falling overboard and drowning while we make the agonizingly slow adjustments of the rudder that are necessary to redirect the way our community assists them.

It requires a special sort of person to stay positive in the face of these daily human tragedies. Hanging out is a great skill when you're working with kids—but *hanging in* is just as important.

HOW'S YOUR VISION?

While leafing through the reading material in a dentist's waiting room years ago, I saw a children's book called *Magic Eyes.* I no longer recall the story, but the title has always stuck with me. It's a perfect name for that special quality that a Champion for Children must have in order to get the job done for kids.

When you have magic eyes, you see things differently. You notice solutions and assets, not problems and liabilities. *Every* situation children face in your community is an opportunity, and you discover the possibilities, not the drawbacks. It's like trying to start a campfire: You see those little sparks, and instead of focusing on all the wood that's not catching, you blow carefully on the glowing specks. Pretty soon you have a flame, and then the fire overcomes the coldness.

This kind of leadership, in my opinion, starts with the heart, not the head. It's about "care providing," not caretaking, and caring isn't a job but a way of life. It's a calling, and it comes from an acute perception of the brokenness all around us, the damaged lives, the broken dreams. Often it comes from the brokenness in ourselves, too—all the ways we've had to learn to go on despite our wounds.

I'm reminded of the time that a friend of mine was in the hospital and quite despondent about it. While I sat with him, a nurse came in and did all the things a nurse does: check the chart, monitor his vital signs and medications, and so on. She was very skillful and very cold. You could tell that she was "doing her job," but she didn't want any interaction with my friend. Her goal was to be efficient, to do what had to be done, and then move on to the next patient.

The next time I visited, a different nurse came in. From the moment he entered the room, he was talking and laughing, making eye contact, touching my friend's shoulder, and asking him how he was—you could tell that he really wanted to know the answer and wasn't just going through the motions. This nurse not only performed all the same tasks the first one had, but he brought joy and healing to that room, and to me, too. There's no way to eliminate all the tension and fear that a sickroom breeds, but he did his best. My friend, who was very ill, was *excited* about the nurse's visit— that's the only word to describe it. His despondency was lifted.

Now, both these professionals were "being good nurses," but for one it was a job and for the other it was a calling. That second one needed the salary—I'm sure he had a family to take care of and bills to pay just like anyone else. But that wasn't why he was doing it. You could tell he loved his patients. There's no substitute for skill, but if you're working with and for people, technique isn't enough.

A good pair of magic eyes will keep you focused on what you *can* do, not what you can't. It will also help you see others differently. When I first began trying to reach out to kids, I didn't know how to build community. I was highly suspicious of the "establishment" and all its works. If you'd asked me what to do about the public school system, I would have said in frustration, "Get rid of it."

But gradually, through the example of others and through my own painful lessons, I came to understand that everybody has a place at the table—and that most definitely includes professional educators and administrators. Once I started hanging out with teachers, I saw their viewpoint and felt *their* frustration. People like me had been pointing fingers at them and lecturing them: "You have to change, and we'll tell you how." I was beginning to realize how arrogant that position was. The teachers I met understood very well that schools had to change and were more than willing to be a part of that change. But they wanted to be *included* as partners with an equal say, not told how to do their jobs.

Arrogance and anger have no place in community building. Do you want to fail as quickly as possible, trying to build a coalition around kids? Just walk into that first meeting and treat your potential partners—especially the ones with resources and standing—as if they aren't as good as you or the kids you serve. As if they've "sold out" or they "owe the community" something. On the contrary, you are *giving* them a precious gift by inviting their help. You're allowing them to be part of something bigger than themselves.

There are times, too, when magic eyes help you see the most basic and obvious realities—simple truths that get lost in the complications of our daily struggles. I remember being part of a team that President George H. W. Bush pulled together to advise him on an upcoming education summit with the nation's governors. I heard some wonderful ideas from this group of national leaders in the field. In fact, I was starting to feel a little out of place since I was the only noneducator in the room.

I kept silent for a long while, but finally my turn came to speak. I complimented everyone on the depth of their insights and told them how moved I was by their concern, which was absolutely true. Then I mentioned what seemed obvious: "The only word I haven't heard is *children*. Shouldn't we be starting with them instead of theories and strategies? How do we connect with them so they'll get turned on to learning?" And—for a while, at least—the conversation changed.

Seeing things differently leads to *thinking* differently, which in turn leads to *acting* differently. Simply trying harder is no longer enough. This doesn't mean, however, that persistence and dedication in the face of sometimes overwhelming challenges can be bypassed or replaced with "new thinking." Over the years as I've watched successful community leaders both inside and outside the CIS movement, the common denominator is always persistence.

Atlanta businessman George Johnson, one of our first board members and one of my closest friends, once told me about a visit he made right after college to one of his city's legendary lawyers and most prominent bankers. As a new graduate, George asked him, "What's the key to success?"

"There are three basic ingredients," the attorney said. "Do I need to write them down?" George asked.

"No, you'll remember them. Number one, above everything else, is 'stick-ability.' It's not about who you know or what you know—it's perseverance. Number two is perseverance. And number three is perseverance. George, you've just got to keep showing up!"

This story means a lot to me because of how George himself has lived it out. He has been one of our most faithful supporters, "showing up" for kids and for CIS for more than 40 years.

Perseverance is an old-fashioned notion. But it's just as essential as seeing and thinking differently. We have to declare collectively that we're completely committed to these kids, that we want to see a broken world knit together and made whole. We're not going to give up, no matter how many defeats we suffer, because love never quits. Love is for a lifetime.

This is a very important lesson. You must never confuse faith that you will prevail in the end—which you can never afford to lose— with the discipline to confront the most brutal facts of your current reality, whatever they might be.

— ADMIRAL JAMES STOCKDALE[1]

NO CHEAP GRACE

My friend Neil Shorthouse has magic eyes. We've been colleagues for more than 50 years, and he's helped me see so many things that I would have missed without his 20/20 vision. There wouldn't be any Communities In Schools without Neil. Here's how it happened:

You may recall from Chapter 2 that our New York Street Academy movement was facing some tough questions by the end of the 1960s. Increasingly, we were wondering how we could reach potential dropouts before they left school. We couldn't address this quandary, however, until we confronted some immediate and serious practical problems. We'd received federal funding for a number of the academies, but by the early 1970s that was withdrawn. Many of our private supporters were also backing off. I don't mean to sound cynical, but there are trends in causes just like in everything else, and street work was no longer as fashionable as it had been. The urban riots were over, the fires were out, and a lot of people had moved on to different social issues.

Our long-range question was: *How do we keep this thing going?* In the short term, the question was even more immediate: Which of our struggling prototypes—by that point launched in five cities in addition to New York—could we use as a new beachhead, a restarting point?

I'd known Neil Shorthouse since we were both teenagers in Pittsburgh. Unlike me, however, he was a star in everything he attempted. He went through the University of Pittsburgh in three years on a golf scholarship. He was involved with an organization called the Fellowship of Christian Athletes, a group that fit in well with the theology of his upbringing, but he also joined Young Life, the same youth organization that had turned me around.

Neil graduated from college in 1963, while I was deep into street work with Vinnie and Harv in New York City. He'd considered a career in law, picturing himself doing Christian advocacy work, but soon decided it wouldn't suit his person-to-person temperament. Instead, he became a Young Life staffer, running youth clubs in Pittsburgh and later becoming the program director in Philadelphia. At first he was based in the Delaware County suburbs, but soon expanded into the tough ghetto of West Philly. It changed his life.

Neil saw that his version of Christianity—which he now calls an "Everything's all right!" viewpoint—couldn't make sense of the poverty and hopelessness that surrounded him in West Philly. "I had a kind of 'Everything's all wrong!' conversion," he says. "The world is wrong, there's no justice, churches are missing the point, and the schools are terrible." It was a necessary swing in the other direction, but a long way from magic eyes.

Then in 1968, Neil learned about a community in Georgia called Koinonia. An IBM executive who was a supporter of ours told him about it. The man suggested that Neil, Dean Borgman, and I might want to learn more about this remarkable Christian agrarian commune that was led by a man named Clarence Jordan.

It turned out that Clarence was going to be spending the weekend at a boys' school in New York State, so a number of us, including Neil, went up there to hang out with him.

I'd kept in touch with my friend over the years, but this was the first time we'd really spent time together since boyhood. Both of us were amazed by Clarence Jordan. He had a Ph.D. in New Testament Greek and a high level of sophistication as a peanut farmer—an unusual combination for a Southern Baptist minister. His take on spiritual matters was unique and so down-to-earth, so focused on social justice and personal transformation, that it was like hearing the Christian message for the first time.

Clarence had been active in the civil rights movement in Georgia, putting his life in danger to help his brothers and sisters.

Koinonia itself was the target of continual violence from those who were opposed to the commune's commitment to civil rights. But Clarence believed that "fear is the polio of the soul—it prevents you from walking by faith." He also introduced us to the German theologian Dietrich Bonhoeffer's concept of "cheap grace": you get saved, but there's no cost, no transformation, and you keep right on as before. That wasn't Clarence's way, and Neil, Dean, and I realized it could never be our way either.

Neil and his family visited Koinonia a few months later, and he was even more impressed with the way the community was living out its spiritual values. He returned to Philadelphia with renewed energy but still angry and frustrated about the failure of the school system and the indifference of society toward its children. Inevitably, he found himself being alienated by Young Life. "They thought I was heavy baggage," he recalls. He and the organization parted ways in 1970, six months after Neil and I had mourned another parting as we learned of Clarence Jordan's death at the age of 57.

What next? Neil and I and our families made one of the most difficult decisions of our lives: we would relocate from New York City and Philadelphia, respectively, to Atlanta, and begin living communally in a way that would reflect the Christian values of peace, brotherhood, and sharing espoused by Clarence Jordan. We chose Atlanta for two reasons: it was close to Koinonia, and our Street Academies were still active in that city.

We decided to incorporate as a nonprofit organization to run the schools. We called our new project EXODUS, Inc. Our first "office" consisted of two desks, one phone, and one file cabinet in the 10-foot-by-10-foot dugout basement of the communal house where 16 of us were living. It was a modest beginning but seemingly all we needed.

The Street Academies in Atlanta had received funding from the U.S. Postal Service and used mail carriers as teachers, mentors, and administrators. An ex–postal worker named David Lewis had been vital in creating the schools in Atlanta, and we were fortunate to be able to team up with him and his partners in our new endeavor.

Dave was another guy with magic eyes. I've never known anyone who could make a connection with kids—any kids—the way he did. (You may remember that he was one of the street workers mentioned in Chapter 1 who helped Reginald Beaty decide to believe in himself and go back to school, beginning his transformation from "loser" to lieutenant colonel.) An African American, Dave could overcome barriers of race and class in a truly extraordinary way. Along with Neil and me, he was the third co-founder of what is now Communities In Schools.

With the withdrawal of federal funds, private dollars had to be raised for what had formerly been the Postal Street Academies. This is when I began to understand another aspect of what "magic eyes" can mean because I watched Neil's indefatigable efforts to partner, persuade, and create community with all strata of society on behalf of the children of Atlanta. This man saw possibilities *everywhere:* small foundation grants, a little state-government funding, loans from generous (and trusting) board members, borrowing from one bank to pay off another. We never knew how we'd meet payroll from one pay period to the next, but somehow Neil kept the ball rolling, and by the mid-'70s we had four Street Academies operating in Atlanta. They were very much on the New York City model: storefront schools for dropouts. We also opened an academy inside St. Luke's Episcopal Church.

From the beginning of our Atlanta adventure, we had a critical ally. Robert H. B. Baldwin was a top executive at Morgan Stanley in New York, someone I'd first met in our Street Academy days and who believed in us from the start. When he learned that Neil and I were relocating to Atlanta, he called a friend of his there, Justus Martin, the president of a major regional stock brokerage firm, the Robinson-Humphrey Company. He asked Martin and R-H board chairman Sandy Yearley to meet with us and learn more about what we were trying to do.

I remember well the looks these ultrarespectable stockbrokers gave us when we entered their boardroom, so I can say without hesitation that it was Bob Baldwin's influence and reputation that convinced them to provide some crucial start-up funding for the Atlanta academies. This was neither the first nor the last time that he would make the difference between success and failure for us. Five years later, he became the first chairman of our national board of directors. From his position as president and eventually chairman of Morgan Stanley, he gave us the credibility we needed in the business and political communities. He also held me personally to a very high standard of professionalism. As an early funder said, "Bill, I've grown to like you a lot and believe in your mission, but I can sleep at night because Bob Baldwin is your board chair."

In 1974, we took a major step: Neil and I convinced the Atlanta public education system to assign teachers to our academies. Dr. Alonzo Crim was the superintendent of schools. Relatively new to the job in Atlanta after having led several other major school systems, Dr. Crim was aware that his students needed help, and he was open to new ideas. He'd met Dave Lewis when Dave was running the Postal Street Academies and was powerfully impressed. So when Neil and I came in and explained that we were teaming up with Dave, it gave Dr. Crim the confidence to back us. I believe he could see that we were for real, that we meant what we said about our commitment to kids, even if our methods were untried locally.

Neil approached Dr. Crim with the idea of repositioning teachers into our academies. "We could call them satellite learning centers," Neil said. The superintendent agreed to roll the dice. We weren't quite *in* the schools yet, but we were getting very close. And finally, Neil, Dave, and I saw the necessity of crossing that boundary and actually setting up a project inside the public schools to reach kids before they became dropouts. With the unwavering support of Dr. Crim, we started working in an elementary school and a high school.

Neil helped me understand how important it was to build positive relationships with teachers at the same time that we connected with students. He used to sketch a little picture: It showed the school surrounded by a moat with the drawbridge raised. Outside the moat were weird-looking blobs that seemed like they could swallow the school in one gulp.

"This is how teachers and principals get to feeling sometimes," he said. "They believe they're surrounded by amoeba do-gooders, all circling around the school and trying to absorb them. Is it any wonder the drawbridge stays up? We need to show them every day that we're partners and allies, not threats."

The magic eyes of a guy like Neil Shorthouse are indispensable to rallying the community around its children. Knowing Neil as well as I do, I can't say that I've *never* seen him discouraged or uncertain. But like the nurse whose job was also a calling, he makes it his business to see life, joy, and possibilities everywhere he looks. "It provides meaning for me," he says. "It's my purpose on Earth." He has remained, next to my wife, my best friend and partner.

SOMETHING'S GOING TO HAPPEN . . .

The good news is there are people like Neil in *your* community. We've located hundreds of them around the country as we search for Champions for Children to fight the dropout epidemic.

I remember one early funder saying to me, skeptically: "This job isn't exactly for your Junior League types, is it?"

Well, you'd be surprised.

In 1985, when I first met her, Cynthia Marshall was president of the Charlotte, North Carolina, Junior League, which had rallied 600 women volunteers to improve the civic life of their city. Cynthia called the CIS office in Washington to ask me to come speak to her group. Somehow I'd gotten through life without ever having heard of the Junior League. When my assistant, Haleh Samii, passed on the request, my reaction was: "Great—I love baseball!"

Haleh straightened me out, and I headed down to Charlotte. Even before I gave my talk, I could tell that Cynthia and I saw things in similar ways, although her beautiful Southern manners were quite a bit different from my urban style.

Cynthia had helped develop Charlotte's Family Center, a resource for abused and neglected children. The idea of creating caring teams of agency personnel to help kids in trouble wasn't new to her. I guess we were fortunate that our paths crossed at the moment they did, because she latched onto the idea of Communities In Schools and vowed to start an affiliate in Charlotte.

I don't think I've ever met a more tenacious and energetic advocate for children. Her magic eyes are supersharp. "Cynthia is one of those rare people who never sees a 'problem,'" says Linda Harrill, CIS of North Carolina state director from 1989 to 2012. "She sees *everything* as an opportunity. She grasps ideas quickly and sees how to implement and expand them. I could say, 'Cynthia, have you ever thought of doing a Mall Academy?' and she'd get that twinkle in her eye and say, 'Oh . . . yes, we can do that,' and you can just tell she's already putting the pieces together in her mind."

One of my favorite statements of Cynthia's is this one: "In any community, if a cross section of key leaders gets together and sees an issue that needs attention, especially one with economic implications, something's going to happen." I agree wholeheartedly, but I would add that the "something" depends on the vision and abilities of people like Cynthia, Charlotte's Champion for Children.

Cynthia Marshall names three principles as crucial for a CIS team:

1. Be wide open to any idea or person that happens to come your way. She says, "You can be talking to a person in a grocery store and find that they know someone who has a call to be connected."

2. Listen with your heart as well as your head.

3. Use the network you have, the people you've known for many years, not just whatever group of agencies or organizations the board of directors may help locate. Find a way for them to understand that *everyone* is part of the big picture, that everyone has a role to play.

It's easy to see how these principles have influenced some of the important successes that Cynthia has achieved over the years. Consider this situation, which took place shortly after she got CIS off the ground and had begun her practice of remaining constantly alert to new ideas and new ways to serve students and families:

Kim, a fourth grader at a Charlotte elementary school with a CIS presence, came from an Asian American family who'd been in the U.S. for just a short time. Kim's CIS coordinator noticed that he was absent a lot. When she asked him what was wrong, he told her that his head hurt. He also didn't seem to be getting enough to eat.

The coordinator took him to the school nurse, who looked in his mouth in the course of her examination. It wasn't pretty: twelve teeth were either decaying or abscessed. I'm guessing that Cynthia's principle about "using your own network" was already being instilled among her colleagues, because the CIS staffer thought first of a dentist who belonged to her own church. She knew that this practitioner was used to treating middle- and upper-income people, but she also knew he had a good heart and cared about the community. And in fact, when the dentist heard about Kim, he was appalled and volunteered to treat the boy for free.

Getting the right dental attention took care of the headaches, and of course once Kim could chew without wincing, his appetite improved, too. The site coordinator was even able to extend the benefits to Kim's family, making a home visit to counsel them on the importance of nutrition and checkups for the other children.

But for Cynthia, the seed of an idea had been planted. *How many more kids*, she wondered, *have the same problem?* The county health department was already one of her partners, providing CIS students with physical screenings but not dental hygiene. So Cynthia forged a new agreement with them to perform dental screenings for every CIS child.

With that program in place, her team was able to gauge the scope of the problem—and it was huge. Many, many students were suffering from poor dental health, and it wasn't hard to extrapolate from Kim's case and assume that a number of the kids' daily academic performance was being affected. The dentist from the CIS staffer's congregation put the word out to his colleagues: Did they realize how bad a problem this was in their community? Shortly thereafter, the number of dentists providing free care for CIS students began to increase.

This was also an issue that Cynthia was able to use to engage the entire community. People could buy toothpaste and toothbrushes and give them to every CIS kid. "They may feel: 'I can't prevent dropouts, but I'll help kids this way.' And the amazing thing is, it *does* prevent dropouts."

One person and one partnership leads to another and another. Cynthia learned that the local community college had a program that taught high school graduates how to become dental assistants. They also operated a free clinic so they could learn their trade—and they needed patients to work on. In short order, dozens of CIS kids were being taken there regularly to get their teeth cleaned. One student got into a conversation with his hygienist, became a dental assistant after graduating from high school, and went to work in the office of one of the volunteer dentists. As a result, he decided he wanted to become a dentist himself. It's amazing how these things come full circle . . . but as Cynthia says, "As we adults learn to be more open to possibilities, that attitude is transferred to the young people."

More than 30 years after its start, the dental program continues in new forms. Mecklenburg County school nurses refer cases to county dental hygienists, who come to the school to screen individual students. If it's determined that the student needs services, the school nurse and dental hygienists collaborate and refer students to private dentists. If a family has little or no dental insurance, the CIS school site coordinator may use part of their small discretionary account to cover the costs. In most cases, the students who are referred by the school nurse are those who have severe problems—poor attendance, headaches—so they're eligible for receiving the limited services. This issue may also surface when site coordinators conduct "check-ins" with parents and a plan of action is set in motion.

The pandemic has created inevitable disruptions in programs like this. Prior to the school shutdowns, the Junior League of Charlotte approved a placement with a small group of volunteers who helped to coordinate the effort and recruit dentists from their private networks. These volunteers worked with a CIS staff member to coordinate the program. A community college dental program whose senior students provided free dental services to some students has also been curtailed. But CIS of Charlotte–Mecklenburg is working hard to get things back to normal—as are we all.

AIM FOR COLLEGE . . . AND STAY IN SCHOOL

Jack Tate, CIS of Charlotte's founding board president, was a former bank president and one of Charlotte's most powerful and respected businessmen. He was also a "consummate child advocate," in Cynthia's words. One day in 1994, Jack walked into Cynthia's office and said, "Okay, I'm done. I've raised $500,000 for a college scholarship fund. So . . . can you build a program?"

This wasn't quite as out of the blue as it might sound. A few months earlier, he'd begun to develop an idea partly inspired by a man named George Lewis, a Charlotte entrepreneur and founder of Cogentrix Energy. Jack had two connections with the other businessman: they shared a common enthusiasm for CIS, and Jack's son John was George's banker. When George mentioned to John Tate that he was interested in doing something to help Charlotte's children, John said, "Well, my dad is really involved in this Communities In Schools program, and they want to start a small alternative high school for hard-to-reach kids on the top floor of a Methodist church. They're looking for someone to 'adopt' the school."

George Lewis paid the lease to the church so the Wesley Uptown academy could begin its work. He got his employees at Cogentrix involved, too, as tutors and mentors. And as if this weren't enough, he declared, "Your mission is to keep kids in school. That's fantastic, but I think we can do even better. Young people need college these days. I'm going to give a four-year scholarship to every senior who graduates from the academy."

When CIS board president Jack Tate heard this, the inspiration struck. He said to Cynthia: "We need a college scholarship program here for the other CIS kids who aren't at the Uptown academy. I'll raise the money." Cynthia agreed that it was a wonderful idea, thanked him, and went on with her busy life.

Nine weeks later, he returned, saying, "I'm done," and CIS of Charlotte–Mecklenburg was half a million dollars to the good. Now Cynthia *really* needed to come up with a scholarship program.

What happened next is a perfect illustration of how to use magic eyes to see creative possibilities. A scholarship is a great thing, she reasoned, but if you're not prepared for college, it's not going to do much good. You have to engage students early on and imbue them with a college-bound mentality—and of course, the academic and social skills needed to succeed in higher education. Cynthia also realized something else: the very process of grooming kids for college could act as a powerful deterrent to dropping out of high school. "You can tell a student that they'll make X thousand dollars more with a diploma than as a dropout, and even more as a college graduate, but it may not mean anything. Words without experiences often don't sink in. You have to *show* them the jobs and *show* them the connection between the education and the jobs. Demonstrate how math and computer skills make a difference in your prospects. Show how punctuality and reliability and courtesy are part of success in life."

A lot of us take these truths for granted because they're part of the culture we grew up in. But children bring a diversity of experiences to school. It's a frequently mistaken middle-class assumption that all kids already know about the values of the dominant culture.

Cynthia and her colleagues matched the money Jack Tate had raised with a grant from the Z. Smith Reynolds Foundation and hired the first director of the ThinkCOLLEGE® program. Kemal Atkins had been an admissions officer at Appalachian State University and was ideally suited to plan an initiative that would identify the best practices used nationwide to prepare kids to go to college.

As of 2020, ThinkCOLLEGE® has overseen scholarships for thousands of scholars over the past 20-plus years. Jack Tate's fund alone has awarded over $100,000 to 132 students. And the emphasis on going to college has continued to intensify. Educational and career coaches provide one-on-one and group counseling, life skills workshops, college and career exploration, job shadowing, internships, and social capital leadership opportunities. CIS of Charlotte partners with Central Piedmont Community College (CPCC) to support their Summer Bridge program, which helps graduating high school seniors get a head start on college classes the summer after graduating from high school. The program lets students enroll in up to two college classes at CPCC for six weeks in the summer, with structured support at one of CPCC's five campuses.

CIS of Charlotte also established the Talent Search program, with a primary focus on college and career readiness. Talent Search is administered by CIS through funding from the U.S. Department of Education and serves about 1,000 students annually. The goal of Talent Search is to support students who have the potential to succeed in higher education and who may be the first in their family to attend college. The students focus on career exploration, college preparation, and social and cultural development. Moreover, the Talent Search counselors continue to assist the students with the transition from high school to college through their first semester in college.

The dropout epidemic *can* be stopped . . . if a Champion for Children with heart, vision, and a strategy is there to rally the community around its schools.

SEEING DIFFERENTLY

Cynthia Marshall retired in 2006 after 21 years at the helm of CIS of Charlotte–Mecklenburg. She left an organization that now serves more than 3,900 young people every year in 48 elementary, middle, and high schools. It's one of the most lauded human-services programs in the nation.

Cynthia has received just about every honor you can think of, including Charlotte's Woman of the Year, the *Charlotte Business Journal*'s Women in Business Achievement Award, and the Order of the Long Leaf Pine, the highest civilian honor given by the governor of North Carolina to reward outstanding leadership.

Looking back on her years with CIS, she told me:

At the start I had so much to learn. I grasped the whole agency-coordination idea, but I didn't really understand how much volunteers could mean to young people. But when our board member from IBM recruited 120 IBM employees in one year, then I understood. The kids can't believe an adult is coming to spend time with them and not getting paid for it! It's a miracle to them, and it changes how they feel about themselves and about adults. And after a while, I learned something just as important: the change is reciprocal. The tutors who gave their hour a week were being transformed in just as great a way as the kids receiving the gift.

Cynthia believes that this two-way transformation will be a lasting legacy to Charlotte's youth.

We've discovered that many of our CIS graduates have either gone into a helping profession or found a way to give back. One former student was a teenage mom in high school. Now she's an executive assistant at Bank of America and mentors other teen mothers. Bill, I've often heard you say, "You can't give away what you don't have"—and these kids got it. They're living it out, and as a result, the positive cycle goes on and on.

Barb Pellin, past president of the Charlotte CIS board of directors, told me: "As I've talked to CIS leaders at the state and national level, it's clear that Charlotte was blessed with an executive director that every CIS organization in the country would like to duplicate."

That's true: Cynthia Marshall was and is a model Champion for Children, an inspiring leader for our entire network. But she would be the first to tell you that her principles and approach are easy enough to duplicate if you consistently see opportunities and possibilities in the maze of challenges confronting schools, kids, and families.

. . . AND BEYOND

In this chapter I talked a lot about CIS's roots in Atlanta, and the magic eyes of people like Neil Shorthouse and Dave Lewis, who helped build the Atlanta program. The current executive director, Frank Brown, is another guy with magic eyes. He's created an alumni association for CIS students that will be a model for the entire network.

Looking around at the students CIS was serving, Frank says, "I started to see patterns." These kids needed continued support after graduating from high school, and they also represented an untapped force for change in their communities. So Frank began to organize his alumni efforts, beginning with just two students. Now there are nearly 200 kids involved.

In essence, members of the association continue to receive CIS case management as they proceed to college, technical school, entrepreneurial projects, and even the military. Any CIS student can join, with two requirements: if they're going on to further education, they have to maintain a 2.5 GPA, and they have to come back and volunteer in their community. The Atlanta program has been able to provide almost $60,000 in tuition assistance, and CIS National has also supported the alumni association with a $100,000 grant.

This vision represents quite an expansion for CIS of Atlanta. Frank Brown asked himself, *Was that my mission?* This Champion for Children saw the need, and his answer was yes. "I call it a cocoon—a cocoon of love," he says. "They go in as caterpillars and come out as beautiful butterflies who can fly on their own. And every one of the children we serve is a butterfly."

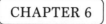
THE THIRD SIDE
OF THE TRIANGLE

In the first edition of this book, published in 2007, I opened the chapter you're about to read with this statement: "'No child left behind' . . . If ever there was a great goal for America's students, this is surely it."

The reference was to the then-current No Child Left Behind Act, which President George W. Bush signed into law in 2002. No Child Left Behind (NCLB) was intended as the cornerstone of a nationwide school-reform movement. Fifteen years later, a new piece of legislation is in place, signed by a different president. But I can use the same words to praise it: "'Every student succeeds' . . . If ever there was a great goal for America's students, this is surely it."

The same, yes, but in some crucial ways very different. The Every Student Succeeds Act (ESSA), which went into effect in 2015, is light-years more responsive and comprehensive than NCLB. It creates an entirely new series of benchmarks for success, and many of these goals are the very ones CIS has been reaching for, too.

THINKING ABOUT FAILURE

When I wrote about No Child Left Behind in 2007, I meant what I said: it really was, and is, an inspiring goal. However, I went on to criticize the legislation on several counts:

- It called for supplemental education services for students but only deemed tutoring and academic coaching as qualifying rather than the whole set of resources needed and available.

- It assumed all kids have the same position at the starting line and come to school ready to learn.

- It overemphasized standardized testing and held schools accountable for "failures" that in many instances were out of their control.

- It championed "school choice" for parents, encouraging the abandonment of "failing" schools rather than a serious attempt to fix them that went beyond "improved performance on tests."

- Most importantly, *the NCLB legislation offered no coherent treatment of the fundamental importance of community involvement as a means of achieving the legislation's goals.*

The Every Student Succeeds Act is a different story. The emphasis on standards and on improving low-performing schools remains in ESSA, but unlike NCLB, "ESSA focuses less on standardized tests, limits federal control over schools, and equips states with the power to measure, identify, and remedy performance and academic inequality," as CIS staffer Afia Obeng wrote when the legislation was passed. She went on, "This is an important victory for Communities In Schools. For the first time in the history of our organization, integrated student supports is now cited in federal education law."[1]

CIS National President Dan Cardinali declared, "This represents our nation's best opportunity to help poor students, who are now the majority in public schools, overcome their barriers to learning. . . . It is gratifying that our leaders in Congress looked at the evidence and determined this is an effective and cost-efficient use of resources."[2]

The U.S. Department of Education frankly admitted that "NCLB's prescriptive requirements became increasingly unworkable for schools and educators." The improved legislation addresses this issue, and many others beyond the scope of this chapter.

Of particular concern here is that ESSA "advances equity by upholding critical protections for America's disadvantaged and high-need students."[3] One innovation that may prove particularly significant for CIS and the students we serve is the section of ESSA under Title IV-A called Student Support and Academic Enrichment Grants. These are block grants to states based on the Title I funding formula, and then that same formula is used by a state to allocate funds to individual school districts. This funding directly addresses the fact that all kids do *not* come to school ready to learn and broadens the scope of the additional resources deemed as academic supports. So it takes into account the nonacademic barriers to success; it supports the whole child.

When President Obama signed ESSA into law in December 2015, he called it "a Christmas miracle" for U.S. students. That's really not an exaggeration, because for years we've been working to gain recognition and support for what I call "the third side of the triangle."

A CHALLENGE TO THE SYSTEM

No Child Left Behind painted a picture of our education system that resembles a triangle with only two sides. The first side of the triangle is about *governance*. Reform in this area involves training principals and teachers, improving school administration, and introducing efficiency and standards-based accountability. The idea is to professionalize the system, often by adapting management practices from the private sector, with the aim of making the school more effective. Improvements to the physical plant—which is often in disgraceful shape—are part of this area, too. And should the school still fail to meet standards, "governance" takes on a whole different meaning, since mayors could take over such institutions and become the new bosses.

The second side of the triangle is about *pedagogy*. Reform efforts focus on teaching strategies, curriculum innovations, and the options we provide students to help them learn. We work to inculcate different teaching styles and fresh approaches (such as distance learning and service-learning), along with proven programmatic elements to more effectively teach phonics, math, and writing. Educators consider the most basic questions about "the project of education": what it's set up to do and achieve in terms of preparation for citizenship and economic empowerment in the growing global marketplace. Broadly speaking, this side of the triangle is about the *content* and *purpose* of education, while the first side is about the *form*.

What was missing, until ESSA was signed into law, was the third side of the triangle: the coordinated involvement of community members who can meet the nonacademic needs of students and help schools truly become places where every student succeeds. Neither of the first two sides of the triangle address the issues of the most vulnerable kids. The best teacher, the top administrator, the most outstanding curriculum, the highest standards—none of these will put food in a child's stomach or a roof over his head. And these "extracurricular" issues are so pervasive in our country that when ignored, they undermine the huge and necessary investment we're making in the other two sides of the triangle.

Think of a business that's run very well, with great employees and a terrific product—except that their intended customers have no money, so the whole thing is pointless. Even if reforms worked perfectly to strengthen governance and pedagogy, you'd still be missing something huge: Are the students themselves coming to school ready and able to succeed?

Integrated, school-based services aren't just an addendum or a support to reform of the other two sides. Rather, they must be welded into the triangle as a firm, equal third side. *Community resources and support are a necessary—but not sufficient—condition for true school reform and for the success of millions of children*, especially those whose social well-being is threatened.

To believe otherwise is to allow middle-class presuppositions about "what kids need" to frame the debate. It may well be that your children and most of the other kids in your community come to school after a good night's sleep, a nutritious breakfast, and a short walk through a safe, pretty neighborhood. Outdated, shortsighted reform perspectives assume that *all* kids come to school this way:

ready to learn and succeed. They think the kids are fine—it's those darn *schools* that are failing them. And if there *is* some inequality among children at the starting line, it can be ameliorated through academic-support services and maybe a mentor.

In thousands of schools across the U.S., that picture is tragically inaccurate and far from reality, and it's about time the reform movement faced up to it. ESSA is a huge step forward in this regard.

Historically, CIS has been something of a thorn in the side of the education-reform movement because we point to these issues that schools aren't equipped to handle, and we refuse to accept that the problems aren't directly related to a child's failure. We necessarily challenge an institution—public education—that isn't set up to respond. A homeless child needs a stable place to live, but getting her one isn't a "school-reform strategy."

It's all too understandable that the education establishment responded defensively to our critique of traditional, "two-sided" reform efforts. That's why it's so important that we approach educators in a spirit of empathy and respect. It's not their fault that they aren't housing experts—or family therapists, nutritionists, or employment counselors. That's not their job. Moreover, most of them know perfectly well that there's something vital missing from the equation. We need to help provide an environment in which they, too, can speak out about the inadequacies of reform efforts that ignore the third side of the triangle. Without this baseline, many kids literally drop out.

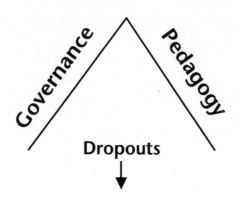

All the school reform in the world won't provide the Five Basics. That's up to the community.

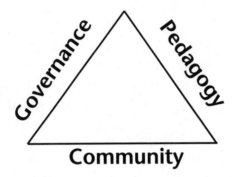

Blaming educators and schools for "failing" is no more helpful than the previous generation's tendency to blame the kids. If you really want to put it in those terms, it's the community that's failing both schools and children. We need to accept our share of the solution instead of expecting teachers to be superheroes. And we certainly can't keep telling our teachers that they aren't any good. Either they'll start to believe it—just as kids do if you criticize them enough—or else they'll get mad and devote precious time to organizing ways to force us to give them respect (and money). And if that doesn't work, many will simply quit the profession.

I'm not trying to let teachers and principals off the hook. They have an incredibly important role to play; they have to be accountable, and if they're not getting results, the next step is to find out why. Some just need to find another job—that's true in every business. But the majority of educators are good; they're just overstressed and under-resourced. I've seen teachers who were considered mediocre become much better once they had an environment created for them that respected them and provided the resources they needed to do their job.

Herb Alpert, legendary musician, co-founder of A&M Records, and one of my and CIS's oldest friends, once came with me to visit a high school in a very tough New York City community. The principal was a former star basketball player; he stood about 6'10" and was pretty tough himself. Everything in that school was neat, orderly, and well managed—not even a piece of paper on the floor. Herb took all this in and then asked the man: "So why do you need CIS?"

"I'm good at my job," the principal replied. "I can keep it calm and professional in here and make sure we have good teachers, high standards, and a strong curriculum. But I have no control over what happens outside the school grounds. The CIS team is my arms and legs to all the housing projects around here. They make sure kids get safely to school with the resources they need." That, in a few words, says so much about how all three sides of the triangle can come together in a coordinated way. Great principals need help, too, and conversely, once the students arrive safely at school, they expect and deserve a high-quality education.

The problem is that most school districts—*especially* those where the dropout epidemic is most dire—don't have any obvious person or group that superintendents can turn to and say, "Please handle the third side of the triangle. Please be our Champion for Children. Please help these young people come to school ready to learn." The goal of a Communities In Schools local affiliate is to be that organization. And our overall "reform strategy" is to articulate this approach, provide effective examples of it, and help create national momentum leading to the day when *every* school district, with or without CIS's presence, will have a triangle with three strong sides.

In this as in everything else, the power of community, of working together, is all-important. Neil Shorthouse has a list of what he calls the Magnificent Seven—seven community sectors that, in partnership, can make the biggest difference in creating change.

The Magnificent Seven

1. Educators (including college-level teachers and education departments)
2. The private sector (including business, labor, the media, and funders)
3. Faith community leaders
4. Government and civic community leaders
5. Professionals (including health services, housing, the justice system, counselors, United Way–supported agencies, and other nonprofits)
6. Parents, guardians, and extended family members
7. Students

Creating an environment in which these seven community groups can be part of the process, bringing the third side of the triangle together with governance and pedagogy, requires the encouragement and collaboration of professional educators. And yes, there can be resistance from school authorities; we'll go into that in more detail later in this chapter. But many community leaders may not realize just how open their school system is to their involvement. Educators can't do it alone, and they will welcome your help.

Let me pause right here to emphasize the word *help*. We're talking about committed, experienced professionals—the thousands of superintendents, principals, teachers, and administrators who've dedicated their lives to the education of our young people. They do not need you, me, or anyone else to stroll into their schools and start telling them what to do. That's a terrible abuse of whatever influence we might wield as a community. (They also don't need politicians passing legislation that commits them to "reforms" without the means to implement the changes, as we learned all too well with No Child Left Behind.) The superintendent of your local school district would never think of walking into Microsoft and telling the managers how to do their work. Why, then, would a CEO—no matter how gifted at running his own business—think he could tell a school system how to do its job?

We're speaking once again of partnership, of the kind of collaboration in which each member of the orchestra offers what they do best. When community leaders—especially those in the business world—approach school officials with this attitude, they'll receive a warm welcome.

"PEOPLE WHO DO WHAT HE'S DONE . . ."

Once upon a time there was a boy named Paul who grew up in a small, poor town called Davis Creek, West Virginia. He was a slow learner in elementary school and didn't learn to read until he was in the third grade. That label "slow learner" stuck with him for years. In junior high, they started calling him an "underachiever" because they discovered he was pretty smart, even though he wasn't doing well in class. Then in high school, his grades shot up, and suddenly he was "gifted."

But in his heart and soul, he knew that he was still little Paul, the slow learner. He didn't think like other people. The school wanted him to conceive of the world sequentially, in order from A to B. He tended to see ideas holistically, metaphorically. He made connections that seemed perfectly clear to him, but when he voiced them, most adults didn't get it. "You're being too random!" they told him. "Stop going off on tangents and then trying to pull everything together into some 'big picture.'"

So despite his good grades and the fancy new label of "gifted," Paul knew he wasn't going to college. *No one* from his high school went to college.

One teacher disagreed.

Mrs. Sang taught Latin and French, and she wouldn't leave Paul alone. "You're going to college," she insisted. "You *are.*" "I'm not college material," he'd mutter, but she showed him and his parents how to fill out the applications and declared that he *would* be accepted.

He was. Paul went off to Ohio State University, and well into his freshman year he continued to get letters from Mrs. Sang, letters full of exhortations to believe in himself, to remember that he was still being formed, that he was young and capable of anything.

A number of years passed, and the adult Paul decided to make a trip back to his old high school. Mrs. Sang was still there and delighted to see him. She'd followed his career with interest and pride. She promptly pulled him into her fifth-period class and sat him up in front of the students.

"Did you go to college?" she asked him.

"Yes, I did," Paul replied. "I went to Ohio State."

"Do you have a master's degree?"

"Yes, from the University of North Carolina."

"Do you have a doctorate?"

"I do."

"From where?"

"Harvard University."

"What sort of jobs have you worked?"

"Well, I started out as a teacher. Then I became a principal, then an assistant superintendent. At the moment I'm superintendent of schools in Princeton, New Jersey."

Mrs. Sang allowed a moment of silence, then asked Paul, "Where did you go to high school?"

"Right here."

And the classroom erupted in disbelieving catcalls and shouts. "You did not!" the students yelled. "No way! Who are you really?"

Mrs. Sang told them to be quiet, then asked, "Now, why don't you believe this man? He just got done telling you he's from Davis Creek, just like you."

One boy raised his hand and said, "People who do what he's done don't go to this school."

Dr. Paul D. Houston has never forgotten that day. "People who do what he's done don't go to this school." It reinforced his passion to work for the day when our public school system would never provoke a student to speak such sad, negative words.

RAISING A VILLAGE

In 1994, Paul Houston became the executive director of the American Association of School Administrators, and until his retirement in 2008, he served as a brilliant and tireless advocate for breaking down the barriers between schools and communities. To this day he continues to write and speak out for equitable education for all students.

It's startling how much we have in common. Both of us were called "slow," and neither of us would have been a good bet for adult success. We're both "right-brain" people, thinking metaphorically and holistically. A caring adult made the crucial difference in each of our young lives, helping us believe in ourselves and reject the negative labeling.

Paul Houston's credo was clear, and it was very good news for community leaders who wanted to be involved in stopping the dropout epidemic:

> The schools have to change, they have to involve communities, parents, the greater world. It's the only way they're going to be able to keep kids in school. I tell superintendents: "You have to stop thinking of yourselves as superintendents of *schools* and start thinking of yourselves as superintendents of *education*, of *learning*." There's a big difference.

Some administrators are unsure and perhaps anxious about what this means for their own school districts, but Paul's words remain cogent:

> We're past the point of people saying, "I don't think it's the right idea." Now the whole conversation is about the right *ways* for this idea to be realized. How can communities step up and support the work school superintendents are doing? The schools are looking to community leaders and saying, "Help—we can't do this alone."

So as Paul likes to ask, if it takes a village to raise a child, what does it take to raise a village? Public schools play two essential roles here. First, if you're looking for a rallying cry, a cause to believe in, you can't do better than the schools. Regardless of what political or social divisions may exist in a community, *everyone* wants kids to do well in this area. It's a place to plant your flag and call others to join the battle. Second, these facilities are physically central to the community as well. A village has to *happen* somewhere—what better place than the schoolhouse? It's right there, it's a place where families are already used to going, it's a public trust, and all too often it's underutilized once classes are over for the day.

Community involvement (the third side of the triangle) is, as I've said, a necessary but not sufficient condition for successful schools. Paul Houston and other advocates for community involvement in schools are well aware that the other two sides of the triangle—the ones for which educators and policy makers are accountable—are badly in need of true reform. Community involvement is not the be-all and end-all, the miraculous solution to every school's problems. We need to reexamine how school experiences—teaching, testing, assessments—are presented to our young people.

"We make kids failures," Paul pointed out, "and then say, 'Why do you want to quit school? You don't like failing? What's wrong with you?' We educators bear a big chunk of the burden for that situation."

During his tenure at AASA, he always saw a particularly crucial role for the business community to play in creating a "tipping point" for genuine school reform.

"Are businesspeople going to read *The Last Dropout*?" he asked me when I was writing the first edition of this book, back in 2007.

"I sure hope so," I replied.

"Okay," Paul said. "Please say this to them: The head of the American Association of School Administrators needs you to be part of the solution to our schools' problems. We need you to speak out and take action on behalf of community involvement with our kids' education. As a superintendent, I could say, 'Schools need this kind of help,' and people think, *There he goes, just bellyaching and whining again.* But if a business leader says the same thing, people are going to pay attention: 'Wow, we'd better do something about this. The president of the electric company said the community has to partner with the schools—it must be true.'"

So business leaders have credibility that they can apply in a positive fashion. They can use their influence in the political process to get politicians to focus on the right set of issues. The basic argument should be that we can't sustain democracy without a strong public school system because citizens need to be literate, informed, and able to participate knowledgeably in civic life. That's why *public* education came into existence in this country, and its mission has, if anything, grown even more critical. Business leaders need to say to politicians, loudly and clearly: "Every one of us has a stake in this. We've got to keep our kids in school."

I hear Paul talking about three things: **awareness, advocacy,** and **action**. Local business leaders and other power brokers must first become **aware** of the true problems confronting their school system; then they must firmly claim a role as **advocates** for the right kind of change. Last, they can take appropriate **action** to support a coordinated community response to the needs of children—and their teachers. These are themes we'll continue to explore in Chapter 9.

I also hear Paul making a clear case for why schools need the third side of the triangle. Without community support, educators and administrators simply can't provide the safety net that will prevent students from leaving school, branded as "failures," long before any reforms in the other two sides of the triangle have a chance to work. If only all kids started from the same place, equipped with the same resources and supports that you provide for *your* children, then school reform alone might be the answer to our troubled public education system. But that's not the case—it's not even close. The majority of kids who drop out are suffering from deficits that no curriculum can make up, and these are *all* our children.

Truly, we put our educators in a terrible bind. "No child left behind" and "every student succeeds" are moral obligations and economic necessities. But the deteriorating conditions that millions of families face make it virtually impossible for the schools to fulfill this mission. They just don't have the resources or the expertise to address all the deficiencies. Without the third side of the triangle, we have an unstable, inadequate structure, and kids literally drop out of it. Once again, the need for the community's involvement as an equal partner is clear.

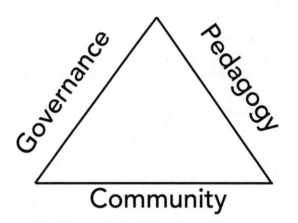

BRINGING POWER, AUTHORITY, AND IDEA TOGETHER

I want to turn to some of the practical implications of what we've been discussing. One problem with a good image or metaphor (such as the third side of the triangle) is that its simplicity and clarity can fool you into thinking that *everything* connected with the concept is likewise simple and clear. But the real-world challenges are extremely complex.

I know that Paul Houston is right when he says that superintendents will welcome your help as an advocate for community involvement. As he says, the debate is no longer about *whether* this partnership should exist. When administrators have questions and doubts, they focus on *how* this should be done, not *if* it should happen, and the Every Student Succeeds Act has come to their aid in crucially important ways.

But just because a school superintendent may be familiar with the general idea of using a school as a delivery point for needed social services for children and families, that doesn't mean he'll be an easy sell on the *specifics*. With the best intentions—and these leaders are overwhelmingly good, smart, dedicated people who are completely committed to the children in their school system— those in authority tend to be skeptical of ideas that arise from *outside* their own area of expertise, especially if those concepts seem to call their expertise into question. And the natural response when you're feeling skeptical is to focus on the negative, to quickly point out all the problems and drawbacks.

What's the result? When a grassroots community leader manages to get five minutes with a school superintendent to "sell" CIS or its equivalent, they may have to spend four of those minutes being told why the ideas wouldn't work in this school system—or worse yet, "We're already doing that" when they aren't.

Superintendents and school boards represent *Authority:* they make the decisions about what will happen in the education system. And a group like CIS is offering an *Idea*, a strategy, a new way of approaching an old problem. The fact is, a one-on-one meeting between Idea and Authority can be a tricky proposition.

Fortunately, there's another way to do this, one that brings to the table the missing voice. This is the voice of *Power*—and it might be *your* voice, if you're a respected business leader, local government official, foundation director, or leader of a faith community. This is one of the most time-tested principles of community organizing: *Power, Authority, and Idea need to sit at the same table.* It's the same principle that Paul Houston invoked when he talked about the critical role of business leaders in advocating for a new approach to the dropout epidemic.

People in positions of power in your area—and again, you may be one of them—have a stake in the community. If there's a serious problem, they want it solved. The dropout epidemic is about as serious as a problem can get. Enlightened self-interest alone would dictate that community leaders need to take it seriously and play a major role in stemming the tide of young dropouts. Unemployment equals crime and unsafe neighborhoods, affecting every family who lives there. And the business sector in particular simply can't afford this constant, worsening drain on the economy and the labor force.

I'm happy to say that for many, many powerful individuals, self-interest isn't the only motivator. Beyond that, these people simply care. They see the human cost of the dropout epidemic, and they feel a moral responsibility to help their community— especially if part of that morality is an ethic of giving back, of making a contribution to society as a way of expressing gratitude for the gifts and benefits they've enjoyed in their own lives.

WHEN POWER SPEAKS . . .

Some people get nervous when they hear the word *power*, as if it's a nasty secret that no good-hearted person should know about. The truth is that *every* community has its centers of power, and everyone knows who those people are. Often they're the ones with money (but not always). Using power simply means using your internal and external resources to get the job done. Those with this strength have respect and influence—when Power speaks, Authority *will* listen.

This idea isn't new or unique to CIS. Almost every successful agent for community change has followed a similar path, and CIS local affiliates are no exception. At some point, there was a "power lunch," convened by Power, that brought Authority and Idea to the same table.

There's a hitch that can sometimes occur when Idea talks to Power about convening a "power lunch." Generous, civic-minded individuals (and corporations and foundations) are often accustomed to exercising their might with their checkbooks. I'm the last person to refuse a contribution in the name of kids, but as valuable as funding is, it's *not* always the best use of power.

Neither is personal involvement in the schools, necessarily. We need volunteers, as many as possible—at this writing, 11,800 people volunteer with CIS affiliates, contributing $8 million worth of volunteer time—but putting you on the front lines to work directly with kids and families may not be the best use of your talents.

A good case in point is my friend Brad Currey. He and I went to the same adult Sunday school at St. Luke's Episcopal Church in Atlanta back when we were trying to launch the first prototype Communities In Schools sites. Brad was the second-in-command at Atlanta's largest bank, and he had a big heart and a strong desire to give back to his community. One Sunday morning we were pondering how the scriptural message of loving your neighbor could be put into action for Atlanta's youth.

"Well, I know you've started these academies," Brad said to me. "Do you want me to be a tutor?"

As much as I appreciated the offer, I already had something different in mind. "Uh, not really, Brad," I replied.

I think his feelings might have been a little hurt, but he hung in there. "Then how can I help?"

"Simple. Give me one hour of your time. Call the superintendent of schools and ask him to lunch at your club—tell him you'd like to discuss a great idea for helping kids succeed. Then bring me along. I'll be the Idea."

So we brought Power, Authority, and Idea together for lunch. And by the time we'd had our coffee, Superintendent Crim had agreed to another meeting with me and my colleagues to explore the CIS idea.

Yes, I could have encouraged Brad to just become a tutor. And who knows—he might have been great at it. But by encouraging him instead to use his power on behalf of *thousands* of kids, not just a few, we took a big step forward. He had a unique gift to give, and fortunately he was willing to share it.

A NEW DEAL IN VEGAS

A revealing case study of how to bring Power, Authority, and Idea together to introduce the third side of the triangle into a school system took place in 2003; the setting was Las Vegas.

You probably associate the city with glitzy casinos and 24-hour action. But Clark County, home to the gaming mecca, also happened to be the fastest-growing school system in the United

States that year. And when you left the Strip, you found thousands of children living in the most dire circumstances imaginable. An estimated 3,500 school-age children were homeless, and more than 40 percent qualified for free or reduced-price lunches, a measure that's reliably correlated with economic disadvantage. These children needed the community to stand up for them, and fortunately we saw that happen.

Elaine Wynn and her husband, Steve, started their hotel-casino company in 1973 with one little hotel in downtown Las Vegas called the Golden Nugget. Over the years, they expanded their business and created some of the city's most well-known spots, including the Mirage, Treasure Island, Bellagio, and the Wynn. Elaine is definitely a force to be reckoned with, a true community Power. She's charming, intelligent, and extremely motivated to succeed.

However, I've had the privilege of knowing Elaine in a very different context. Like most mothers, she wanted to make sure her kids grew up healthy, happy, and well educated. But what makes Elaine special is that she decided early on that *all* children should have these same benefits. And she has walked her talk ever since, working hard to ensure that Las Vegas provides educational and cultural opportunities for all who live there.

We've also had the great good fortune to have Elaine on the CIS National Board of Directors since 1999, and she's served as our board chair since 2007. She got up to speed with our mission and strategies about as fast as anyone I've ever known. She wanted to speak up for Idea right from the start, in addition to using her power in the usual ways a board member might. So her contributions to our work around the country have been enormous, but Las Vegas and its children have always been close to her heart.

She called me one day in 2003 with two pieces of news: There was a new school superintendent in Clark County whom she believed might be receptive to the CIS idea. And the Omidyar family, owners of the very well-funded Omidyar Foundation (as it was then called; now it's the Omidyar Group) had just relocated to Las Vegas. Didn't this sound like a potential "power lunch"?

It did. But I reminded Elaine about our previous experience in Las Vegas, nearly 10 years earlier. It's not a story I like to dwell on, but it's instructive in this context. It's a great example of what happens when Power, Idea, and Authority do *not* find a way to talk.

HOW TO REJECT A GOOD IDEA

In the mid-1990s, CIS was keen to offer its services in Las Vegas. Naturally, Elaine was spearheading our efforts there. Well, one of the drawbacks of being a Power is that sometimes you get into a power *struggle*. That was what happened almost immediately. It wasn't Elaine's fault, and at this late date the details really don't matter. But the result was that Authority—represented by the school board—was unwilling to give the CIS idea a fair hearing.

Of course, a reason was needed for rejecting the idea. When you're looking for apparent negatives, you can always find one. Certain people pointed out that among dozens of other services, CIS affiliates offered health clinics in some schools. And didn't these do family-planning counseling? Did they make birth control available? What about abortion referrals? In short, the CIS idea was turned into an official "pro-choice" platform, which went over very badly in this largely traditional community.

Now, none of this was accurate. As I've described in previous chapters, the whole essence of the organization is that it's locally accountable to the community. *Nothing* can happen through CIS that isn't approved by the board of directors and the school system. We have no "laundry list" of required services that a local affiliate must provide to the schools; it's entirely up to the stakeholders. So this notion that CIS as a whole—as an Idea—was somehow pro–teenage sex or pro-abortion was absurd. We're just pro-kids, pro-parents, and pro-communities.

So it was up to us as holders of the Idea to convince Authority in Las Vegas of the truth of this. Power, represented by Elaine, had gotten us a seat at the table. The players were staring at us, waiting to hear what we had to say.

And we failed. We couldn't find the right words, the right arguments, to convince them that CIS had no political ax to grind. Authority was unable to accept Idea, was ultimately threatened by Idea, and rejected it. Maybe there were no right words; the political infighting and power struggle may have been insurmountable. But 10 years later, when this same issue came up again, we were a decade wiser and knew that we would take a different tack . . . and this time Authority listened.

SHOWING THE RESULTS

I said that I "reminded" Elaine of our failure in Las Vegas when she called me with the news about the new superintendent and the Omidyars, but that's not really true. She didn't need any prompting. I could tell from her voice that the memory was still vivid—and distinctly unpleasant. Yet she was convinced that things were different now, that we could reengage with the Clark County school system without repeating the mistakes of the past.

I agreed. I also pointed out (not that she needed reminding of this either) that we now had a terrific asset in our favor. Daniel J. Cardinali was our executive vice president for field operations, and he went on to become the president of the national Communities In Schools organization. I told Elaine that Dan wanted to personally represent us in Las Vegas, side by side with her. He was one of the hardest-working, most gifted community organizers I'd ever met. All of us at the CIS National Office were coming to rely on him more and more. I knew that if anyone could bring CIS to Las Vegas, he could.

Dan flew off on what would be the first of many trips for this project. Reviewing the situation with Elaine, he learned that the new school superintendent, Carlos Garcia, had come to Clark County from Fresno, where he'd heard good things about CIS through some mutual friends. Elaine was right: Carlos was predisposed to give us a hearing, and she was also correct that the Omidyars were willing to listen. But she warned Dan: This foundation is *tough*. They expect all their potential grantees to treat the process like a business deal. They want a plan and outcomes—don't think you can go in there and sell the Idea without a clear, solid strategy to back it up.

So Dan devised an incredibly detailed three-year business plan. It laid out exactly what CIS's mission in Las Vegas would be and how we'd go about achieving it. He matched the goals of the Clark County school system with the kinds of outcomes a successful CIS affiliate can achieve. Then he showed how both of these supported the Omidyar Foundation's mission. If approved, CIS would begin at just one school, Reynaldo Martinez Elementary, whose desperately underserved students were struggling against the most basic, heartbreaking deficiencies. They lacked food, clothing, shelter . . . and hope.

Now Power, Authority, and Idea were ready to sit down together. Dan and Elaine spoke with Carlos Garcia and the Omidyar Foundation's representative in a series of three meetings. A couple of things soon became clear. One was that the new superintendent was keenly aware of Clark County's status as the fastest-growing school district in the country. Carlos had his hands full just trying to find qualified teachers and administrators to handle the burgeoning enrollment. But he also felt a moral responsibility to see that every child got the knowledge that he or she deserved. "No child left behind" was already his motto. Second, Carlos wanted to be what Paul Houston called a "superintendent of education," not just a superintendent of schools. In other words, he was open to the idea that the schools can't do it alone. He wanted a way for the community and the educators to work together—the only question was how.

Dan also discovered that Elaine's role as a champion of the Idea was invaluable. She had the respect of all the movers and shakers in Las Vegas, and here she was, able to put the CIS argument in the clearest and most compelling terms. Moreover, her role as the Power member of the trio was ideal: She and her then-husband, Steve, could easily have written a check to help get CIS off the ground and left it at that. But instead she insisted upon using her influence as a convener, as the one who could get all the others to talk to each other, and to take seriously the ideas being proposed.

Hopefully, the Omidyars would exercise the power of the purse and other foundations would follow.

These meetings were hard. Dan would call in and say, "Yes, they're still grilling us. Gotta run." Authority and Power wanted to know exactly what CIS was doing around the country, and Dan had the data that pointed to concrete results. *He was backing up Idea with evidence.* For Carlos, the plan was starting to look attractive: This independent, nonpartisan group could leverage significant resources on behalf of his students. Dan and Elaine weren't asking him to come up with "development dollars" or, in fact, any start-up funding at all. The flow would go the other way, *into* the school system. As for the Omidyar Foundation, they could see that the CIS Idea wasn't just theory. We had an idea about how to get things done, too.

There was still the school board to win over. The head of the board came from a highly respected—and highly conservative—family. Her name was Sheila Moulton, and she was a wonderful leader, by all accounts. She was there at Dan and Elaine's next "power lunch."

Her very first question was: "What's your formal relationship with Planned Parenthood?"

Dan responded truthfully that we had none. Local CIS affiliates around the country often developed relationships with Planned Parenthood, but that was up to them and those they served. "We function *by invitation only,*" Dan explained. "We can't exist without the superintendent's permission, and we do nothing that hasn't been approved by the community." The head of the school board seemed pleased with that answer, so Dan decided to follow it up: Why not make a personal visit to a CIS community as similar as possible to Las Vegas?

As I look back on our failure to start CIS in Clark County 10 years earlier, I can't help but wonder if an offer like that might have turned the tide. Sometimes you have to give voices and bodies to Idea—you have to show Authority the flesh-and-blood results, the daily operation of a successful initiative.

Sheila Moulton took Dan up on his offer. A month later, during a meeting of the Council of Great City Schools in Chicago, the two of them were in the office of Chicago CIS Executive Director Jane Mentzinger. Jane laid out the precise strategies that allowed her CIS affiliate to operate in 138 Chicago schools, connecting more than 150 local service providers with children and families in need.

She also made a telling point about local ownership versus some kind of official "CIS line." As it happened, Chicago CIS partnered with Planned Parenthood in a number of school sites. But at the time the Chicago school system had an "abstinence only" policy in regard to what can be taught to young people about sexual activity. Both Chicago CIS and Planned Parenthood rigorously respected this policy, and the latter's role was limited to teen-health issues that did *not* involve reproduction. CIS is committed to getting the best possible resources in place for young people, but we always respect the political and ethical sensitivities of the schools who invite us in.

To put it another way: CIS has an Idea about local ownership—we think it's critical to success with schools. What Sheila saw was the Idea in the flesh. Thanks to Elaine Wynn's superb "convener" skills, an important Authority was getting a close-up look at how a good Idea really works. Sheila was willing to give it a try.

Back in Las Vegas, Superintendent Garcia gave a thumbs-up, too, and we had funding in place from the Omidyars. We held a big community meeting, at which, among many other issues, we expressed our desire to hire a local liaison. Almost immediately we found a fantastic candidate in Louise Helton, who went on to become CIS of Southern Nevada's first executive director.

This is a very abbreviated version of the entire process, of course. I don't mean to imply that it was all smooth sailing once Power, Authority, and Idea were in the same boat—it never is. But I do hold this up as a fine example to illustrate the crucial importance of such a trio.

CIS of Southern Nevada officially launched in June 2004, and as of school year 2020–21, it served 53 schools and over 55,000 students. More than 10,000 students each year still experience homelessness in Clark County.[4] But there's good news, too: during the 2021–22 school year, breakfast and lunch were available at no cost to all students in the county under the federally subsidized National School Lunch Program.[5]

Is it the job of the Clark County school system to meet its students' housing needs or to provide health care for them? Of course not. And yet the lack of these basic human needs was destroying the ability of students to succeed in school—and in life. So the community had to step up and bring its helping resources into partnership with the schools. All the "school reform" in the world wouldn't have accomplished this. But as we know, a triangle needs three sides. Integrated, school-based services are the missing third side, and when they're in place, we can foresee the day when, truly, *every* student succeeds.

. . . AND BEYOND

Let me again quote Rey Saldaña: "As we look out into the future, our goal is clear: we want to see a CIS site coordinator in every Title I school in the country."

In short, we intend to build the third side of the triangle into every school that serves children living in poverty. As Rey goes on to say, "It's not an easy goal, but it's an understandable one." The new education legislation, ESSA, goes a long way toward supporting this goal. And overall there is a much greater understanding of the importance of providing integrated school-based services to students.

Some states are ramping up their support for this model, as you'll read in Chapter 9, where I focus on West Virginia's implementation of the CIS licensing concept. I have to say, it really touches my heart that this huge change is taking place in Paul Houston's home state. Davis Creek, West Virginia, the town where Paul grew up—where all the kids refused to believe he had really gone to school—is in Kanawha County, home to six "CIS schools." We haven't gotten to Davis Creek yet . . . but I bet we will.

PART III

FROM CHARITY TO CHANGE

CHAPTER 7

A NEW WAY OF THINKING ABOUT SCHOOLS

HOW FAR CAN CHARITY GO?

The United States is very good at charity. We're a generous people. After the Gulf Coast hurricanes of 2005, there was an outpouring of support from institutions, foundations, congregations, entertainment and sports figures, and ordinary American citizens. Millions rallied round the survivors of the disaster. And thankfully, this is typical of how our country responds to unexpected tragedy.

But charity only goes so far. The problem is that every call on our help and generosity eventually moves out of the headlines and off our screens. We go back into our ordinary world—some of us to our gated communities and "safe neighborhoods"—and life goes on. It's similar to the aftermath of a funeral: someone close to us has died, and neighbors and relatives all come and give us cakes and casseroles and surround us with love . . . but six months later, we're alone.

How could it be any other way, really? No one wants to be a perpetual "charity case," and even the most generous givers have priorities in their own lives.

If we treat the grave challenges that our public school students face as opportunities for yet more charity, I know the same pattern will occur. There may well be an outpouring of giving amid

statements of support for public schools, families, and students—
but life goes on . . .

The fact is that **curing the dropout epidemic will demand
change, not just charity.** We have to alter our fundamental way
of doing business where schools are concerned, although it's
extremely important to understand that such a shift doesn't *replace*
charitable support. A generous personal response that reflects our
deep desire to give and help is always needed. But systemic reform
is essential, too. It does no good to keep putting resources into a
failing system; instead, the plan has to change. But once the switch
is successful, that doesn't mean that we suddenly stop funding it.
Instead, we keep giving as before, the difference being that now
the resources are used effectively.

This word *charity* is really a synonym for *giving*, for providing
resources. In the business world, no one calls it charity, of course,
but every time a CEO approves a budget item for a particular
project, he or she is making a decision to *give*, to *invest*, to allocate
resources in the expectation of accomplishing an objective.
Similarly, a local government agency that approves a grant to fund,
say, a reading initiative in the public school system, is approving
a particular type of gift.

But if the *system* needs to change, all of the giving and investing
won't make enough of a difference. When people talk about
the uselessness of "throwing money at a problem," this is what
they mean. Always remember, though, that once the necessary
transformation has been effected, the resources must continue.
Now we're no longer "throwing money"; we're *using* it to fund a
truly effective plan.

In a sense, the Five Basics are charity. A positive one-on-one
relationship with a caring adult, a safe place, a healthy start, a
marketable skill, and a chance to give back—these are all things
we can and should *give* every child. But the coordination of these
resources around the schools is *change*. In fact, it's the necessary
difference that will allow the Five Basics to be effective in meeting
the needs of kids and families.

People in your area who give to or work for charities often have
an appetite for systemic change and feel frustrated because they

don't see the opportunity to be part of it. They're tired of Band-Aids applied to specific problems that crop up again and again, with no vision to stem the flow of young people bleeding out onto the streets. They're fed up with commissions and meetings that investigate some tragic circumstance and make recommendations about how it could have been better addressed—without asking why it happened in the first place.

A FIRST STEP TOWARD CHANGE: UNITED <u>ALL</u> THE WAY

Businesspeople can have an enormous impact on turning charity into change on behalf of kids. Many such leaders either support the community through corporate-giving programs or sit on the boards of charitable foundations. The vitally important thing you can do if you're one of these decision makers is to *fund cooperation and coordination* among your grantees and in the community at large.

This is the efficient way to operate, not only for its desirable results but also in terms of the investment you make. Your money will go a lot further when organizations are able to use the leveraging power of the grant to secure in-kind support from others. A truly cooperative community effort creates a convergence of resources and energy that's far greater than the sum of its parts.

When I speak to groups of business leaders, I'm often asked, "What sorts of changes are you asking us to implement?" In response, I request that they think about the United Way, which has done a truly exceptional job of changing how people make contributions to social causes. What if the process was united *all* the way? That is, what if the money was not only collected together but also allocated so as to encourage integration and collaboration among the many community charities? We need to *reward cooperation* and stop the bad habit of giving funds to 20 different groups without creating conditions and incentives for them to work together. The new expectation should be: *Okay, we're funding you—now how are you going to help each other do your jobs more effectively?*

Let's say that your corporate or nonprofit foundation decides to fund Teach For America, which places recent top college graduates as teachers in troubled schools. You also want to support New Leaders, which recruits, trains, and supports talented principals. And perhaps there's a local health clinic that badly needs a way to expand its outreach to poor children.

Each of these organizations is worthy of your support. They'll know of each other and respect each other's missions, but realistically they aren't going to find time to *work together* unless you make that a condition of their funding. And at this point, you may decide that you need to add a Champion for Children into the mix as well—an organization similar to CIS that knows how to broker and coordinate all the players together into a holistic team for youth.

But one way or another, it's critical that social service and volunteer agencies understand that they'll be supported and rewarded *to the extent that they not only talk and work together but truly integrate their resources.* The aim is to create a safety net for children and families based on shared goals, information, and supplies. In effect, the various local organizations are being asked to think of themselves as part of the same "company." There's no competition, no hoarding of assets or data. What CEO would willingly permit that from the various departments of his or her business, all supposedly engaged on a single project? We need to foster the same attitude in the community.

This is genuine institutional change at several levels. Not only are you changing the way your organization gives its funds, but you're shifting how the grantees view their mission. Even better, when Teach For America, New Leaders, the local health clinic, and CIS are all working efficiently as one, they're affecting the most important institution of all—the public schools. Educators no longer have to go it alone, overextended and ill-equipped for the demands being placed on them. They can now confidently rely on a coordinated community team to meet students' nonacademic needs. It's a fundamental shift in the relationship between the school as an institution and the community it serves.

This is easy to recommend but often difficult to implement. No one likes to change, and many a book has been written about why this is so. When I was working on the streets, I used to believe there was a conspiracy on the part of the powers that be, a deliberate plan to maintain the status quo and keep poor people poor. That was before I moved to Washington, D.C., and saw that many federal government bureaucrats had enough trouble understanding and navigating through this red tape themselves without also trying to launch a scheme to oppress anyone. I now believe that our failure to support systemic change results largely from two factors: the natural inertia of people and institutions when called upon to do things differently, and a deeply felt uncertainty, bordering on despair, about *how* to change.

This despair leads to a retreat into small areas of personal responsibility, just as we saw in the example of Tara Larson and the many social services available to help her. If people can't feel good about changing, they at least want to feel good about doing their own jobs. This has the paradoxical effect of making the work tougher because we create little silos of expertise that often fail to communicate—let alone integrate—their efforts and end up pointing fingers of blame. Everyone's trying to "outgood" everyone else.

Philanthropic and corporate foundations unwittingly contribute to this mindset when they select a single organization—no matter how worthy—to address a problem that by its nature demands cooperation from many sources. Instantly, potential partners become competitors, first in their grant applications and then in the inevitable turf battles that follow. "Looking good" when you file your end-of-grant report becomes more important than truly *doing* good. And, sadly, this often means demonstrating that your organization is better than A, B, or C. If only A, B, and C were working *with* you! The combined results would be truly impressive.

It's important to note that cooperation and coordination are nonpartisan values that transcend political ideologies. Given my roots in the social changes of the 1960s, my organization and I frequently used to be accused of being "left wing." In the mid-1990s when the Republicans achieved their majority in Congress, I was asked by a leading politician to attend one of a series of meetings he was holding among some of the new members of the House and Senate. He invited people whose ideas interested him, offered them a chance to present some of their key concepts, and then opened the floor for a question-and-answer session.

After I explained some of what CIS does, one of the first questions came from a first-term congressman. Actually, it wasn't a question so much as a complaint: "You sound like a Kennedy liberal," he told me. I protested that nothing I'd said was remotely connected with either liberalism or Senator Kennedy. "Well, how *do* you feel about the conservatives taking over Congress?" he retorted.

"I'm disappointed," I said.

"See? That's what I mean. You're a liberal."

"Not at all," I replied. "I'm disappointed because I was hoping that all this talk about 'the new conservatives' would bring a truly conservative spirit to Congress. What I've heard here today doesn't sound conservative *enough* to me. The best way I know of to conserve resources is to spend them wisely on programs that produce the kind of synergy and leveraging effects I was just describing to you. But that's not what's happened, as far as I can tell. You believed that the previous Congress was spending too much money and spending it inefficiently. So now you want to spend *less* money in an equally inefficient way. It's not about how much money you spend, Congressman. It's about spending it to support personal, accountable, and coordinated responses to our students' needs."

A SECOND STEP TOWARD CHANGE: TAKING THE TIME

Another important aspect of turning charity into change takes us back to the basics: the necessity for personal relationships. If institutions are to cooperate and work together on behalf of children and families, they really have to spend time in each other's company. Much as we depend on and value the new technologies of the 21st-century workplace, we all know that a Zoom exchange is never the same as a face-to-face meeting. E-mails and texts are short and (hopefully) sweet; they're efficient; they get the job done. But I'm not sure how well they build community.

Communication serves two purposes, one informational and the other relational. We rely on our face-to-face interactions with others to build a sense of trust and even love, not just to provide facts. Only proximity can create the all-important relational aspects of community.

Remember, we adults have a call to build this environment for our young people. It's something that far too many kids never get to experience. So all our talk of cooperation and working together has got to result in action that *models* community. Children learn from what they see—and so do adults. If you want staff and volunteers from a half dozen different agencies to work together at a school site, demonstrating community for kids, then you'd better be willing to demonstrate it for the staff yourself. Physical propinquity— actually getting leaders into the same room together to talk and learn from each other—is an essential step in changing institutions.

A THIRD STEP TOWARD CHANGE: PATIENCE IS A VIRTUE

Change takes time. In particular, the positive *results* of change take time, and the bigger the problem, the longer it can take. We aren't going to see the last dropout this year, or next year, or the year after that—not even if every district in America changed overnight and used the schools as delivery points for personal, coordinated, and accountable services. We all understand the importance of persistence and patience when trying to turn around a huge social issue—or a huge corporate one, for that matter. CEOs need to be patient, too, as long as the signs are clear that they're on the right track toward making their company profitable.

This is all to say that systemic change shouldn't be *evaluated* as if it were a scientific experiment or a small demonstration project. In other words, we've got to stop basing our funding cycles on three-year grants (as many foundations do) or on four-year administrations (whether federal, state, or local). It's like planting a delicate new tree and then digging it up a year later to examine the roots. It hasn't completely developed yet? Oh well, throw it away and try something else. Our educational system didn't get to where it is overnight. Reversing its negative aspects will also take time, and the last thing we need is a series of short-sighted benchmarks based on timetables that aren't relevant to the problems.

So we need to urge our partners and funders to stick with us for the long haul. This isn't the same thing as sitting back while no progress is made in the hopes that "something" will improve. Every local CIS affiliate has specific benchmarks for success, and funders rightly expect these goals to be met. Rather, it's an attitude of commitment and perseverance.

We mustn't promise any quick fixes or magic bullets. What we can predict is change in—finally—the right direction. And if a funder is truly determined to get a quick result for its investment, we can suggest a donation to any of a number of veteran CIS affiliates where the infrastructure for change is already in place and the school system is partnering with the community to create a new way of delivering services for its students. In such a community, an infusion of new funds can lead to CIS coordinators at new schools and hundreds more young people who are connected with needed resources.

The Communities In Schools movement ultimately aims to put itself out of business. Our vision of change will be realized on the day when our concepts are so institutionalized, so truly a part of how every community responds to the needs of its children, that no special "neutral third party" is required. No one has to advocate for cafeterias in schools. They're just *there* because everyone knows that kids have to eat lunch. Do we need a special Gymnasiums In Schools organization? Of course not. Gyms are taken for granted and planned for in every school system. It's my hope that someday all of the Five Basics will be similarly available, delivered by caring adults who view the students as human beings, not statistics.

NEW ORLEANS: EVERY CHILD A "CIS STUDENT"

When the levees broke in New Orleans in August 2005, the devastation triggered an outpouring of charity. Especially in light of the disgraceful response to the initial disaster from all levels of government, the private sector and individual givers were willing to dig deep and commit themselves to getting the Big Easy back on its feet.

Once again, the charity was there when it was needed. But something else began to stir in the city, as the region's education leaders recognized that their broken community had been handed an opportunity in the midst of tragedy.

The New Orleans schools, which served between 50,000 and 60,000 students, were on the brink of failure before Hurricane Katrina arrived. The state was preparing to take over and restructure the system. A small CIS affiliate was operating in one school, but its efforts were overwhelmed by a chaotic and bureaucratic structure and a huge dropout rate for the city's students.

Then the hurricanes hit. Thousands of young people and families were displaced, many to be absorbed by nearby school systems, as I described in Chapter 4. But students gradually began to return to a city and a school system that were starting from the ground up. Every one of these kids, along with their families, would need special attention and a variety of social services just to recommence their ordinary lives.

Suddenly, *every child was a "CIS student."*

By this I mean that there was no longer a perceived division between haves and have-nots, between young people who might need additional help to succeed in school and those who presumably already had the necessary resources. It was a citywide educational emergency, and if anything good could be said to have come out of the floods, it was this: We now had a situation in which the coordination of social services around kids and families was a *must*, not just a nice idea. All eyes were on the problem. It was truly a golden moment for systemic change.

The state of Louisiana stepped in to run the New Orleans school districts—a move that likely would have occurred anyway, given the difficulties the system was experiencing before the hurricanes. The state offered an open door to a variety of models, charter schools and parochial schools included. Basically, anyone who was ready and willing to operate classrooms and could measure up to state standards was welcomed. Finding undamaged buildings was a major challenge. In the midst of this unprecedented attempt to meet students' needs as rapidly as possible, CIS of New Orleans stepped forward to act as a service-delivery coordinator that could operate in any or all of these environments.

In the weeks immediately following the hurricanes, the CIS National Office outside Washington, D.C., had organized a hurricane relief fund that raised $437,000 from corporate, foundation, and individual givers. Most of these funds were transferred to 21 local CIS affiliates in six states to provide direct services to 19,000 displaced students and their families.

During this same period, CIS of New Orleans, whose staff and board members initially had to evacuate the city, began to return as services were restored and plans implemented to begin opening schools. Education officials asked CIS to coordinate services beginning in December 2005 with six newly opening schools serving 3,555 students. Success in these locations led to requests for additional support as more opened. CIS brought free mental-health and general medical care to students and their families one day per week, using Tulane University School of Medicine's mobile unit. Family Services of Greater New Orleans offered help for students referred for post-traumatic stress and anger management. A variety of tutoring and cultural enrichment programs started to cope with the deficits and challenges of the interrupted educational lives of these children.

At the height of coping with Hurricane Katrina, CIS of New Orleans put more than 500 local and out-of-town volunteers to work, producing 7,200 hours of community service over eight months, in projects such as repainting classrooms and landscaping campuses, one-on-one tutoring and mentoring, and painting murals and planting gardens. In-kind donations of office and school supplies were also matched with the needs of different institutions as they prepared to reopen.

A year following the floods, New Orleans was still a city in crisis, but when I attended a series of meetings and events commemorating the first anniversary of the disaster, I saw many signs of hope, indicating that systemic change for the region's children could now become a reality. CIS President Dan Cardinali was with me and recalled speaking with a doctor who served on the board of directors of a local private school.

"This man had a reputation for charitable giving, for truly caring about the issues confronting New Orleans children and families," Dan said. "He told me that for the past several years, he'd been increasingly frustrated by the sense that his efforts and those of his colleagues, no matter how generous, were simply not making enough of a difference. He said it was the system that had to change, that New Orleans had to get serious about figuring out how to stop kids from failing in school. I urged him to get involved with our CIS initiative, and after we'd talked a little about it, he said it was the first real sign of hope he could remember in a long while. He wanted a way to change the system, and he told me he wasn't the only one—that plenty of local leaders would rally behind this idea."

Another New Orleans leader told me the same thing in a simple and memorable phrase: "We have a fresh canvas to paint on. We want to get it right this time."

By 2018, CIS of New Orleans (now called CIS Gulf South) was serving over 7,000 students in 24 schools. These students were provided free mental-health and general medical care, academic enrichment programs such as tutoring and leadership development programs, and family enrichment and engagement services.

I continue to hope and believe that a *new* New Orleans rose out of the ashes. I don't want to exaggerate the ability of a single small entity like Communities In Schools to create the many partnerships necessary to meet the needs of all of the city's children and families. It isn't just about schools. A personal, accountable, and coordinated response at *every* level of society is critical for this great city. The principles we've been discussing as a strategy for stopping the dropout epidemic can and do apply to other social institutions. *Everyone* needs community—especially when their former way of life has been shattered beyond repair.

Maintaining the momentum of a community coming together in times of crisis depends on careful planning and management of resources. Hurricane Katrina brought forth the *idea and practice* of that vital third side of the triangle. I haven't talked to a single local or state leader who didn't acknowledge—indeed, *assume*—that ongoing coordination of community resources into the schools was necessary in order to re-create an educational system that the city can be proud of.

Do we need a catastrophe to focus our attention in this way? Can cities and towns across America really stand still until the next opportunity arises to build a school system from scratch in the wake of tragedy? For the sake of our children, the answer has got to be *no*. Instead, I encourage you to think—and advocate in your community—as if the catastrophe has already happened. *Because it has.* The dropout epidemic is doing more damage, ruining more lives, and costing more money than any natural disaster. With one-third of our young people quitting school without a diploma, the levees aren't holding—we're in the midst of a national emergency.

There's great potential and enormous promise for true systemic change in your community and others across the U.S., but you'll need to begin by acknowledging and helping others see the rising waters that are turning our children into evacuees from the America we've known and loved.

. . . AND BEYOND

Fifteen years after Hurricane Katrina, our country—and the entire world—experienced another natural catastrophe: the COVID-19 pandemic. The 2020 shutdown of public schools was an almost unimaginable challenge, especially to the students whose lives and education were disrupted.

CIS rose to the challenge, using all its relationships and resources to keep kids on track. During the school closures of spring 2020, CIS organizations served 400 school districts,

2,681 schools, and an estimated 231,655 families across our network. They contributed 270,756 hours and $7,488,249 of in-kind support to address basic needs, and provided 1,012,849 items related to critical resources.

These resources varied according to demographic and local needs. Public/financial assistance was more likely to be provided in urban communities, while clothing distribution was more common in rural and suburban settings. Whether urban, suburban, or rural, the local CIS affiliates provided food, hygiene products, and school supplies, while connecting community members to other local resources during the early months of the pandemic.

Once again, "every child was a CIS student"—we were all in it together. I pray that with the end of the pandemic, we do *not* go back to normal, if normal means continuing the inequitable public education that millions of students receive. Instead, let's use the lessons learned to forge even stronger networks of support for *every* student.

CHAPTER 8

GOING TO SCALE— THE EVIDENCE IS IN

Fourteen teenagers, most of them former dropouts and disciplinary problems, sat in a math class taught by Harold Finkelstein, a Ph.D. from Emory University.

The subject was the addition of positive and negative numbers—an invitation to instant boredom in the enervating heat. But the young teacher, swinging his gaze from the blackboard to the desks, rallied his students with rapid-fire questions. There was the same intense involvement found in the last 30 seconds of a tight basketball game, everyone on the edges of their seats. And there were cheers, groans, and laughter as they caught the excitement of the properties of additive inverses.

"You wouldn't believe that most of these kids were classified as functional illiterates by their schools, would you?" said a member of the staff.[1]

That was how *Washington Post* columnist David S. Broder described the action at one of our Atlanta Street Academies in the 1970s. The excitement—and success—was real. We knew we'd created something important.

By 1974, our EXODUS program was operating in two Atlanta public schools, as well as four Street Academies and the academy at St. Luke's Church. We had some key local business leaders on our side; George Johnson and Anne Cox Chambers in particular were tirelessly opening doors for us, holding "friend-raisers" and luncheons, and showing up personally at the schools to see firsthand what we were doing. (Anne, who was head of Cox Communications, made it a real "family thing," introducing her son Jim to us.)

Largely thanks to Neil Shorthouse and Dave Lewis, the Postal Street Academies co-founder who joined us in starting the program, we felt we had a prototype that could be expanded to new communities and cities—anywhere in America, really, where kids were dropping out. That had always been our dream. We wanted to take this thing to scale, to affect the entire system, not just the young people on the street. Our vision was to help schools work better so that kids didn't drop out in the first place.

For me, there was an element of conflict, too: On the one hand, I loved street work and found it very difficult to adjust to the establishment's ways. But on the other hand, I knew that if I stayed on the streets forever, our exciting, precious new prototype would probably never grow beyond those streets.

So Neil, Dave, and I set our sights on replication. We had no idea what an important—and challenging—principle was at stake. With near-perfect hindsight, I can see now that *replicability is the precondition of any truly transformative action*. If your program can't be adopted by others in new places and new circumstances, it's at best a limited, localized success. And even replicability doesn't guarantee that the program will "go to scale"—that is, provide a means for change that's large enough and powerful enough to meet and overcome a major social problem head-on. ***Scalability, sustainability,*** **and** ***evidence-based strategies*** **are essential to creating permanent change in the way our education system combats the dropout epidemic.**

Bringing the community "inside the system," creating a model for coordinating services with the school as a "community center," weaving a safety net of "wraparound services" for kids, providing "asset-based resources" to keep students in school . . . these concepts sound familiar now, even obvious, because a lot of people use that language, and a great deal of research has demonstrated their validity, but in 1974 it was all new.

When Neil, Dave, and I made the decision to try to take our Atlanta program to other cities, we were regarded by Power and

Authority as energetic idealists at best and upstart hippie radicals at worst. We quickly learned the reality of what *catch-22* means. We went to potential donors and said, "Please fund us to expand our prototype to new communities and prove our theory that the principles can apply in many different circumstances and settings."

And the funders replied, "We've never heard of this approach before. We'll give you money once you've replicated it and shown that it can be done."

We'd tell them: "But we don't *have* any money to replicate— that's the whole problem!"

One foundation head made a memorable remark: "Bill, we're worried that this thing is built on charisma and unusually dedicated people." My short fuse nearly burned all the way down. *Charisma, huh? Gee, maybe I should get the Centers for Disease Control to look into this. Is it some kind of virus? What's wrong with passion, caring, and fresh ideas?*

"In the '60s," I said to the guy, "I saw that we had a whole country full of 'unusually dedicated people,' and now you're telling me that they're all in one school? They're everywhere, and sometimes all they need is the vision to show them how to act differently and not just try harder. This is *not* about us—any community leader can use these principles."

In today's language, we were *social entrepreneurs*, a phrase invented by the innovative humanitarian Bill Drayton to describe people who "are not content just to give a fish, or teach how to fish. They will not rest until they have revolutionized the fishing industry."[2] This may sound like a fine thing to be, but it turned off a lot of folks precisely because we were so passionate. We still had to find a way to convince potential supporters that our dedication to keeping kids in school was based on principles that, when shared, would evoke similar passions in communities across the country.

I had little patience for requests for research or evidence. Just come see a school, I urged those who asked. You want evidence? Look: These kids are making it, they're getting their diplomas or GEDs, they're not in jail, on drugs, or dead. *There's* your "evidence-based evaluation."

I'm amazed by how much we didn't know—about the expectations of big foundations confronted with a small, experimental program and about the building of community with these potential friends. But we were still driven more by passion than professionalism. For years we'd distrusted the system and bitterly resented attempts to evaluate us.

Equally amazing, though, is what happened next. A combination of God-given opportunity and perseverance on our part took us from the projects to the White House, and it all started when a peanut farmer got himself elected governor of Georgia . . .

CATCHING THE DREAM

President Jimmy Carter was addressing a national Communities In Schools conference in 1998, reflecting back on a hot Atlanta day in 1974. "These two scraggly-looking guys came into my office at the governor's mansion," he told the audience, "and I had to turn to my state policeman and say, 'Are these the people who are supposed to help the school system? They look like *they* need help.'"

Okay, I suppose Neil and I were a pretty scraggly pair. We were also desperate and could hardly believe we'd been given this chance to speak with the governor of Georgia to share the dream of replicating our EXODUS program beyond Atlanta.

The meeting came about thanks to Dr. Wayne Smith, a minister who had become interested in our attempts to create a Christian commune and had broken bread with us a number of times. Dr. Smith was also Carter's liaison with several communities in South America as part of a plan to create "sister city" relationships with municipalities in Georgia. After listening to me describe our frustrations with funders, Dr. Smith took pity on me and said he'd get us a meeting with the governor on two conditions: we'd only stay for 20 minutes, and we wouldn't embarrass him. We were still from the streets, looked it, and acted it. He was worried about how we'd relate to a powerful man who also happened to be his friend.

So Neil and I showed up at the governor's office (not knowing until years later, of course, how dubious Carter was about our initial appearance), and he got right down to it. In the nicest possible way, he looked at us and just asked, "What do you want?"

We answered, "We need resources to replicate what we're doing with kids here in Atlanta." The governor said nothing, but made a gesture that invited us to go on. So we gave him a brief explanation of our commitment to young people and our strategies and goals— what today would be called the "elevator speech."

We could hardly believe our ears when he nodded and said, "All right. Let me see what I can do." By God's grace, we'd managed to intrigue Carter in two ways that were extremely important to him. He could hear the passion we had for poor kids, and he had the same feelings. Moreover, as we later learned, our program appealed to his intellectual side because he could see we'd thought about the principles and had a replicable way to address the dropout problem. That meeting was the beginning of a relationship that has continued to this day, and has included the privilege of knowing most of the Carter family.

Not long after that initial visit, I was presenting at a conference, and one of the other speakers was the late Ruth Stapleton. We hit it off, and she said, "The next time I'm in Atlanta, I'd like to have dinner and hear more about your work." So when she and her husband came to town, they took my wife, Jean, and me out for Chinese food and intense conversation. When the meal was finished, Ruth said, "Let's go back to my brother's place and hang out with them."

Her brother, of course, was Jimmy Carter, and his "place" was the governor's mansion. When we arrived, he was sitting on the couch reading. He remembered me and was friendly but clearly had work to do, so he excused himself to go to his study. But Rosalynn Carter was there, too, and she stayed up half the night talking to us. She really seemed to understand the concept of what we were trying to do.

With Rosalynn's support a major factor, we were soon the grateful recipients of $5,000 from Carter's emergency fund and a letter of endorsement from him that opened the door for us to raise the then-unbelievable sum of $100,000 from Atlanta leaders such as Bert Lance, George Johnson, and Anne Cox Chambers.

Then, in December 1974, I got a call from Phil Alston, a leading Atlanta attorney who had become a member of our fledgling board. He said, "The governor is going to announce for president."

"President of what?" I asked.

Phil explained, and I was excited but, to say the least, skeptical. He asked if I could get some of our folks to come to the press conference at which Carter would make the announcement because the governor believed it was important that some grassroots supporters be there. Neil and I and our families were living communally at the time; I showed up at the press conference wearing sneakers and jeans and looking very grassroots indeed. When it was over, Rosalynn invited me back to the mansion for dinner along with a number of other friends and supporters.

I rode over in a car with Frank Borman, the astronaut, who undoubtedly thought I was the gardener or somebody. It was one of those nights I'll never forget: I was chatting away at the dinner table with Ruth Stapleton, Rosalynn, and Miss Lillian (the governor's ebullient mother). His sons, Chip and Jack, were there, too, and you could tell what a strong, close family they were. Then the 11 o'clock news came on, and we all watched Jimmy Carter say he would be the next president of the United States.

That same night, he told me that he wanted something in writing about our dreams of a national program. I agreed, thinking that if by some amazing chance he got elected president, then *maybe* we'd actually have a shot at achieving those dreams.

ANYTHING BUT A PLAN

And a year later . . . Governor Jimmy Carter was the president-elect. Neil and I just shook our heads in wonder. It's the kind of thing that confirms my belief that our journey was a response to God's invitation to do good work. We can't take credit for it.

Years after these events, I was interviewed by someone who had a chip on her shoulder for some reason. She kept asking, "Come on, really, how did you invent this thing and get it to be so successful?" What she meant was, how did someone like *you* do it? I told her, "Well, I'm brilliant. In 1974 I figured out that our first-term governor in Georgia was going to be elected president two years later, so Neil and I wrote a strategic plan based on that."

The point is that it wasn't brains or political experience that got us together with a future president. We were simply staying open to possibilities, following our hearts and our faith, and Jimmy Carter, a man of faith himself, could hear our message and it was part of his dream, too. You can call it synchronicity, luck, or humility—anything but a plan.

After Carter won, I got a phone call asking me to come down to his home in Plains, where he was interviewing people for cabinet positions. That was definitely not why he wanted me there! It turned out that he just wanted to ask, at Rosalynn's urging, how he could help. This is when he told us how intrigued he'd been by the ideas and principles we were trying to replicate. They appealed to his intellectual side, his "scientist's mind" (for science and engineering comprised his original training). Everyone knows how big Jimmy Carter's heart is, but he's also one of the smartest people I've ever met. He reads constantly and remembers everything. Mutual friends would meet him and come away telling me, "He knows more about my area of expertise than I do."

Still, there were mixed feelings about suddenly being in Jimmy Carter's world. Part of me had never expected to leave the streets and my one-on-one mission with kids—and that was fine with me, because I loved the work. But Neil and I knew that we had to make our commitment bigger than that. Well, there I was with the next president of the United States. It was hard to believe he wanted to help us, but it was true.

I came to Washington for the inauguration and wound up staying the night at Blair House. Later, I went to the prayer breakfast, and in the middle of it I received a message to call Rosalynn. She told me that she'd decided to make "Project Propinquity" (as we were then calling our national program) her personal cause. That was why *Post* writer David Broder did a long story about us later that year. "Bill Milliken has shaved his beard," the piece began, "but he slides in and out of the Executive Office Building in Washington dressed as casually as he did when his hangout was an abandoned church building in the shadow of Atlanta Stadium." Thank God, the story went on to focus on our work and not on me. It ended: "The combination of faith, fund-raising, and the First Lady is putting Project Propinquity on the move." That was absolutely true.

Jimmy and Rosalynn let me use space in the Old Executive Office Building (OEOB) whenever I was in town. I had a title, too—Advisor on Youth Issues—but no paycheck and no place to stay in D.C. The first time I came up as an "advisor," Rosalynn said in that warm way of hers, "Oh, why don't you just stay with us?" So that night I called my mother in Pittsburgh and said, "Guess where I'm calling from? The Lincoln Bedroom!" I couldn't resist; even at the age of 37, I was still trying to prove that my parents' low expectations of me were wrong.

At the OEOB, I was working on the document the president had requested with help from two friends and colleagues: Landrum Bolling, former president of the Lilly Endowment, and Dean Overman, who'd been part of the Street Academy movement and was now the managing partner of the Washington office of a major law firm. I sent Rosalynn memos on our progress every week just to make sure she didn't forget about us. I needn't have worried. She was a wonderful and dedicated friend, opening so many doors for us in the new administration. Rosalynn told Broder: "I have asked the department heads to see Bill because I think what he's doing is so important. We spend money, money, money on these problems, and so many of the services don't even reach the people who need them."

In May 1977, Rosalynn, Senator Richard Lugar of Indiana, and Bert Lance, our Atlanta supporter (who had become director of the Office of Management and Budget), sponsored and spoke at a breakfast intended to introduce Project Propinquity to the private sector. We had more than 200 businesspeople there, and out of that morning grew some extremely important relationships. Around the same time, Harv Oostdyk and I began to sketch out what a national organization might actually look like. We had the invaluable help of Burt Chamberlin, head trainer for the Postal Street Academies and one of the key players in our fledgling movement.

Together we spent what seemed like endless days on retreats and in planning sessions, trying to figure out how to launch an organization that would stay true to our principles and still be able to affect the dropout problem nationwide. We didn't want to be seen as "just another charity" but as a movement for change. In Atlanta, corporate leaders would say dubiously, "Well, I help a lot of charities . . ." We'd answer, "This isn't a charity; it's an *investment*—in kids and in the future."

At this stage, we needed to create an independent board of directors that would still carry weight with educators. Dr. Crim was on our board in Atlanta—would other superintendents also join us at the national level? How could we build a structure that would last, that could survive changes in administrations and economic climate? And what roles would each of us take? How would we *pay* everyone?

In the end, the consensus was that Neil would continue to refine the Atlanta prototype and I'd head the national office. Burt agreed to be executive vice president. Harv stuck with us until the office was launched, then moved to Dallas to pursue his dream of using these principles to address the way entire neighborhoods coordinate services.

Bob Baldwin at Morgan Stanley came through for us once again, taking on the chairmanship of the national board of directors. Despite also serving as the chairman of Morgan Stanley, Bob always found the time to give back. Without him, there would have been no Communities In Schools. But his involvement wasn't a blank check: he made it clear that while he respected our passion and vision, we had a long way to go in learning how to run a business—caring wasn't enough.

Bob insisted that we become *professionals*, and although it took us some time to accomplish this, I'll always be grateful to him for setting the standard. He also *passed on* these principles: shortly after he agreed to lead our board, he introduced me to a colleague of his at Morgan Stanley named James M. Allwin, who would eventually succeed Bob as chairman.

But in 1977, all this was far ahead of us. We finished our white paper, turned it over to Rosalynn and the president, and held our breath. When the answer came, it was better than we could have hoped for: $2.7 million in federal funds to expand our prototype in Atlanta, Indianapolis, and New York City.

SMALLNESS ON A LARGE SCALE

One of the first decisions we made was to change our name from Project Propinquity to Cities In Schools. It seemed to capture the essence of what we were advocating: bringing the resources of the city into the schoolhouse to help kids graduate. The "cities" part was a given. We were city boys and felt comfortable in that environment, and we believed that the majority of the youth problem was urban. We watched country people in Georgia coming to the cities, full of hope for the future. Instead, the next generation of kids was "fresh meat," falling into drugs, crime, and unemployment. They were naive, and they were preyed upon.

As we launched our national movement, the question was: *How will we manage something so big, a multi-city effort?* The answer was: We won't. We decided that we'd replicate smallness on a large scale. Every unit would have its own sense of community rather than being run from Washington. Each city would incorporate as a separate, locally owned nonprofit. Our role would be to supply the model, the experience, and—as best we could—the initial funding. But we knew that sooner or later these new programs would have to survive on their own. Their boards needed to be able to raise their own budgets.

It's become a hallmark of the CIS movement and a key to scalability and sustainability. If local leaders aren't able to take ownership of the problem and the solution, then the effort will ultimately fail.

With the benefit now of over 40 years of national replication, I can say that the Communities In Schools model is demonstrably adaptable to just about any location that wants it—urban, suburban, or rural. The key is to retain the *form*—integrated student-support services delivered at the school site—while leaving the *content* flexible, depending on each community's particular strengths and challenges. Like hot wax, we take the shape of whatever place we become part of. It's not as if we're saying: "In order to change the way you deliver services to kids, you have to have Big Brothers Big Sisters, AmeriCorps, and the local university involved." The particular players in each orchestra are up to you—or rather, up to the community—and any effort to create a CIS-like initiative has to start with a really good assessment of local needs and wants. We must scratch where people are itching. We need the input of parents, faith communities, the students themselves, and the helping agencies, not just the school or local-government authorities.

Similarly, funding sources can vary enormously. The relative percentages of funding from public, private, and foundation sources run the gamut in our 117 organizations and licensees. Local CIS executive directors show amazing creativity in finding funders who really do work as partners, because again, we're looking for a change in the way we do business around kids, not just a collection of givers, no matter how generous.

Far too many projects aimed at improving schools are unique—in the worst sense of the word. They may be successful, but they depend on a special set of circumstances that others can't replicate or adapt. Sometimes these situations involve a particularly generous amount of financial support. Sometimes it's a "model program" with many experts focusing their attention on one school. And indeed, the result may be genuine institutional change at that location. But how do you do the same thing elsewhere? How does the change become systemic? The licensing model, which CIS has recently developed thanks to decades of learning among our affiliates, and which I discuss in the next chapter, is one promising response to this question.

Replicability should be the goal within districts, too. If you succeed in bringing a personal, coordinated, and accountable team of adults into one high school, consider how to adapt that same configuration to the elementary and middle schools whose students will go on to attend that high school—and to other high schools as well. Ideally, an unbroken continuum of services should go beyond K through 12 and be available from preschool through graduation—and then continue through the postsecondary years.

This "P–16" (preschool to college graduation) movement is reminding us that college students often need the same kinds of integrated services to assist them with their educational goals.

A JUSTICE ISSUE

We were hoping for—even expecting—eight years of President Jimmy Carter, but it was not to be. After his defeat in 1980, we were left with six half-developed prototypes, limping along. The plan was always to let these sites go once they were strong enough to survive on their own—rather like young people. But without federal funding, it was extremely difficult to keep them alive. We were considered "Carter's program," even though I tried to show how CIS was completely independent of political ideology. By now my wife and I, with our children, Sean and Lani, had moved to Washington, and the national CIS office was officially located there. We were committed to finding a base for our work in the nation's capital.

Our big break came when I was introduced to Barbara Bush, wife of the then vice president. I poured my heart out to her about needing assistance, and she said, "I'd like to help, but my particular cause is adult literacy."

"So is ours," I replied.

"But I thought you were a youth program."

"We are—we're trying to keep young people from *becoming* adult illiterates."

I was afraid she'd be offended, but to her credit she just nodded and said, "You're right. Okay, I'll help you."

She connected us with Ed Meese, President Reagan's attorney general, at my request. This was for two reasons: First, we could argue for the impact CIS had on juvenile justice in the communities we served. It was simply another illustration of how dropouts affect *everyone*—the fewer kids on the streets, the less crime. (In fact, we used a very similar argument 10 years later when the Clinton administration supported us through HUD: How are you going to get any successful urban development if half your city kids are dropping out?) Second, I wanted someone on our side whom *nobody* would expect to support us. That way we couldn't be accused of being Jimmy or Rosalynn Carter's pet program anymore. I'd done my homework on the attorney general, and I knew that in addition to his well-deserved reputation as a hardcore conservative, he cared a lot about kids and was committed to helping them.

He became our champion and succeeded in reinstating our federal funding through the Department of Justice. He knew Bob Baldwin, our board chair, and Bob had him come up and speak at Morgan Stanley. It helped our standing with the business world a lot, and people were really starting to see that this wasn't a Democratic or Republican issue—it was about all of us.

Under Meese's leadership, we crafted the "Partnership Plan," an arrangement in which four cabinet-level departments—Justice, Health and Human Services, Labor, and Education—all put money into a pot that was used to support CIS. This was an almost unprecedented interagency approach at the time. The cooperation of these four groups made a strong statement about our basic philosophy. All along we'd been saying that the dropout issue was *not* just about education; it affected every segment of society. Its roots were often outside the academic world, and it would require the participation and coordination of resources far beyond the school building.

The Partnership Plan was a vote of confidence in this approach. The federal government was saying, loud and clear: "If your mission is juvenile justice, you have a stake in helping kids graduate. If your mission is health and human services, then keep these young people healthy. If your mission is jobs and a vibrant economy, you've got to stop the dropout epidemic. And we need to work *together* and coordinate our efforts."

Slowly, painfully, the CIS movement grew through the 1980s. Our Partnership Plan funding helped us attract matching privatesector and foundation grants. Barbara Bush's stalwart support continued to help us publicize our work. Had we learned all we needed to know about replication and sustainability? Our prototypes were now in 25 cities and all independent of us, which was exactly what we wanted. Yet this very success created the next challenge in our understanding of how to take CIS to scale: how to turn it into a solution that was truly national in scope and commanded the respect of a wide diversity of partners.

The problem, put simply, was this: Why did local CIS affiliates and prospective CIS communities need *us*? What did the national office bring to the table? I used to fend off that question by saying: "Why do you need a United States? Why not just be the Country of Illinois, the Republic of Florida?" But I knew that was too easy. CIS National really wasn't much like the federal government, which could do things that no state could—such as print money, amend the Constitution, and declare war. So what precisely *were* the things that we as a national organization could uniquely contribute?

The issue came to a head shortly after George H. W. Bush was elected president in 1988. To our astonishment, he'd mentioned Cities In Schools in one of the presidential debates as an example of what he meant by a "Point of Light." He'd visited one of our school sites at Bob Baldwin's request and remembered us, and out it came when the question about volunteerism was put to him and Democratic candidate Michael Dukakis. Then, less than a month after the election, he videotaped an endorsement for us to use that sounded like something we'd written ourselves. After drawing attention to the gravity of the dropout crisis, he said, "I urge all of you—business leaders, educators, parents, human service providers—to give your support to Cities In Schools, and to find out how you can become involved."

One of our founding board members was Dan Burke, the head of Capital Cities/ABC. Dan was close to the Bushes, and he, too, could see that we were poised to make a big leap—*if* we could take the necessary steps. Early in 1989 he invited me to his office for a talk.

"CIS is starting to take root in more and more states," he pointed out. "New communities are asking for our help. President and Mrs. Bush respect our work. And yet you and Neil still act like nobody wants you, like you're outsiders banging on the door. That's no longer the situation. What's more, you're killing yourselves trying to get this message personally to every community in the country.

Do you two ever see your families anymore? How much travel time are you logging every month? Bill, you need to get all this down on paper as a training program so that others can use it. And if you don't, I'm going to leave the board and suggest you get a real job."

FLEXIBILITY—WITH STANDARDS

Dan Burke's caring directness was the right voice at the right time. I realized that he was pushing us to a new understanding of what "replicability" means. With a curriculum and a place to conduct training sessions, we could empower hundreds of others with the CIS concepts. We could say, in effect, "We're not going to control how you implement the ideas. We'll share this set of values and principles, framed around implementation parameters that are very wide, so you can adapt and benefit from them."

Capital Cities/ABC and the Department of Justice provided initial funding for our training curriculum, and Lehigh University in Bethlehem, Pennsylvania, got the contract to develop it. Jim Hill, our vice president of administration at that time, worked tirelessly and creatively on shaping the words and ensuring that a generation of firsthand knowledge was captured in print. Lehigh produced one of the first "hypermedia" curricula in that proto-computer era. It used laser discs, interactive video, a variety of groundbreaking teaching tools.

The actual training was done at the Iacocca Institute at Lehigh. Lee Iacocca was on the university board and had just launched this institute to focus on what he saw, correctly, as the imminent danger to America's competitiveness resulting from our failure to educate our young people.

Dan Burke set up a meeting for me with Iacocca, telling me: "Just don't try to 'explain' hypermedia to him, all right?" I had no desire or ability to do that. I just told Iacocca that in my opinion, our efforts to train new CIS practitioners would strengthen his own mission. How can you foster competitiveness if you're losing 30 percent of the kids? After visiting one of our school sites in

Atlanta, he agreed to let us affiliate our work with his new institute. And when he learned more about our successes through the
1980s, he gave us a ringing endorsement: "All of us in the business
world like a program that gets results. CIS gets results. I am solidly
behind it."

The CIS Training Institute rapidly became essential to our
expansion. To the question, *What does CIS National offer?* we could
now answer, *A flexible, practical training program that equips you with
strategies you can take home to your own community and use to begin
fighting the dropout epidemic.*

There was another side to this "value-add" as well. In creating
our training materials, we inevitably found ourselves emphasizing
certain standards, both of program quality and of management,
that we believed were necessary for success with kids and schools.
It was the flip side of flexibility: Our model was highly adaptable,
but it wasn't "whatever you wanted." There were bottom-line
practices that we knew had to be embraced.

So here was something else we could offer as a national organization: the criteria that would allow a fledgling local initiative
to call itself "CIS." This led directly to our Quality & Standards
program, now called the Accreditation Standards, which we developed throughout the '90s and continue to improve to this day,
and which resulted in "accredited" CIS affiliates. These organizations had been peer-reviewed by others in the CIS network and by
our own trainers and could be demonstrably shown to adhere to
the highest standards of nonprofit management.

The emphasis on standards also helped us make what was
probably a long overdue decision in 1996: to change our name from
Cities In Schools to Communities In Schools. We were striving for
more uniformity among our local affiliates and that extended to
their names. They were getting very creative with what they called
themselves, but we could hardly blame a small community in east
Texas for not wanting to be "Cities In Schools"!

Increasingly, affiliates in Texas and North Carolina were
choosing the name "Communities In Schools" instead. Not only
was this more accurate demographically, but we realized that the
name captured a whole other level of meaning. Yes, we bring the

city—or the community—into the school, but our fundamental mission is to *create* community where before there was none. This is at the heart of our whole approach to integrated, caring delivery of resources. So when it came time to settle on a single name for the national organization and all the state and local affiliates, "Communities In Schools" was the overwhelming choice.

Throughout this period, it was fascinating to watch the interplay between flexibility and core standards. To our surprise, we learned that they weren't truly opposites. Codifying our bottom-line principles actually encouraged innovation because new affiliates had a stronger base to stand on. And once they'd come up with innovations that worked for them, they could communicate them to other affiliates because we all shared the common language of core beliefs and standards. It was like jazz players improvising on well-known tunes: everyone could hear what you were basing your creativity on.

The goal, always, was replication on a national scale. We didn't care much about the philosophical question *Why does CIS National exist?* for its own sake. We just wanted to be the best, most effective organization we could, the better to spread the CIS movement to as many schools, families, and kids as possible. And this in turn would create a "tipping point," a change in the way communities thought about their schools, whether or not CIS was present. We never imagined our organization in every school district in the country. Our vision—then and now—was to engender a critical mass of successful affiliates that would inspire and instruct others and eventually transform how our nation delivers resources to students and families.

Business expert Jim Collins's book *Good to Great* talks about "inflection points," those moments in a corporation's journey when some key decision is made that spells the difference between middling success and a fantastic upswing in productivity. There's no doubt that the decision to replicate through training was one of those inflection points for CIS, and I think it led directly to a second such moment for us.

As we began to train hundreds, rather than dozens, of people every year, we saw that some of our most cherished, time-tested implementation strategies were going to be questioned and reworked by these talented trainees. And so we didn't try to contain innovation, even at that basic level. We took a deep breath, swallowed hard, and *encouraged* the questioning and creativity. Our ideas had to be malleable enough to work in urban centers such as New York City, Chicago, and Los Angeles, as well as in rural North Carolina, in Appalachia, and in the suburbs of Washington, D.C. That just wasn't going to happen if we beat people up about not doing it "the way Neil and I did it in Atlanta in the good old days."

A direct result of encouraging such an entrepreneurial approach among our local affiliates was a willingness to fall flat and an acceptance of the missteps of others. Failure can lead to greater and deeper learning than success. Bill Gates has often said that he built Microsoft by fostering a culture in which it was *expected* that everyone would risk, fail, and risk again.

Being okay with failure wasn't something new for me personally. I couldn't count the number of mistakes and losses that marked my journey since 1960. But there was a key difference at this point. In the beginning, our defeats often resulted from a lack of understanding of key principles—the very ones we had to learn, codify, and eventually share with others, such as the Five Basics or the idea of personalism, accountability, and coordination. We were like musicians who didn't know our scales. But by the '90s, we had those scales down cold and could teach them to others. We'd still permit and even encourage failure, but within a context of excellent musicianship, so the improvisations were more intelligent and even the errors provided information. You can see that this is directly tied to that yin-yang relationship of flexibility and core standards.

MANAGING FROM WASHINGTON

One of our most informative failures helped us clarify even more precisely just what a national-level organization like CIS can and can't do for its local network. Throughout the '90s, we'd routinely accept funding from corporations that had a specific agenda relating to kids, families, or schools. In effect, we'd act as a contractor for them, and if we didn't know quite how to do what they wanted, we assumed that we'd figure it out as we went along. But it turned out that the uniformity of results that these businesses expected wasn't something we could always deliver.

A classic example of this misguided approach was our three-year partnership with a major retailer. Its CEO sat on our board, and his support was generous and consistent. When he suggested that we talk to his corporation's charitable foundation, we were happy to do it. They had 10 markets they wanted us to work in, and we agreed to regrant their dollars to our local affiliates in those areas. The plan was to encourage the retailer's employees to volunteer at CIS school sites. While the foundation let us set the indicators of "success" for the kids involved, they wanted these benchmarks to be uniform. They intended to grant the same amount of money to each of the 10 affiliates and expected the same results in all locations.

There were so many reasons why this couldn't have worked. Most important, none of the 10 affiliates had even *asked* for the partnership with the retailer, which went against the core principle we'd taught them of responding to community needs from the bottom up, not by bringing in programs from outside. In addition, we had no business trying to manage the work of the local affiliates, but that was exactly the position we found ourselves in since we were responsible for the results of the grant money.

So we learned that we would never again direct a local series of initiatives out of the national office. With 25 affiliates, we might have a shot at doing that effectively, but not with a hundred. If this same retailer (which, by the way, was extremely understanding and forgiving about our failures) had asked us for a partnership again, we'd say, "We have a strategic plan that emphasizes a few clear goals. These are achievable because they're based on the things we do well. If you can suggest a partnership that fits, there are a lot of options for working together. But if not, it's better for all concerned that we part ways."

We're still willing to regrant money to local or state CIS affiliates because many corporations are simply not set up to manage 15 or 20 small grants themselves; they want to deal with one larger organization. And we often fundraise for the national office with an eye toward driving strategic priorities within our network by coupling such a gift with pass-through funding. But we won't do it just to subsidize the grantor's particular programmatic ideas. They have to be interested in supporting our core business, as well as the particular goals of the grantee in question. By agreeing to administer their resources in subgrants to local affiliates, we're making a pledge that those gifts will be used effectively and will show measurable results. We're offering our guarantee that an investment through the national office will be used in a high-quality way by a high-quality network.

THE STATE STRATEGY

Another key inflection point that occurred in the 1990s made a huge difference in our ability to replicate and sustain the CIS movement. We decided to emphasize independent, state-level CIS affiliates as an efficient way to grow and institutionalize our work, rather than using a regional structure staffed by employees of CIS National. Our original idea had been to manage replication from five regional offices. But we discovered that whatever benefit this structure might confer in terms of national leadership was more than offset by the "top-down" headaches involved and, ultimately, by the simple fact that Georgians should replicate in Georgia and Floridians in Florida.

Our first state office, which was in Texas, had been successful from its start in the mid-1980s, thanks to our original state director, Jill Binder, and the support of Democratic governor Mark White and First Lady Linda Gale White. This was a case where public-sector support led to a degree of institutionalization that in turn spurred rapid growth of CIS within Texas. CIS wasn't quite part of the state education department (as would occur decades later in West Virginia), but most of its funding came from the state legislature and there was no question that CIS of Texas was able to operate effectively and independently from the national office.

Around the same time, Neil convinced John Clendenin, chairman of BellSouth, to approve funding for statewide CIS operations in Georgia, North Carolina, South Carolina, and Florida. John was also chair of the U.S. Chamber of Commerce and a conservative Southern Republican, and he saw the value of replicating and sustaining CIS at the state level. Thanks to the superb leadership of the four state directors—Neil Shorthouse in Georgia, Linda Harrill in North Carolina, Martha Gale in South Carolina, and Lois Gracey in Florida—the investment quickly paid off.

The success of the "state strategy," as we came to call it, rested on several factors. First, it placed ownership and control of the dropout issue where it belonged: not with us in Washington but with the state decision makers directly affected by the performance of their young people. Second, it encouraged information sharing and networking among communities that operated in the same educational environment, especially in terms of funding and academic standards. And third, state CIS directors found that they could become important players in the education policies being developed by state legislatures and boards of education.

All these factors led to a strong surge both in numbers of new CIS communities within the states with CIS offices and in the success rates of the local affiliates. There's no question that the state strategy took the CIS movement to new levels, and it was an important precursor of the licensing model, which we'll look at in the next chapter.

PROFITABLE NONPROFITS

Nonprofits in America provide a way for citizens to mobilize to address social problems that the government can't or won't work on effectively. This blunt truth may in part explain why it's so difficult to sustain a national nonprofit network. In the 1970s, there were around 300,000 nonprofits in the U.S. Today the total number of nonprofits has soared to about 1.6 million.[3] CIS remains one of the very small group that has a network-wide annual budget of $50 million or more (actually, about $303 million as of the 2020–21 academic year).[4]

Looking back on our story, I think it's clear that we had a great vision and many good ideas going in. And without false modesty, I can say that Dave Lewis, Neil Shorthouse, and I—along with Harv Oostdyk, Burt Chamberlin, Jim Hill, and so many other early leaders of the CIS movement—worked our tails off to keep the dream alive for children who had no hope and no future. But by themselves, good ideas and dedication to kids wouldn't have done it. We had to become a *replicable, effective, sustainable* process that communities across the country could adapt as their own.

To summarize what we learned:

- CIS used decentralization as a key to "going to scale," with each community taking ownership of the problem and the solution.
- Replicability involves a tension between adaptability to unique community conditions and fidelity to successful, proven models.
- Being nonpartisan is a precondition for scalability— the future of our children is not a partisan issue.
- Replicability involves training others and letting others take ownership of the results.
- Scalability and sustainability require core standards for the national network to follow.
- Replicability demands risk and a tolerance for failure, whereas scalability calls for innovation and refinement.

I think these lessons apply well to the nonprofit world in general. There's no question that they made the difference for us. They were the result of the collective intelligence of many, many CIS practitioners. This isn't the same thing as consensus, which tends to water down principles and strategies. Rather, it allows a high level of risk and disagreement.

Ultimately, we just have to stay open to the right combination of elements coalescing at the right time. The combination of circumstances and personal traits—collective intelligence, the right leadership, a tolerance for risk, the ability to learn from success and failure, and trust in God and each other—creates an almost-magical alchemy. If one element is missing, nothing works.

BUT DOES IT WORK?

Scalability and sustainability are two of the vital ingredients necessary for creating a permanent change in the way our education system combats the epidemic. The third is one of the most challenging yet essential aspects of fighting the dropout epidemic: a reliance on *evidence-based strategies*. Communities In Schools has become a national leader in this area.

As I've said, my colleagues and I came from a street culture that had little patience with the rigors of formal evaluations. We could see with our own eyes that young lives were being turned around, and that was all the proof we needed. Many of the original Street Academies were funded by corporations that regarded their dollars as "investment money." They basically said, "We don't understand how you do it, but we love what you do, so just go to it!"

I'm sure that my personal experiences with "standards" back in high school also contributed to our dislike of being evaluated. I was one of those kids who was set up to fail by the school system—not out of any malice on the part of teachers, but because I learned differently and never did well on tests. So I had a strong negative reaction to the idea that objective, measurable standards could ever really capture the worth of something I cared about. Whether I realized it clearly or not, my own self-worth was tied up in the issue.

That attitude is unacceptable today, and rightly so, for an organization that claims to be going to scale on combating the dropout epidemic. Corporations, foundations, and government leaders at all levels want to know that their funding dollars are being well spent and that nonprofits like CIS are truly making a measurable difference. The kids we serve are almost exclusively those young people who, without intervention, would likely fall far below the national averages for student success.

For now, though, there's still plenty of evidence to rely upon. The Five Basics, for instance, are recognized today as an early, prescient example of an "asset-based model": if you provide kids with these assets, they will do better in school. A wealth of research is available to validate this approach (see Appendix 3: "Research on Asset-Based Approaches").

Asset-based strategies have been the focus of great attention, and so have prevention-based models—which it turned out we had also been doing all along. Some kids are in such deep trouble that the immediate goal is to keep them from getting worse. Most CIS affiliates offer access to services and resources for the entire school—broadly, the Five Basics—while also providing targeted, case-managed services to a smaller, more at-risk group. This work tends to be preventive—interventions that can turn around a potential drug addict or criminal, for instance.

Our local affiliates submit end-of-year reports on student outcomes in areas such as attendance, behavior issues, promotion, and academic achievement. These are self-reported data, but we hold the affiliates to the highest standards of such accounting. At this writing, we have data from the 2020–21 academic year, and the numbers are remarkable:

- 74 percent of students met or made progress toward at least one of their attendance goals.

- 86 percent of students met or made progress toward at least one of their academic goals.

- 83 percent of students met or made progress toward at least one of their behavior goals.

- 96 percent of K–11 students were promoted to the next grade.

- 93 percent of 12th-grade students graduated or received a GED.

- *99 percent of students remained in school through the end of the 2020–21 school year.*[5]

Remember, the majority of these students are often underserved and at risk of falling below the national averages for measuring student success. This makes the results all the more impressive.

We also have a lot of data about the cost-effectiveness of this approach. Here's the statistic that says it all: the average cost per student to connect him or her with the needed resources and services, including both our whole-school and case-management models, is $188 a year. That's what I call a bargain.

Another excellent measure of our cost-effectiveness is the average *yearly* cost of implementing the CIS model at a school site. While the range is large, given the demographic diversity of the CIS network, the average cost is about $87,000.

Now compare both those statistics to the latest figure on K–12 public school spending *per pupil*: $14,455.[6] CIS is clearly producing a huge result for the dollars spent.

In 2012, a study on the economic impact of CIS was commissioned by the Annie E. Casey Foundation, Edna McConnell Clark Foundation, and Capital One. Economic Modeling Specialists Inc. (EMSI), one of the nation's leading economic modeling firms, found that:

- The average annual rate of return to society resulting from CIS's investment is 18.4 percent.

- The benefit-cost ratio is 11.6, which means that every dollar invested in Communities In Schools creates $11.60 of economic benefit for the community.

- High school graduates will be net contributors to their communities for an average of 44 years of their working life, using their increased income to purchase homes and cars, and paying taxes that will support police officers, firefighters, and teachers.[7]

I want to emphasize once again that the majority of these young people bring enormous problems and needs to school with them. They've already been stigmatized and abandoned by many in our society. Not to put too fine a point on it, these kids are *supposed* to drop out. The percentages above are nothing short of astonishing for this group, but we're committed to doing even better.

In the midst of this rather dry discussion of rates and percentages, let's pause to remember what's at stake. These children aren't statistics. Consider, deeply, the words I used to describe them: *stigmatized and abandoned . . . kids who are supposed to drop out . . . enormous problems and needs.* We're talking about a tremendous human toll, a legacy of deprivation and hopelessness being visited on the most innocent members of our society. If you can't feel heartbroken and outraged about this, you're probably reading the wrong book. These young people could be contributing incredible gifts, talents, and ideas—a legacy that would enrich their own lives and the lives of everyone around them—but that is being thwarted because of circumstances they had nothing to do with.

So when we seek evidence about practices that help these children succeed in school and in life, it's not just a matter of pleasing funders or adhering to sociologists' standards of what counts as "evidence-based strategies." We have a moral obligation to collect the very best proof—a point I didn't always understand but now believe passionately. We can't give ourselves any slack. If something works, it's our duty to demonstrate it objectively and share the news as widely as possible. And if something doesn't work or doesn't do the job well enough, we have to either adjust it accordingly or stop doing it. Our children are too precious for anything less.

CHANGING THE CLIMATE

Looking past the percentages for a moment, we can also say that CIS, through its interventions, is aiming to change a school's entire climate—admittedly a difficult thing to measure, but a reality nonetheless. We believe that when a team of caring adults is creating community in a school, the institution becomes a safer place, both physically and emotionally. When the most pressing needs of the hardest-hit students are being addressed, everyone breathes easier. Teachers can devote more time to teaching, discipline is no longer a daily crisis for administrators, and families reconnect with the school, seeing it as a place where other adults believe in their children, too. These "climate changes" will be reflected in the hard numbers—but also in a growing sense of optimism and empowerment.

For sure, we can show the *correlation* between CIS-provided services and improved student outcomes and school climate. What we're now studying is the role CIS plays in improving these outcomes.

Thirty years ago, I would have laughed at such a distinction, or maybe lost my temper. Of *course* CIS made the difference—what else could it have been? Today, I'm a little older and wiser, and I see the importance of this point. To really nail down our effectiveness, we have to show that CIS was the deciding factor, the catalyst for change, not just a wheel turned by some other, more important wheel in the school system.

Here's what we can say, based on the most recent independent evaluation of CIS: We know that CIS case management positively impacts nonacademic student outcomes, including improved relationships with adults, better-quality relationships with peers, and improved engagement with school, educational attitudes, and student belief that education has value for their future. Research suggests that these outcomes are behaviors and attitudes that are linked to students' success in school. We also know that high schools implementing the CIS model with fidelity experienced improved on-time graduation and dropout rates. Elementary schools implementing the CIS model improved the average daily attendance rate of their students.[8,9]

There are many other outcomes that I wish this evaluation had demonstrated, but it certainly helped us implement some important changes. We've improved our ability to home in on levels of need when we assign students to caseloads and also on the degree of support required. We have new assessments we can use to measure students' developmental relationships with adults and also their social and emotional growth. Our internal research capacities have also been brought to a new level of strength and sophistication.

So when we claim that our strategies and principles are evidence based, we know that decision makers will be able to rely on that statement.

But what about programmatic tactics? Are there, for instance, better and worse ways of providing the Five Basics? Shouldn't we be able to offer communities some guidance on content, too, not just process?

In partnership with the National Dropout Prevention Center at Clemson University, we identified risk factors in elementary, middle, and high school that may lead to dropping out. We then went on to examine programs that are successful in mitigating those factors. Then we analyzed what the best programs have in common and extracted the "critical elements." Now we can say to a local community, "If you want to create or 'broker in' a mentoring program or a family engagement program, make sure to incorporate these six elements and you'll have a much greater chance of success."[10]

Throughout much of our history, we stood firm on the Basics. They formed our only criteria for partnership (remember that national retailer?) and our message to communities across the nation: provide the Five Basics and you're doing good, as long as they're part of a personal, accountable, and coordinated effort on behalf of kids and families.

But after all, what doesn't fit the Basics? They're like world peace: of course everyone agrees they're good, but they're also extremely broad. We had to make a decision that merely "fitting the Five Basics" could no longer be a criterion for endorsement by us. We now won't settle for just *any* caring adult, *any* tutoring or skill-building program. If it really works for kids, there has to be evidence for it.

Today, Communities In Schools reaches more than 1.6 million young people annually in 26 states and the District of Columbia, along with 293,000 family members. That's not nearly enough.

As an organization, we can't possibly expect to stop the dropout epidemic alone. I've written so much about the scalability, sustainability, and evidence-based approach of CIS for one reason— *to convince you to take these principles and make them your own in your community.* I want you to agree that this approach not only makes sense; it also *works* and is capable of creating a lasting impact on the education system. You don't have to call it Communities In Schools as long as you're committed to the principles.

In the next chapter, we'll consider what the thorough adoption of these ideas would really mean and how you can help us get even closer to that day when we see the last dropout.

. . . AND BEYOND

When we discussed the P–16 (preschool to college graduation) movement earlier, I pointed out that college students often need the same kinds of integrated services to assist them with their educational goals. That's going to be a big focus for CIS as we go "beyond."

The "cradle to career" concept is the latest version of this vital response to helping high school graduates succeed. As of 2020, we have 15 college campuses in Texas with a CIS program manager. Dropping out doesn't only happen in high school. The first six months of trade, technical, and two-year college also see high numbers of dropouts.

And keep in mind Rey Saldaña's story of how he stayed in contact with his CIS coordinator when he went off to study at Stanford. He's not alone—many high school graduates feel the same fears and uncertainty and need a caring adult in their corner. That's a role that more and more CIS programs can take on going forward.

CHAPTER 9

FROM AWARENESS TO ADVOCACY TO ACTION

You don't have to call it Communities In Schools . . . or maybe you do call it CIS but train another dedicated group to implement the model in their community. This simple concept is the basis for one of the most exciting and potentially game-changing strategies we've developed. We call it the licensing model, and in the state of West Virginia, it's already helping us go to scale in 30 counties.

OUT OF ONE, MANY

Back in 2018, CIS had exactly one local program in West Virginia. But CIS of Greenbrier County was getting great results, and one of their board members happened to know First Lady Cathy Justice, who is passionate about education and improving opportunities for young people. West Virginia's children endure some of the highest rates in the nation of so-called adverse childhood experiences—including sexual abuse, domestic violence, traumatic divorce, and exposure to drug abuse.

The Greenbrier board member knew about Mrs. Justice's determination to end this and suggested that someone from CIS National meet with her and explore a statewide expansion. So what started out as a cup of coffee with the First Lady turned into something that has changed public education in West Virginia.

Essentially, Mrs. Justice said, "I want this program expanded into many more counties in my state, and I challenge you to figure out how you can make that happen quickly, given that your process of replication is resource- and time-intensive." We had to think harder and bigger, and eventually we came up with the idea of *licensing* the CIS model to the state education authorities, and then providing training and accreditation in implementation of that model.

We'd done some tentative exploration of the licensing concept in other settings. Licensed partners pay a fee to receive personalized training and technical assistance from the CIS National Office. The existing school district, nonprofit, or state department of education manages the administrative aspects of implementing the CIS model, including hiring site coordinators and a program director.

The result is still very much a CIS program. Site coordinators deliver the full CIS model at the school, including all aspects of site coordination, case management, and partner/resource development and integration. The use of CIS's data management system is required, as well as adherence to all Student Support Standards under Accreditation Standards. Licensed partners undergo a certification review after three years (similar to the accreditation process that CIS affiliates undergo) and at regular intervals thereafter.

In West Virginia, three counties were chosen to pilot this concept in the 2018–19 school year, adding 9 new schools to the 10 previously served by CIS in Greenbrier County. Establishing a new nonprofit in each county wasn't necessary. The West Virginia Department of Education directed public dollars to the local school districts to hire school-based site coordinators who would identify students with the most challenges, case-manage them, and connect community resources to the schools. The site coordinators would also deliver school-wide supports to affect the entire school climate. Governor Justice donated his salary, and a system of state grants to local counties was established.

All this happened in an amazingly short period of time, and before we knew it, we had to devise our training program with about two weeks to spare. Laura VanDeusen was a new hire at the national office, and her first assignment was to create a training—yesterday! "Fortunately, I could call on veteran CIS site coordinators and trainers," Laura remembers. "Thanks to the strength of our network, we had all the pieces we needed, and the training materials and resources just came together."

Principals, site coordinators, and counselors from the new schools received the training, and the expansion was underway. Results that year exceeded expectations, and the next thing we knew, we were being asked to expand into *another* 37 new schools in eight additional counties for the 2019–20 school year.

THE SPEED OF TRUST

I want to pause here to highlight three things that I think are very important.

1. Yes, we had great numbers that first year, but CIS can only go where it's wanted, whether as an independent affiliate or a licensed model. Governor Justice authorized a statewide community engagement and research effort called West Virginia's Voice. It included data from over 20,000 interviews with West Virginians, and the report highlighted a shared goal that CIS could fulfill: "Forum attendees overwhelmingly recognized a need for greater social-emotional supports for students. Additionally, the need to take significant action . . . was expressed due to the effects of increased drug use, including the opioid crisis." Further, the report noted that "stakeholder support for embedding social services in schools is widespread." Seventy-five percent of respondents saw embedded social services as "a worthwhile investment of tax dollars." And CIS in particular was lauded in the report: "Students with poor physical or mental health, who are homeless, who experience instability at home or who come to school hungry do less well in school than students who feel safe and secure. For 40 years, the

Communities In Schools (CIS) model has proven to be a cost-effective model that district leaders recognize as a critical component of successful school turnaround."[1]

I have to say, it's deeply gratifying to see that the case we were making 40 years ago—when school systems were not as receptive to inviting outside organizations into schools—has now become the accepted wisdom. If you come to school hungry, you'll do less well . . . We didn't think it took a genius to discover this. Maybe the real challenge was in convincing school systems of the *solution*: what West Virginia and many other states are now calling "embedded social services in schools." For me, that is—and always has been—the CIS model.

2. Once West Virginia counties recognized they were ready to welcome a program like CIS, the phrase I started to hear a lot from the folks working in West Virginia was "We're moving at the speed of trust."

This idea captures so much of what Communities In Schools does. Relationships, not programs, make the difference, as we've said over and over. People tend not to trust a "program," especially if they've never seen it before. But they can very quickly come to trust the individuals involved, and that was the real reason for our quick success in West Virginia. The kids trusted the site coordinators, and so did the parents and the administrators. The new trainees trusted the CIS staff, because they could see we'd been here before, we knew all the problems and pitfalls, and we were absolutely committed to equipping them with the skills and support they needed.

Moreover, it was going to be all about local control. The CIS model would be implemented in the same way throughout the state and is measured by the same rigorous standards, but local practitioners would have control over that implementation. This made a big difference. Clayton Burch, state superintendent of schools, told a West Virginia Public Broadcasting interviewer, "Even though CIS has a framework, a system that's put in place, the ability it has to grow to what the individual community and families need is amazing." So we discovered that thanks to our model and experience, "the speed of trust" in West Virginia was pretty darn fast.

Laura VanDeusen says, "A lot of that first year was just showing up and having conversations, taking the time and being intentional at the beginning of every meeting, to talk to people and build in those relational pieces. We were able to do a lot of things virtually, but we learned that year how important it was to adjust and respond when the trainees said, 'We really need more in-person time with you.'"

3. Lastly, the licensing model in West Virginia is the latest and most comprehensive example of what is now called braided funding, which we have championed all along under the heading of "public-private partnership." Braided funding is the use of multiple sources of funding to achieve a common objective, fund a specific initiative, or pay for personnel. Typically, you'll get a mix of federal, state, local, and private dollars in this way. The initial grants to the counties to implement the CIS model used state-identified and legislatively approved funding. These funds allow a school district to get started and can later be augmented by local funds or other braided sources, including federal dollars. In fact, as CIS's population and outcomes grew in West Virginia, counties came to the table with their own general operating and federal dollars first, even without the state grants.

    I should also note that this kind of partnership happens at the individual school level as well, with investments by private supporters. Just to name one example: Walmart donates paper, pens, pencils, and snacks to 11 schools in the southern part of the state.

Chris Rockenstein, a Walmart marketing manager who grew up in the West Virginia school system, says, "You go on a school visit, see the innocence, see the fun, and just look around and observe what the need is. Then you jump in and help out."

INSIDE THE SYSTEM

The big question for the future of the licensing model, as Laura VanDeusen saw it, was, "Can we support another organization and build their internal capacity such that they no longer require CIS National to direct them in how to use the model? And to me, the answer from the West Virginia project has been a resounding yes." This is indeed the key question for our CIS leadership as we look to the future—and I agree that the answer is yes.

Once again, institutionalization was the key in West Virginia. In the spring of 2019, First Lady Justice created a statewide advisory council to help unlock additional resources that counties and schools might need. She made sure that this council was connected to the state board of education, in keeping with the "all hands on deck" approach to education championed by the Governor and First Lady from the outset. A nonprofit organization was also formed to accept and distribute philanthropic support more easily.

How did we know this new model was working and actually getting results? The data confirmed it: For the 2019–20 school year, the CIS case-managed students were improving attendance by 70 percent, academics by 81 percent, and behavior by 82 percent. Ninety-eight percent were being promoted, 99 percent graduated (including GED completion), and 100 percent of these students stayed in school.[2]

When the pandemic shutdown came along in March 2020, West Virginia's school system, and its children, needed more support than ever. With buildings closed and teachers and staff unable to reach families and students, CIS site coordinators filled the gap and, in fact, are credited by the Department of Education personnel with driving more positive outcomes than were found in other schools that did not have CIS. Deputy superintendent Michele Blatt declared, "Schools which had CIS facilitators in place had developed strong relationships with their students and the community and were better prepared to take care of their students during the pandemic."

As of March 2022, CIS is reaching 70,000 students in 171 schools, comprising 31 county school districts in West Virginia. It's well within reach for us to be in all 55 counties in the near future. And best of all, if you Google "CIS of West Virginia," you'll be taken to a page that gives a fantastic account of our work there, all the lives we've affected, and the constant expansion . . . and that page is housed on the West Virginia Department of Education website, because we are *part* of their mission. We have gone inside the system and changed it for the better.

"It's Communities In Schools, but it's truly West Virginia," says Laura VanDeusen, now our senior director for licensing at CIS National. "Sometimes it feels a little jarring—they're not calling me as much as they used to. Did I do something wrong? But it's the opposite. Because we did things right, they don't need us."

STOP THE EPIDEMIC!

The story of our licensing model's success in West Virginia opens the door to a huge and fascinating vista: Where is Communities In Schools going next in its quest to serve children, families, schools, and communities?

This much we know: the day when all school systems routinely connect community services for students who need them as an ordinary part of their commitment to educate *all* children will be the day we glimpse the last dropout.

It can be done—it *is* being done. And now is the time to start getting it done in *your* community. **Our children need three things from you: your *awareness*, your *advocacy*, and your *action*.**

The most important thing to be *aware* of is exactly how serious the dropout epidemic is. We're losing about 1.2 million young people every year. The fiscal and human consequences are huge. The epidemic is costing our society billions of dollars in lost economic productivity. It's catastrophic for the workforce, and it's dooming millions of young adults to lives with little hope for a future.

What's the dropout rate in your local school system? In your state? The U.S. Department of Education's official publication that contains state-by-state figures, "Trends in High School Dropout and Completion Rates in the United States," is available online at nces.ed.gov. An inquiry to your local school board or superintendent of schools should also produce a helpful response—and if it doesn't, that, too, will be informative. It's particularly important to ask questions about poor and minority student success. The dropout epidemic is a *justice* issue, in large part because the least advantaged young people in our society are bearing the brunt of our systems' failures.

What steps are schools taking to respond? As you become aware of the facts that reflect the extent of the dropout epidemic in your community and state, find out what resources and strategies are already in place to stem the flow of students leaving the classroom. It's a most unusual school system that isn't doing *something*. Our challenge is to help educators and administrators apply the principles of integrated, school-based service delivery in a way that will maximize their already-existing efforts.

Charter schools, for example, are operated independently of the traditional public school system and tailor their programs to community needs. According to the U.S. Department of Education's Charter School website, 7,427 new schools have been launched since state legislatures began passing charter legislation in the 1990s.[3] "Policy makers, parents, and educators are looking at chartering as a way to increase educational choice and innovation within the public school system," says the Department of Education.[4] It's an excellent opportunity to include integrated, school-based service delivery into the mix of choices.

When it comes to *advocacy* and *action*, the choices are many, all of them rich with possibilities. These possibilities depend on personal circumstances, and of course I don't know yours. Writing a book is an odd experience, especially for someone like me who thrives on one-to-one relationships. If only I knew exactly who you were, reading these words! In that case, I'd be better able to offer very specific recommendations about how to move forward on behalf of the kids in your school system, based on your level of energy, time, commitment, and standing in the community.

Since that's not possible, I'll try to suggest some general paths to follow. If I've done my job well in writing this book, most readers will close the covers with a new understanding and, I hope, new energy and willingness to advocate, to speak out, to join a movement dedicated to ending the dropout epidemic. These readers, in short, are willing to be part of the solution.

In addition, there are probably a few of you—a much smaller number—who are in a position to *take this on* as a major life activity, a cause to which you can devote considerable energy and commitment. The Communities In Schools movement is nourished by people like you, and I certainly want to connect with you.

But for that other, larger group of readers, I offer two ways to explore and get more information about the advocacy and action possibilities in your community. First, I invite you to visit the CIS National website, communitiesinschools.org, to find out more. And second, in Appendix 3 you'll find a list and brief descriptions of many national programs that are walking parallel roads with us that would welcome your help.

ADVOCACY AND ACTION IN CIS COMMUNITIES

Certainly we need your support, wherever we are and wherever you are, but most school districts don't have a CIS affiliate. At this writing, the nationwide CIS network consists of 117 organizations and licensees in 26 states and the District of Columbia, providing services at 2,860 public schools and community sites. (See communitiesinschools.org for a complete list of CIS communities.) If you're one of that smaller group of readers who really wants to put significant time and energy into combating the dropout epidemic, and you find that CIS is already in your community or state—welcome aboard! We'll surely find plenty of work for you. Among other things, you can:

- Visit a school with a CIS presence to observe directly the work we do with and for students

- Serve on a school or community committee, sharing your expertise to make a difference

- Build and support relationships between schools and community programs and businesses through your CIS local affiliate

- Identify appropriate funding sources or contribute to needed school and community programs through the CIS affiliate

I can't emphasize strongly enough that along with specific advocacy, we need to change our attitudes and responses to solving our education system's greatest problems. If you're a businessperson, rethink how your company is using its influence in the community. If you're involved in social services, take a look at how your people are positioned. If you're a faith-based leader, use the brainpower and influence of your congregation, not just their charitable impulses.

The most important action you can take is often within your own sphere of activity. The responsibility for stopping the dropout epidemic rests with each one of us. Communities In Schools former president Dan Cardinali put it this way: "Americans will never have a strong, successful education system unless they take more of a role in their schools than just paying property taxes."

THE LAST DROPOUT

There's an old saying: "You can't appreciate the good news unless you know what the *bad* news is." Well, if you're looking for bad news about the frightening outcomes that millions of our children face, you don't have to look far. But I believe there is also an unprecedented appetite for some *good* news about what we can do to turn this around.

The nine principles I've described and the Communities In Schools success story represent that good news. We can work together to make these values a reality:

1. Programs don't change kids—*relationships* do.

2. The dropout crisis isn't just an education issue.

3. Young people need the five *real* basics, not just the three *R*'s: a one-on-one relationship with a caring adult, a safe place to learn and grow, a healthy start and a healthy future, a marketable skill to use upon graduation, and a chance to give back to peers and community.

4. The community must weave a safety net around its children in a manner that's personal, accountable, and coordinated.

5. Every community needs a "Champion for Children": a neutral third party with "magic eyes" to see things—and people—differently, and coordinate and broker the diverse community resources into the schools on behalf of young people and families.

6. Educators and policy makers can't do it alone . . . and they'll welcome your help.

7. Curing the dropout epidemic will demand *change*, not just charity.

8. *Scalability, sustainability,* and *evidence-based strategies* are essential to creating permanent change in the way our education system combats the dropout epidemic.

9. Our children need three things from you: your *awareness*, your *advocacy*, and your *action*.

If we succeed in practicing these principles, change *will* come. I would add only one caution: you can't pick and choose which principles you "like better" or the ones that you think will be easiest to implement. A *holistic, coordinated* approach is at the heart of what we're advocating, and that has to start with a big-picture commitment to institutional change. Only by adopting (and adapting) all nine of these principles to meet each community's challenges can we have any hope of seeing, someday, the last dropout.

I've called this book *The Last Dropout* because it *is* a phrase full of hope. It's Utopian, and it's "impossible," sure—but it's also the *only* morally acceptable vision for us Americans to endorse. And is it really impossible? I wonder . . . My grandchildren's kids might attend a high school where *no one* drops out. Not because it's such a wonderful place, but because . . . well, we just don't let that happen to our children anymore.

CONCLUSION: THE GOLDEN TRIANGLE

I grew up in Pittsburgh, and by God's grace I met and married my wife, Jean, there. The two of us and our wonderful children, Sean and Lani, don't get back to the city as often as we'd like now that our birth parents, extended family, and friends have moved on, and our lives remain so busy. My work at Communities In Schools always seemed to involve 60-hour weeks, even after I made the transition in 2004 from president to vice chairman. Jean has been an Episcopal priest since 1980 and has a doctorate in pastoral counseling, so she's extremely busy, too. As she likes to remind me, it's a good thing that she's a priest *and* a therapist, because her husband needs both!

I do love to visit Pittsburgh when I can, though. I still have great friends and CIS staff who are based there—and besides, I'm a huge Steelers fan. I never tire of driving from the airport into the city and, as I emerge from the Fort Pitt Tunnel, seeing "the Golden Triangle." That's what a lot of folks call this great place, once known as America's steel capital. They call it that because it's where three rivers merge: the Monongahela, the Allegheny, and the Ohio. Pittsburgh produced a lot of golden times, with those three rivers bringing prosperity and fame.

There is a Golden Triangle that can bring prosperity to our children, too. If we can align the three sides of the triangle as I've proposed in this book, a Golden Triangle of reform will make our schools environments of learning and nurturing, keeping our young people on track for graduation and preparing them for life. It's going to take all of us—the entire community—to make it happen.

I remember an occasion when I had the privilege of speaking at the Chicago Communities In Schools annual meeting. This vibrant CIS affiliate now has a presence in 190 schools, with approximately 150 community partnerships bringing much-needed services and caring individuals into the schoolhouses. After my speech, Chicago's CIS executive director thanked me and then quickly said that she wasn't going to give a speech herself, but just wanted to take time to thank "the orchestra" of more than 200 people sitting before her. The crowd included representatives from the mayor's office as well as the superintendent's. There were health-care providers; corporations; parents and students; volunteers and leaders from the YMCA, Boys & Girls Clubs, the Urban League, Big Brothers Big Sisters, and many more.

I could feel my joyful tears starting as I watched them stand and applaud one another for bringing their gifts to the table on behalf of children. These men and women had come out of their various "silos" to weave a safety net of relationships and resources, freeing teachers up to teach and creating safe, caring environments in the schools they're privileged to serve.

After the meeting ended, I did what I love to do most, which is to visit a local CIS school site. The middle school I went to was a beacon of hope in the midst of a very poor neighborhood. Just walking in the door made me feel good as I took in the renovations, the new paint, the glistening clean walls. Students' art hung in the halls leading to their classrooms. This place had a great principal who'd taken over a failing enterprise and begun to turn it around. The teachers were energetic, and the administrators felt very much a part of the growing success of this wonderful school. They boasted of increased reading and math scores. The young people also seemed to love this environment of learning and care—they had smiles on their faces and a bounce to their walk, treating us visitors with respect and dignity. They weren't only studying the curriculum; they were also learning *community* and how to be part of it. The Golden Triangle was in place, and anyone could see the results.

A couple of people from the corporate community who'd also been at the Chicago CIS meeting were with me that day. At the end of our tour, we had a roundtable discussion with some of the students, a couple of parents, the principal, and some teachers. One of the businesspeople asked a student named Clarence who was halfway through eighth grade what his experience had been like so far. Clarence responded that when he'd first arrived, he'd wanted to drop out after a couple of months. He said that he was behind in his grades and didn't feel comfortable at school.

Our business friend asked him what made the difference. Clarence replied, "I found out that there were a whole lot of people who believed in me and were willing to help me make it."

And what had Clarence gained from this experience? "I feel ready for high school, and *I got me a future*."

There are millions of young people in our schools who are close to giving up. They're desperately searching for a future. By coming together as a community in and around our schools, we have the capacity and the resources to help every student succeed.

My prayer is that this will happen in your community. I pray that we all may have new minds to think differently, not simply try harder—that we may develop "magic eyes" to see the incredible assets already in place throughout our schools and communities. And may our hearts be filled with love that never quits until there truly is hope and a future for *all* our children.

AFTERWORD

Communities In Schools . . . and Beyond:
A Conversation with Rey Saldaña
and Bill Milliken

From the desk of Rey Saldaña:

I got the call one morning in November 2021. A few days previously, an e-mail had showed up at my home office in San Antonio. It was from a name I didn't recognize, someone who said he worked for an unnamed philanthropist, asking if I could find a few minutes to chat about a client who wanted to make an anonymous gift to CIS.

I said yes, though half of me knew it had to be a scam. The other half was hoping it might be for real.

The caller said, "I have a role on the team working for a client who I'm still not going to identify yet, but if this call goes the way I hope it will, by the end of our talk you'll know who it is." The call did go well, and the mystery client was revealed. When I heard the name MacKenzie Scott, I took a deep breath before starting my next sentence . . . and realized I didn't know what to say.

Everyone in the nonprofit world knew about Ms. Scott's philanthropy. She had donated somewhere around $12 billion to nonprofits since 2020. You couldn't "apply" for a gift. Her method of selecting recipients was unknown, though she always picked organizations of the highest reputation.

I was flooded with thoughts and images and feelings from my time with CIS over the last year and a half—students and families and staff who've been working so incredibly hard and who needed some good news.

So I just let Ms. Scott's representative keep talking, and gradually the details emerged. First: They'd be making a gift to the national office and also to our affiliates. Another individual on the team would be calling to give the actual amount. Clearly they were very concerned about confidentiality, but I had no doubt from the way he was talking that the amount involved was a large one.

I was trying to remember all the articles I'd read about MacKenzie Scott's other mega-gifts. I thought some went as high as $8 million, even $10 million. So I dared to hope this gift might be in the same range.

A few days later, the second call came. I heard this: "MacKenzie Scott believes in your work and your leadership, your team and your research, and she'd like to give $20 million to your organization." After trying to express my thanks, my next thought was about how exciting it would be to share the news, but I was told, "No, we need to roll this out in our own way. You have to keep this completely confidential for a month and a half."

And then . . . "Actually, we're not done with CIS this year. We're also going to make investments to your independent affiliates." Before he said this, I'd already started thinking about how to get the affiliates involved and get it distributed in the right way for them. My first notion was, maybe we'll keep half at National for our own efforts, and half can go out to the network. But now I was hearing a whole new opportunity. I asked the Scott representative how much money might be added for the affiliates.

He replied, "Here's how we do this. We're going to talk to each of them individually and tell them what our gift will be. Then you can contact them yourselves and ask them. It's up to them how they choose to share the news. But we may need your help in one area: We're going to start sending those e-mails out tomorrow, and you'll probably be getting calls from the affiliates asking you if this is for real. So please just tell them, yes, it's legitimate, and make sure you respond to that e-mail."

Over the next couple of weeks, I got calls from Houston, Memphis, Chicago, Los Angeles, East Texas. "Hey, have you heard of this name?" I answered, "I can't share the news with you. They want to tell you themselves. It'll make much more sense when they talk to you. But call them back!"

Gradually we started to get a sense of who in the network was getting these e-mails. I had hoped that perhaps as many as 10 of our affiliates would get gifts. But when we totaled it all up four weeks later, the number was 40. Still the MacKenzie Scott folks wouldn't give us the individual grant amounts. "It's up to them to share with you. I can give you the cumulative total, including the gift to CIS National, which is . . . $133.5 million."

One hundred and thirty-three million dollars is one of those phrases that almost literally won't compute when you first hear it. You could do nothing to prepare for this, and there's just no basis of comparison for this kind of news.

I was running a marathon in Dallas that day. It put some gas in my tank, that's for sure. I ran my best time ever.

AND BEYOND . . .

A month or two later, Bill Milliken asked me if I would lend a hand in updating The Last Dropout, his book about the founding of Communities In Schools. I wasn't sure exactly what he wanted me to bring to the party. Bill said, "Well, it would be great if you could write a new piece to open the book, introducing yourself and telling your story. And then we could conclude the new edition by having a conversation between the two of us about where CIS is going. We can discuss that phrase we both love so much: 'Communities In Schools . . . and Beyond.'"

What follows is our best shot at picturing the future of CIS. We hope it informs and inspires you.

Rey Saldaña: Bill, you once pointed to the "Communities In Schools . . . and Beyond" sign behind me and said, "You guys have really figured this out." We were in the midst of the pandemic, asking, "Do we have a future in this work?" especially because we had just sent 50 million students back home and shut down schools. What's the future of Communities In Schools without being "in schools"?

What we recognized to be true was that we've *always* worked beyond school, as students brought to us the challenges that they faced beyond the classroom. We've always been willing to go outside the school walls to ensure that we're meeting the needs and removing the obstacles our students face, whether that means helping with doctor appointments, dentist's appointments, mental health specialists, access to college programs, or anything else.

So as we think about "and beyond," it's important to articulate that this is something we've always been doing. We're just trying to get a little more scientific, if you will, around what works with the hardest-to-engage students. It's not just a question of finding students who are disengaged. When you find them, can you actually connect with them and reengage them with their school, or with other relationships that are important for that student and their family?

Traditionally, our job is to get students back into school and make sure they graduate. We do that very well, and that continues to be true. But there are multiple pathways now for our students, especially those who are juniors and seniors in high school who say, "Look, I need to be in school, but at the same time, I need to have a job to make sure that I can bring some extra income into the house." Or maybe the student is getting close to graduation but their path still feels uncertain, and they say, "I still need your support." There are challenges around college or career or military or housing assistance. These things don't dissolve just because you've got a high school diploma. I know that very well from my own experience.

And those are just a few measures and concepts that go "beyond." We need to envision a future where that is standard operating procedure for us. Of course we want to expand into more schools and continue to achieve excellent metrics around attendance and graduation and academic improvement. But in trying to figure out that journey toward success in life, we need to create an escape velocity for the students so that at some point they're doing things on their own. And that takes a little more than just getting them beyond the high school graduation stage.

I wonder if you'd agree with this direction, Bill?

Bill Milliken: I agree 100 percent; I just would add to it. The "beyond" is also about the "cradle to career" concept that's out there now in the world of education, and which is totally suited to CIS.

Here's an example. We've signed a memorandum of understanding with Head Start, and we're already working in West Virginia and Virginia with *Sesame Street*. We're linking *Sesame Street* and Head Start with CIS as a continuum of service from cradle through K–12. CIS doesn't need to "do *Sesame Street*" or re-create a similar program; we can be the connector, the orchestra leader, to reach young preschoolers.

Rey: When you first hear the phrase "and beyond," you tend to think of the "beyond" as meaning "the future." But the picture you're drawing includes preschool as well. We need to reach beyond the schools to start embracing kids even before they're school age—literally cradle to college, cradle to career.

Bill: Right. On the other end of the age spectrum, we need to maintain our support all the way through to young adulthood. In Texas, there are now 15 college campuses with a CIS program manager. We know that the highest dropout numbers post–high school are in the first six months of trade, technical, or two-year college.

If you're fortunate enough that the support system called "a family" provides the resources your children need to flourish, then that's a delivery system. The CIS site coordinator creates this same kind of delivery system to make sure that a kid who may not have that support system at home is known all the way through the process and isn't lost in the system.

Rey, you and I went to Shaq O'Neal's fundraising event for CIS and Boys & Girls Clubs in Nevada. The Nevada chapters of CIS and Boys & Girls Clubs are already thinking about a more meaningful partnership: CIS alumni as mentors to the Boys & Girls Clubs kids, all in the same building together. That's another "beyond" idea.

Rey: Yes, these examples are perfectly clear indicators of how our work continues to take us where we've always needed to go, whether it is "beyond" to community colleges or to career pipeline pathways. Just yesterday I had a conversation with the CEO of the Big Brothers Big Sisters program about their trajectory of growth and CIS's trajectory of growth, and how we continue to be strong partners together.

I like to use the term "Swiss Army knife" to describe the approach of building linkages. The goal would be to provide whatever tool the young person may need. It can be difficult when you're living in poverty and you don't have a person who you can count on to help you find those resources or assets. Even when they're located down the street from your community, it can feel like it might as well be a thousand miles away without an access point, a delivery system, or a person to help you walk through the process.

Bill: We have to remember our history. We went into schools because that's where the kids are for a large portion of the day. We knew if we didn't "turn off the faucet" of dropouts, the rest would be irrelevant in so many high-dropout areas of the country. If you have a million kids on the streets, then you're going to continue to create more pockets of intergenerational poverty. People don't want to put their stores there, they don't want to live there, they don't want to invest there, because there's too much danger in these communities. So we "went beyond" and partnered with community groups to get the tools for the CIS site coordinators to use in the schools, where more and more young people were looking to us.

It's important not to lose sight of organizing around the Five Basics, because everything we're talking about now can still be connected to those five critical needs. "A safe place to learn and grow"—we said that from the beginning. And when you create school-to-work support, that's the Fourth Basic, "a marketable skill to use upon graduation." We keep our core principles and continue to build on a solid basis of what we know works, and at the same time we're realizing that we have to meet kids wherever they are and respond to their changing needs to make sure that they are launched into a successful life.

Rey: Yes, and it's another key point in thinking about "CIS and beyond"—our whole conception of ourselves as a "dropout-prevention program." This is nuanced; it's not a simple answer. Certainly that label is a good way to make sense to the world about who we are: "What is our work? Yes, we keep kids in school." We do measure that metric, and we will continue to do so. But I think the future of this work is going in a much broader direction.

CHANGING THE SYSTEM

Bill: We're about changes for kids, but we're also trying to change the delivery system. And there are two ways to do it. One is to work on the connections, making them stronger and more all-encompassing. The other is to affect *policy*, where you reward people to work together rather than in their own silos of expertise.

In the federal education legislation, the Elementary and Secondary Education Act, there's language written into the law that allows school districts to use Title I money to pay for a site coordinator. You can't have an integrated system without an integrator any more than you can have an orchestra without a conductor. This is a major breakthrough in supporting our model. When you combine it with new validation from the private sector, you begin to see how public and private together are creating a whole new "beyond" for kids.

Rey: We want to be more than just a vaccine for some students. We want to improve the health of the whole school. And this invokes two other concepts that I think are worth talking about with respect to "and beyond" for CIS. Any nonprofit is sometimes working at the whims of its consumers, or the person who pays for its work, or the funder who helps support the infrastructure that you're building. And sometimes the tail wags the dog. Nonprofits can get themselves into a position of saying, "Whatever our donors are telling us they need from us, we will conform to that."

So a school system might say to us, "Look, stay in your lane here. We need you to be a small program that impacts attendance and graduation rates." But from the earliest days of CIS, we were saying that things like food, shelter, basic needs—the Five Basics, as you were describing—are in fact *more* than just what schools said they needed from us.

As we think about our future as an organization, the question becomes: How do you get a system to pay for its own disruption? Because that's what we're asking schools to do when they invite us in. We're saying, "Look, it's not just that we need to be here to support a student who's trying to navigate the speed bumps or the land mines. We will do that. We've become very good at doing that. But the bigger question is, why are those obstacles in front of that student to begin with? How can we *remove* barriers, not simply guide students around them?"

Sometimes the policies that need to change are inside the school or the school system. But other times those policies are a reflection of what's going on *outside* the school—this is the "beyond" idea again—whether it is access to affordable housing or overdisciplining of our students of color. It could be an overpoliced community, or a community without proper infrastructure, so students can't safely walk to school in the early mornings because the lights are out. All of a sudden, you're talking about really changing the environment that students are breathing in, rather than just saying, "Here's an oxygen mask to help you breathe through this really thick, toxic environment."

At the same time, we acknowledge that it can be a challenge to the system. Every system is designed to want to defend the results it's currently getting, and every system is designed to resist change. We need to be able to sit at the leadership table with the principal and the staff and the counselors and say, "Here's our caseload of students. But notice that this caseload of 50 or 60 students has a very distinct pattern around, for example, access to mental health services. There's nothing they can access within a two- or three-mile radius within the school. So we need transportation for them; we need to talk to our city council or county commissioners about bringing such a service into the community." That's a "level beyond" where I think our work has begun, and where it will ultimately evolve to.

Bill: I once took a group of businesspeople on a site visit to a school with a CIS coordinator. The principal invited some of the kids to talk to us. One young lady had been a really tough kid. Now she was the head of the student council. One of the businesspeople said to her, "It seems like you have everything you need here, and the CIS approach is really working." She said, "Oh yes, I love this place. I love coming to school." He asked, "Well, what's the main obstacle for you now, what's the part that causes you the most fear?" Her answer was: "When I go out that school door and have to walk home. Because it's *not safe* from here to my house."

That's exactly what you're talking about, Rey. That's why we need to partner with groups outside the schools. There are organizations that create "safe passages," for instance. Better yet, how can we change policy and infrastructure in that neighborhood so the streets become safe to walk?

Here's another example. Raj Chetty, the Harvard economist, visited our Charlotte, North Carolina, program and loved what we're doing. He said, "You've gotten all these kids out of poverty, you've broken the poverty cycle. That's fantastic. But what do you do about the parents that are left behind? They're still there."

He's right: "And beyond . . ." has to mean connecting to parents and caregivers. Neil Shorthouse, former President of CIS of Georgia, created a program called Partners In Change to respond to this. There's a story I just heard, about an Atlanta woman named Sandra who was homeless, a struggling mother with three kids. She heard about getting a free life coach through Partners in Change from one of her kids' CIS site coordinators and signed up. She describes her coach, who's a volunteer from BlackRock, the huge asset management firm and longtime partner with CIS, as her *personal accountability partner.* She knew that's what she needed to help her persist in her education and increase her chances of landing a better job. Now she says all the kids talk about her being in school and are trying harder as students to be "just like Mommy." Sandra's plan is that after one year with her coach, she'll be ready to train to *be* a coach for another CIS parent.

This is just one example of one of the blades in your Swiss Army knife, Rey. The CIS site coordinator in that school is a broker for services for both students and their parents. To me that's definitely a "beyond" concept.

Rey: Yes, and it's another example of how we recognize that we're not trying to re-create the wheel; we want to partner with those who are already doing good work.

I mentioned two ideas earlier. The first was the issue of how to work with a school system to make fundamental changes in the community. The second is a vision that we're still struggling to articulate, but we know we're all committed to it: finding a role for some of our alumni, especially in the context of the Fifth Basic, "giving back to peers and community." We want to get our alumni reengaged with CIS and their community, providing leadership and support for students moving toward college and careers.

Of course, we can find other partners who do that really well, too. We don't have to build an entire system like this ourselves. In fact, we shouldn't, if we know other organizations are doing this well with a population of students who look like the students that we serve. But I think our alumni could have a unique role to play. We're still designing this, drawing on local CIS alumni programs. Some of the local alumni efforts don't do the kind of scholarships, for instance, that CIS of Atlanta is offering. But again, this is about local control. We want to support what folks are doing at the local level. But I know there is a yet-to-be-determined role for the CIS National Office in supporting the alumni programs.

One place I know we have to be careful is in fundraising for the organization. You can introduce a face like mine, a young person of color, and say, "This is the successful result we get," or use a sad story and say, "This is why you should support us." It comes from a caring place where we're trying to raise appreciation and support for the organization, but it can, in some cases, be harmful. You don't want young people to relive trauma just to "tell their story" at a fundraising gala. They're not exhibits.

GROWING THE SOLUTION

Rey: The goal of having a CIS site coordinator in every Title I school gives us a target, a North Star to shoot for. As we think about our growth as an organization, we need to make sure that if we know we've got a solution and the evidence *does* show that it works, we get it to as many schools and students as possible. It's our moral obligation.

We need to be strategic and creative here. There are about 70,000 Title I schools, and currently CIS is in 2,860 of them. It could be that CIS grows into, say, 20,000 schools. But the bigger vision is that *all* schools serving a high-poverty population need to recognize the need for some version of the CIS model. This is just the way the U.S. has to do public education going forward. It has to include the ingredient of integrated supports and an integrator, somebody who is trained to do the work and focuses exclusively on those nonacademic supports a student needs, coordinating all the resources in a school that maybe wasn't designed for that in order to truly meet the needs of all students.

Our role is not just to grow our own network, but to really teach the field what an equitable public education system looks like, especially in those communities—Title I being our target population—where we know we have to turn around the bottom third to ensure that we're lifting all boats.

Bill: Yes, this is critical. In the "hundred-year plan," you have to have the aspiration. You'll perish without a vision. And the vision is never going to be perfectly achievable. You have to be flexible. In some bigger schools, you're going to need three or four site coordinators—that's a tougher goal. But you set out your big, audacious idea. That's what gets big resources behind it. We may not reach Utopia, but we have the goal, and we can inspire others.

Back in the Reagan administration, they held a summit with the governors, and out of that came a commission on education that produced the report "A Nation at Risk." There was a lot of information and thought in that report, but if you read the thing, you'd say, "Gee, public education sucks, it's done for." I said, if you look at it through that lens, you're going to fail.

Poverty is the issue, not K–12 public education. Show me a hundred of your best prep schools in New England, private schools where the wealthy send their kids. I'll find you a hundred public schools that are turning out just as many kids going to Harvard and Yale—because those schools are in communities with a good tax base, all the families have houses, they have resources, they have all the economic incentives, so the schools are free to do their job of education.

The issue is, there's an "anchor," the bottom third of kids, the ones that are poor and don't have the resources: that's the anchor that's keeping the ship from sailing and has huge public policy significance. If you can free the anchor, then the ship of public education reform is freed up to sail.

This is where I'm most passionate, and it's been clear *forever*. If we could get national policy zeroed in on poverty as what's pulling down the education system, we could start to turn it around.

Rey: I think the majority of Americans today agree with you on that. True, there's a contingent working against that concept that is well organized right now. They're saying no, schools should not be added to, and you should not bring extra resources to a school or bring somebody in to do the job that a parent should be doing. Leave those issues to the parents, and focus the school just on math, language arts, reading—only academics. I'm sure, Bill, you've heard this before, in earlier decades.

Bill: Oh yeah, many times.

Rey: This attitude completely ignores all of the other issues facing the student, but it particularly ignores how badly some of our students are suffering through the effects of poverty. It just assumes that they've got two parents at home with stable jobs, and they have access to whatever resources are needed to build resiliency skills, to really make it and write their success story.

In some ways, I almost welcome that debate: "What is the role of schools?"—I believe we have the facts on our side, and we make a very strong case. Yes, there's well organized opposition to this, people with very fixed ideas about "this is how you do school, and you can't change it." We've been making this argument for the last 45 years, and I think we're finally breaking through at the scale we need to really meet the problem head-on. Sometimes that's how you know you're on the right track: when folks on the other side are really pushing against progress.

Bill: You say you love God? And you love children? What if you're talking about a community where most students don't have two parents, where the nuclear family is fractured? So you're going to make the *kids* suffer because of *your* philosophy that education should be a certain way? If your own kids have the necessary resources, and the other kids don't, then you can't say you're "caring about all kids."

Rey, I'm happy to pass on the baton to you. I'm glad you've got the youth and energy to take on this fight—I'm getting too old for this! But we need to hold strong. We have to keep the question focused: If you care about your kids and *all* kids, tell me how we can solve this.

It's a social justice issue. I get tears in my eyes, Rey, when I hear you saying, "We're not only about helping kids overcome obstacles; we want to *take the obstacles down*." That is major. It's hard enough to overcome the obstacles. That's a full-time job. But you're challenging us to spend more and more time on policy and creating an entirely different climate in schools and neighborhoods. Talk about "beyond"—you can take CIS to a whole new level.

AND JUSTICE FOR ALL

Rey: In a community where we consistently get the same outcomes for the same population of students, whether they be poor or students of color, the question is: What must "system change" inside a school look like? If we maintain the status quo, we get the same results. So it has to change.

And that's how we define "equity" in this era: We say that there are some schools, particularly Title I schools, where we should be adding extra resources. (And bear in mind, "Title I" is just shorthand for schools that are serving high numbers of students who are from low-income families.) CIS should just own the fact that we're saying, "Yes, some of these schools need to get more resources because they've got more ground to recover in a system that oftentimes held and pulled them back."

We know inequity around funding exists. We know inequity around who gets disciplined exists. We know there are inequities around who gets access to site coordinators, or college access programs, or quality health care. Those things are all true. Sometimes we're silent about those justice issues because that's what gets us in the door. We can't start an acrimonious debate about this right from the start. We don't get to work in schools unless we have *permission* to work in schools. Yet it's equally important for us to be honest about our values.

The first year of my tenure was at the beginning of the racial reckoning prompted by the death of George Floyd and so many others. Many people were protesting in the streets. The executive director of one of our Texas affiliates found the courage to say, "Look, we've been working in this rural Texas community for a while. And we've been pretty silent about how our staff members who are people of color, and our students who are mostly people of color, get talked about and treated. Frankly, we think there's fear and racism embedded into the community that we're working in." The executive director decided to make sure that the school board and the staff heard this, because it needed to be corrected and changed.

Well, it turns out that they didn't like that truth being spoken, and so decided that our CIS contract would not be renewed. We would not continue to serve these students. To speak this important truth about justice, about fair treatment of our students, meant that we couldn't work in that community.

But for the sake of the students, it had to be said. Racism affects how they view themselves, their value, their contributions to their community. They're affected when somebody is calling them the N-word or telling them that they're useless or violent people. So what good were we doing, continuing to be in that environment, working with those students and saying, "I know you're being treated this way; I know you're being talked about in this way. But you just have to grit your teeth and bear it and just try to get through it all and find success"? That's not what we want to be doing in our schools and communities. We want to be able to confront these sometimes uncomfortable truths.

Many more of our affiliates, and our executive directors, are seeing this throughout the country. We can choose to just grow and stay and be silent. Or we can stand up for important values that we hold about who it is we serve, where we come from, and what we want to be able to offer these students. We can nurture their spirit about who they are as people and what they can accomplish. If we don't, we're really just navigating the students around these obstacles. "Don't question them, just move past them."

I come from a background where I found a way to thread the needle and walk a razor-thin line, where I had very little margin for error. And that's great, that I was able to squeeze through and be one of the statistically very small number who do, in this story of who gets to make it out of my zip code. But I can tell you the stories of 50 other students just like me, who were probably smarter than me, much faster than me, more talented. But they ran into those obstacles and fell off their track. It's just not true that "the best will survive." At CIS we're working to try and make sure that all of those obstacles are taken down. It shouldn't be just the lucky few.

This is very relevant to the justice issue, the haves and the have-nots. I still live in the same zip code that I did growing up, and it's the community I represented when I was on the San Antonio city council. I used to have debates with my colleagues on the city council who often wanted to deprioritize or defund programs that support students who grew up like me. It's because their young people are living in a completely different world. In that world, they can make 20 more mistakes than I did and still achieve the same or better measures of success than I did. They have access to college counseling and career counseling. Their parents have access to resources, access to medical care, even access to lawyers if they get in trouble.

That's the inequitable world that we're in. We have to make sure that we don't stay quiet about it. Of course, we want to be respectful. We're not confronting people with fists in the air. We're saying it would be helpful if our staff was not referred to in derogatory ways. We're saying we'd like to work with the community to put a stop to the names that our students are having yelled at them, or the negative descriptions they're given, or the biased policing they experience. These are legitimate issues that need to be addressed.

Bill: From the Street Academies on up, we were about justice. There was one period in particular, in Atlanta in the '70s, when the social unrest was so hot and heavy. I remember thinking, should we drop everything and join the marches, be full-time protestors? It was John Lewis who really helped me here. He said, "You *are* part of this; keep doing what you're doing on your road, and make sure that road runs parallel to ours. We will do the marching. But there can't be mass emancipation without education. That's your part." And that's what we did. We weren't distracted from doing the hard work of loving kids and being in the trenches with them and helping them through their pain.

Rey: Advocating for social justice, for equity, for diversity, for inclusion, has been part of our story from the beginning. And it will be part of our continuing evolution. The events of the last several years, the protests around issues of racial equity, put the question front and center for us: Are we only about *educational* equity, or are we willing to say that we stand for social justice across the board? We believe our work in the schools has a role to play in the larger fight for social justice. We're not afraid to own that. In a way, this might be the biggest "and beyond" of all. Yet, as you said, in another sense it's nothing new—this is how we started.

BEING "JEFFERSONIAN"

Rey: Bill, I just had the thought that in this entire discussion, we haven't said anything about Republicans or Democrats, or red and blue states. That's always been our approach as an organization. We're on the front lines to address challenges in terms that are not about conservative or progressive. It's about making sure a child is fed and gets access to medical care. And so in that way, we've always been nonpartisan, because these are not partisan issues. And as you well know, Bill, we've always gotten really great support from both sides of the aisle. Both parties see what it is we're trying to do with these students.

Bill: In Virginia, Republican governor George Allen sat next to Democratic senator Mark Warner as co-chairs of our CIS of Virginia board. I talked to Governor Allen the first time when he was a senator, because I needed him to help us with an earmark in some legislation. He said, "I love what you're doing. You're Jeffersonian." I said, "I didn't get a really good education; what's 'Jeffersonian'?" "Well, you believe in local control. It's the local level that's making the decisions rather than your people in Washington." And that's true, but then Mark Warner would point out how important it is to help *supply* the resources from Washington once the local community has decided what they need.

Rey: I'm hopeful that this kind of true bipartisanship will continue around CIS. But I also think I have a very realistic perspective about the volume of political division, even at the local level. You've got national politics influencing local, school board, and city council decisions. But when it comes down to it, people need their streets paved and their parks maintained, and in the same way they recognize that students of all colors and backgrounds need to have equal access not just to a great quality education but to the support they need to succeed. That is a winning argument.

Headlines will fly, people will write articles in very academic terms, or very polemical terms, about the role that educators should or shouldn't play. When it comes down to a superintendent making a decision, though, about what is best for their students and their families, they know that what we do works. Dan Domenech, the executive director of the American Association of School Administrators, is on our national board. Educators see the evidence and evaluations of what we do, and that's how we've been successful entering new communities. Let the partisanship turn up to the highest level that it possibly can—at the end of the day, every student has to eat. We want to be sure to be there for them, and that's going to continue.

Bill: Time after time, we see the same thing. No matter their politics, parents say, "Hey, that site coordinator loves my kid. She's here for me; she wants to make our lives better." It's the power of the personal. That's where you win.

Rey: Right. We don't treat any hungry student differently based on whether their family is Republican or Democrat. In fact, some of our greatest successes are in places where a majority of the elected officials are Republican—Texas, North and South Carolina, and most recently West Virginia. In no way do we insist on how students should be taught, or what the content or the curriculum should be. Of course, we would have some opinions on things that we think are important for students to know.

LICENSING THE VISION

Rey: So let's talk about the licensing model for CIS, which we're now seeing go to scale in West Virginia. This is going to be a milestone when we look back in 10 years. It's about growth with quality. The First Lady of West Virginia, Cathy Justice, who has spearheaded this work on our behalf, challenged us to see if we could grow from the original 20 schools that we started with into 50. We did, and then the challenge was to get to 100, and at this moment we're in 171 schools. We're also on track to get into every county in West Virginia. That will represent the first time in our organization's history that we've been able to saturate an entire state.

We essentially took the lessons learned about how we design the model, how we test at the beginning and end of every school year, how our data system is built, and brought them to West Virginia by *training others* to do the work that we do. The results was: 171 schools in three years. Compare that to 169 schools in Houston, a process we began close to 40 years ago. This is new but very promising.

I hope that in 10 years we'll know that West Virginia wasn't just lightning in a bottle, that we captured something important here and were able to replicate it. And it would be incredibly significant for the big goal, the big vision, the North Star of getting into every Title I school. We can train teachers within their existing system to be a site coordinator and to go through our assessments. And often, the assessment reflects not just the school but the community around them.

We still use our quality standards and accreditation process in the licensing model. In many ways, we have even more quality control than we do with, say, a state CIS affiliate. The CIS state office have their own independent staff who keep them on track with standards and accreditation, because they need to be reaccredited every three years. In the licensing model, we go in with a partner, such as the West Virginia Department of Education, and they're saying, "We care at least as much about outcomes as you do, CIS National. You show us how to train our folks, and we will make sure that they are held accountable for how they deliver the model, how they report the data, how they're functioning inside the schools." The point is, the Department of Education has direct supervision of their employees, so they can carry more weight than even some of our CIS affiliates inside the schools.

Bill: The goal is to institutionalize it, so it's there no matter who is governor or in the legislature. Imagine a future in which it was just common practice to hire a site coordinator when you hire a principal. Every school needs a principal, and every school needs someone to help connect resources with kids.

And let's not forget that an important part of institutionalizing something like the licensing model in West Virginia is the involvement of the private sector. You need to build bridges that will outlast any particular administration. Setting up a private foundation to support the Education Department's work might be a great way to go.

The private sector still has a big role to play in all this. Look at it from a business viewpoint. Where is their workforce going to come from? A lot of business executives are absolutely about justice and equity, and wanting to lift people out of poverty and create a pipeline of jobs for the future. But even if they don't share those views, they still need a workforce—it's enlightened self-interest. Business and philanthropic leaders have always been the drivers of the CIS movement, and from my viewpoint, they have to be—but they have to understand their role. It's not about charity; it's not about giving money. CIS received an incredible, game-changing gift from MacKenzie Scott, just unbelievable, and of course we're grateful, but there's another, equally important role for them here: Use your money as *leverage*. Let the private-sector wheel help turn the big wheel of government and change policy.

Initially, that was the big selling point when you went into a new community to establish Communities In Schools. The private sector loved the fact that they were going to be able to be a sort of counterweight for how public money is spent, and how those resources are devoted to kids in schools. And more recently, they've also loved the return-on-investment study we commissioned, which showed that every dollar invested in CIS creates more than $11 of economic benefit for the community.

Rey: We are at our core, and must continue to be, a public-private partnership, for one very specific reason, which is that we are still in only half the country. How did we get into 26 states plus the District of Columbia? It was because we made the argument that the private sector is looking for maximum leverage for early investments. They saw CIS as a very good bet, to get to a larger "market" of schools and students, in the same way that seed investment provides a pathway to future sustainable funding.

Think of it this way: the goal of finance is maximum profitability. In philanthropy, it's maximum *impact*, or at least that's how it should be seen. And of course this speaks to your point, Bill, about using the power of the private sector to best advantage, as more than just a source of funding. An effective philanthropy will find and support organizations that are best able to create that impact and are turning your initial investment into something sustainable.

One thing that's gratifying, 45 years on, is that we're no longer an organization that needs an initial investment just to keep the lights on. Bill, I know that wasn't always true! We're an established, respected leader, and we're widely perceived as a model backed by evidence. Again, think of it as an investor would: you don't invest in an organization that *needs* your money; you choose the one that will *make* you money. In philanthropy, it's about making the most impact. That's the return on investment.

And that leads us naturally to MacKenzie Scott's gift. That gift does something that's incredibly important. It sends a message to the world of philanthropy about how and why to make this kind of huge investment in a nonprofit like CIS. We are a long-standing institution in the school-support movement. We're a "late-stage organization," to use a term from the business world—we've demonstrated that our concept and model work, we're ahead of the competition, and we can focus on expansion and scale. We've made the investments into research and development, and we have proven examples of how to go to scale.

Because this gift is unrestricted, it means that we can go past that old model of philanthropy, where the foundation would say, "Here's a million dollars, and here's how we want you to spend it. We want you to focus on this demographic. And we want you to get them this kind of result." We've been part of that, certainly, in our long history. The attitude becomes, "Thank you, we'll take the money, we'll create the new initiative you're asking for. It'll cost us more than we're actually receiving from you, but we're going to say yes anyway!"

In general, I think philanthropy has recognized that it's better not to create these "niche" or "boutique" gifts but just provide the kind of unrestricted freedom that leads to creativity and imagination. That is so valuable in the nonprofit world.

But with that said, a $133.5 million unrestricted gift is still unprecedented. It's unbelievably generous.

MacKenzie Scott's team did a lot of research into our structure and recognized that they should give the gift in two ways. First, a portion to the national office, so we can focus on branding, research and development, and supporting the infrastructure of the national network. But they also gave individual gifts to 40 of our affiliates to empower their local decision-making, help them create endowments, and reach more schools.

Our affiliate in Memphis wants to use their $2 million gift to create an endowment. If you take a survey of all nonprofits in the country and look at how many have endowments, it's a minuscule number, something less than 10 percent. So they want to use an endowment to sustain their basic operations, and when somebody subsequently gives them a donation, the giver will know that more of their money is going directly into the schools and the services. It's oftentimes really hard to fund that back-office operation. This is a path to being creative at the local level, using future gifts to develop new strategies and resources.

Bill: People are so hungry for hope right now. The MacKenzie Scott gift is like a light breaking through. Everyone is hungry for good news.

Rey: Well, we can't downplay the challenges that lie ahead for us. We still haven't seen "the last dropout." But with this kind of booster, our CIS rocket is really going to take off. And that will be great news for hundreds of thousands of kids.

Bill: Rey, along with our entire CIS family, I'm thankful to have you at the helm! I am blessed to be a part of your team, and I am humbled to continue to serve on our talented board of directors.

It's often been quoted that "it takes a village to raise a child." I also believe it takes an entire orchestra of caring and committed adults to create and sustain a movement. Your "CIS orchestra" surrounds you as you lead us as our outstanding conductor, continuing the vision of hope for every child having a healthy and successful future.

APPENDIX 1:
CIS STUDENT
SUCCESS STORIES

So many students have been able to overcome enormous odds and reclaim their futures because they found themselves in caring communities where the principles described in this book were solidly in place. These kids—and their families, teachers, counselors, and other providers—are often willing to share their experiences so that others who are struggling with similar issues might find hope and a way forward on the path toward their own successes. Here are eight such stories. For more, visit www .communitiesinschools.org.

UNWAVERING COMMITMENT

Talitha Halley is a proud graduate of Howard University and an alumna of CIS of Houston. She has also been a member of the CIS National Board of Directors since 2020.

Talitha found her passion for activism when her family was uprooted from their home in New Orleans due to the devastation of Hurricane Katrina. It was then that Talitha decided that she would live a life of service and that she would not let the tragedy that happened to her dictate her future.

Talitha's CIS journey began her freshman year of high school and continued well into adulthood. She's had the opportunity to experience CIS as a student receiving services, an intern, a spokesperson, and an advisor to the last two CIS National presidents. She is passionate about CIS because the organization has afforded her opportunities and a life that would have been extremely difficult to obtain without it.

Talitha was an athlete and magnet student at Sharpstown High School. During her junior year she applied to the Congressional Page Program and was selected by Congressman Al Green out of 500 applicants to represent Houston. During her time in Washington, D.C., Talitha decided that upon graduation she would obtain her bachelor's degree in political science from Howard University. With the help of CIS and her site coordinators, Donna Wotkyns and Eric Johnson, Talitha made all of her dreams come true.

Her experience at Howard would help shape her worldview, and during her senior year Talitha decided that she would no longer attend law school but instead pursue an alternative career path in branding and fashion—focused primarily on transforming the industry through diversity and inclusion for people of color. Talitha runs her own boutique creative and style consulting firm, and additionally, she has served at a number of positions at Planned Parenthood Federation of America, where she is currently working as an administrative manager.

Talitha has never wavered in her commitment to work with Communities In Schools. With 13 years of involvement in the organization, Talitha's commitment has always been rooted in gratitude and ensuring that she can reach back and pull other students forward. She has been a devoted member of the Alumni Leadership Network since its inception, helping to ensure that students don't feel as though their CIS experience is over once they graduate.

"ELECTING" SUCCESS

Rasheedah Phillips started her secondary education at Washington High School in Philadelphia, transferring to Lincoln High by her second year. "I was pregnant my freshman year of high school," she said, adding that she wasn't the first person in her family who became a parent early in life. "I come from a family of teen mothers. It has been a cycle in my family." At Lincoln, she was referred to a special program offered by Communities In Schools.

Education Leading to Employment and Career Training (ELECT) is a statewide initiative of Pennsylvania's Departments of

Public Welfare and Education, administered locally as a partnership between the School District of Philadelphia and CIS of Philadelphia. Through this program, Teen Parent Classrooms provide pregnant and parenting teens with the academic, health, and social-service supports needed to complete their education and make a successful transition from high school to entry-level employment, additional training, or postsecondary education.

Despite her situation, Rasheedah had a desire to achieve her dream of becoming an attorney. "Before getting pregnant, I had aspirations," she said. "But after I got pregnant, I didn't think I would achieve my goals. For a year or two, I found it difficult . . . but then something clicked and I started to do better."

She credited CIS staff members with helping her move forward in life. "The counselors and social workers provided a safe place for me," she explained. "They would continually encourage me to go to school." Through the CIS program, she also received access to parenting-education classes, child care, and health-care services.

After Rasheedah had her daughter, she began to work hard to improve her grades. "The program has made me a model or example of what teen parents can do to be successful in high school," she said.

She graduated from Lincoln and then went on to complete undergraduate studies at Temple University in three years. With her daughter now seven years old, she then completed her first year of law school. "My first year was difficult," she said. "But no matter what I do, my degree is going to be an asset. I've also been doing a lot of public speaking through community programs, which helps me." She participated in a summer internship at a public law firm affiliated with Temple University Beasley School of Law. "When I finish law school, I want to work with families and teen parents."

Rasheedah shared the following words of wisdom for teen mothers who know they're destined for greatness but unsure of their direction:

Regardless of your circumstances, your goals can be achieved, even if it takes you longer than you hope or expect. So many teens get discouraged because they think they are not good enough or cannot afford college. But I try to be an example of how you can use your situation to your advantage. There are a lot of resources out there for young parents. You have to work hard and look for them . . . no one is going to hand you anything. So many doors are open to you if you go out there to find them. Not everyone wants to go to college, because college is not meant for everyone. But whatever you want to do . . . just do it.

HOPE FOR THE FUTURE

Denise Cook, a student at Communities In Schools of Atlanta's West End Academy Performance Learning Center®, was one of six students who received awards for Student Achievement Month sponsored by CIS of Georgia. At the awards ceremony, she presented her contest entry, a poster-sized piece of artwork, and explained it to her audience, saying, "This poster represents the past, present, and future for me. Before CIS, my life was like death. Everything around me was dead. The CIS staff have been my heroes. Now I have a future and I know that I'm going to make it."

Denise had given up any hope of a successful future when she dropped out of Grady High School. Just a few weeks before the school's graduation ceremony, she found herself short on academic credits, unable to pay her senior dues, and homeless. Denise's mother had substance abuse problems that resulted in a long period of unemployment and the eventual loss of their apartment. What should have been a happy time for Denise became a time of loss and uncertainty.

While Denise's mother entered a shelter, Denise opted to live on the streets. "I was out by myself. Sometimes I stayed with friends, but I was never in the same place for long," said the Atlanta teen. After months on the streets, Denise decided to enter the shelter with her mother. "I got tired of not doing anything. I wanted to get help so I could go back to school. I knew that going to school was the only chance I had to get where I wanted to get in life," Denise said with quiet determination. With assistance from counselors in the shelter, Denise entered the West End Academy PLC in August.

The West End Academy PLC operates as a partnership between Atlanta Public Schools and Communities In Schools of Atlanta. This nontraditional school helps children who have dropped out or who are at risk for dropping out earn their high school diplomas.

Four months after entering the Academy, Denise was just one semester away from graduating. When asked about her plans for the future, the soft-spoken 19-year-old smiled, saying, "I'm going to Georgia Perimeter College for two years, then transferring to Florida A&M University. I want to study journalism because I love to write." (Reprinted with permission of Communities In Schools of Atlanta)

SUSPENDED, EXPELLED . . .
THEN "STUDENT OF THE WEEK"

Upon moving in the third grade from Chicago to La Porte County, Indiana, to live with his grandmother, Barron Moore struggled academically and socially as he adjusted to his new environment. He transferred in and out of three different elementary schools before arriving at Kesling Middle School for what proved to be a very challenging sixth-grade year. After being suspended and then expelled from school due to poor grades and reports of fighting and disrespect toward his teachers, Barron needed to repeat the sixth grade.

Thanks to the strong partnership between Communities In Schools of La Porte County and the local Youth Service Bureau Big Brothers Big Sisters program—part of the oldest and largest mentoring organization in the United States—Barron gradually began to make a remarkable turnaround. Big Brothers Big Sisters of La Porte County was instrumental in bringing Barron together with his mentor, Dan Kaminski, vice president of General Insurance Services in La Porte County.

During Barron's expulsion from school, Kaminski continued to meet with him on a weekly basis. Allison L. Middlebrook, executive director of CIS of La Porte County, noted: "Barron would ride his bike to the Youth Service Bureau to meet with Dan. Even though there were times when Barron would not show up for their sessions, Dan patiently stood by Barron and helped him keep up with his studies."

When asked to describe his relationship with Dan, Barron responded, "Dan talks to me about sports and how to get out of problems. He's an awesome guy, and it's been great having Dan around."

The boy ultimately came to an important realization while expelled from school. "The revelation that there were so many things he couldn't do when he wasn't in school, such as play sports, really made a strong impression on Barron," remarked Middlebrook. "He recognized that if he didn't start making better decisions soon, he would risk repeating the sixth grade again."

Kesling Middle School principal Bill Wilmsen was thrilled by Barron's newfound triumphs in school, including being named Student of the Week. "It is so rewarding, seeing all of the successes that he has had this year," said Wilmsen. "Most important, I am proud of the choices that Barron has made for himself. His story personifies what can happen when agencies are working together toward the common good of the child."

The sixth-grade teachers echoed their principal's sentiment. Kelly Troy, Barron's reading teacher, commented, "I have noticed a huge change in Barron this school year. He is not argumentative, takes pride in his work, and is respectful." Pam Miller, his language-arts teacher, summed it up: "Barron appears to care about his life and always has a smile on his face."

THINKING ABOUT COLLEGE

Acton Archie moved from one government housing development to another as a child—12 times in 12 years, in fact. His father was murdered when Acton was a second grader; his mother was a drug addict. Each day was a struggle, walking past drugs and crime on the way to and from school and waking up with no power or water in the house. He remembers that many days he worried about whether he'd even have a home when he returned.

As a teenager, he made some bad choices as he struggled through the ninth grade, often absent and with no direction, personal interests, or career expectations. A caring grandmother and a strong faith in God kept him going—and Communities In Schools provided a helping hand as well. The CIS site coordinator at Acton's high school in Charlotte, North Carolina, made sure he had transportation to school, dental and health care, and connections to community-support personnel. She also became a mentor and a friend. He was exposed to college and career experiences and encouraged to form goals for himself. "I probably would have dropped out without that support," he said.

The CIS ThinkCOLLEGE® program helps high school students find scholarship opportunities and qualify for higher education. Acton became a ThinkCOLLEGE® participant and won two scholarships, renewing them each year he attended college. Acton graduated from North Carolina State University with a B.S. degree in business management, a concentration in information technology, and a minor in accounting.

SMALL IS BEAUTIFUL

Although he's from a large family, Robert Guy appreciated the value of a small one when it came to his education. Robert and his seven younger siblings were homeschooled for a number of years, in part because the family moved so often. But there came a time for him to move into the public school system, and the first public school he attended was brand new, with a low student-to-teacher ratio. He was active and successful there, but when the family moved again, this time to Athens, Georgia, Robert (then 16) was faced with attending a much larger, traditional high school.

This challenge, added to the economic and personal struggles of divorce that his family was going through at the time, led Robert to the Classic City Performance Learning Center® (PLC) in Athens, a Communities In Schools of Georgia alternative high school. "I've always known that my education comes first," Robert said. "After visiting the local high school and doing some research, my mom and I went to check out the PLC. We met with the principal, who talked to us and showed us around."

Robert was sold. He applied for admission to the school, which offers the advantage of being a small, self-contained learning environment with a low student-to-teacher ratio, high academic standards, personalized programs, and a flexible schedule. With his positive outlook, strong academic track record, and ambitious goal of graduating ahead of time, Robert was a natural choice for the Classic City PLC.

Once there, Robert fell in love with it. "It was like a family and became like home," he said of his two years there. "At the PLC, they get to know you as a person. They cared about what was going on in my life, and how it impacted my education and ability to focus on learning." Jaya Chauhan, Robert's learning facilitator and advisor at the PLC, said that building relationships with classmates and teachers was what attracted the teen to the school. "Robert's life wasn't always smooth, but he had an incredible inner strength and burning motivation to achieve his goal of graduating from high school. He was determined to succeed and be a positive role model; he was persistent, disciplined, organized, meticulous—and very caring," she said. "He was well liked by everyone."

His first year there, Robert had a lead role in creating the student council and, not surprisingly, served as president. "Robert also excelled in the creative arts," added Chauhan. "He was very interested in writing, producing, and acting. He produced a musical rap presentation in collaboration with two other students, and it aired on a local radio station."

In a personal essay about his experience at the PLC, Robert wrote: "I have teachers who genuinely care about me and who would do anything to make sure I succeed. . . . I am at a place where people care about my dreams, goals, and future. Without this school, CIS, and Classic City PLC, I doubt I would have made it."

Robert *did* make it, achieving his goal of graduating from high school and becoming the first in his family to do so. He received scholarships to attend Morehouse College in Atlanta—one of the most prestigious historically Black colleges in the nation—with a grade point average of 3.5.

Jaya Chauhan said, "I feel certain that Robert is going to do really well in life. He has embarked on his journey and is going to just fly."

AROUND THE WORLD WITH SWEET SUCCESS

Lasheeda Perry grew up just outside of Philadelphia, one of eight children; her family moved often and suffered many financial hardships. When she was just 15 years old, Lasheeda and her twin sister became the primary caregivers of their terminally ill mother. It was difficult to juggle schoolwork and family responsibilities, but Lasheeda persevered with a little help from Communities In Schools.

"CIS was always involved in activities at my school. When I was a student at Frankford High School, my teachers exposed me to so many new experiences," she recalled. "While I was at Frankford, Mrs. Stephenson introduced me to the Careers through Culinary Arts Program through CIS . . . and that changed my life. I knew that I had to work really hard to be in the program, but the payoff has been incredible. They helped me go to China! I also won a competition that awarded me a two-week trip to Australia, where I explored culinary delights. Many of my high school friends had never been outside of Philadelphia, but I was given an opportunity to see and experience whole different cultures. My mother pushed me to finish high school, although most of the people around me did not finish school."

Unfortunately, the teen's mother didn't live to see her daughter graduate. She died just weeks before commencement. But by that time, Lasheeda had already been awarded a $75,000 four-year scholarship through Communities In Schools of Philadelphia, and she was on her way to pursue a bachelor's degree in baking and pastry arts, with a minor in food-service management.

"When I was growing up, college wasn't an option," said Lasheeda. She never imagined that she'd be attending one of the country's most prestigious culinary schools, Johnson and Wales University in Rhode Island, on a full four-year scholarship. While at Johnson and Wales, she participated in a three-month internship at the Adare Manor Hotel and Golf Resort in Ireland. During the summer, Lasheeda worked at Sweet Jazmines pastry shop near Philadelphia.

"I love to learn, and I love baking and pastries. Thus far, it has taken me literally around the world."

UNRAVELING AND REAFFIRMING

Steffan Barahona's senior year of college was quiet. The pandemic emptied out Washington College's Chestertown, Maryland, campus and classes were virtual, leaving him a lot of time to think about how he could most meaningfully apply his psychology degree after graduation. He kept coming back to a big reason he was graduating from college to begin with, his CIS of Northern Virginia (NOVA) site coordinator from high school, Amanda Gallardo.

Steffan met Amanda at a Free Application for Federal Student Aid assistance night at Wakefield High School in Arlington, where she was guiding families through the federal aid application process. "I was in her office like, twenty times a week. For the first time in my life I felt like someone was listening to me," he says.

Amanda's open-door policy is something Steffan is replicating as a site coordinator specializing in reengagement at Wakefield. "The number one thing I tell my students when I first meet them is that I am an alum of CIS," Steffan says. "I still live in the community, too, so I can really relate to what my students are experiencing."

Steffan currently spends most of his week at Wakefield and one day at Arlington Community High School. He case-manages 25 students who are most at risk for dropping out after the extended period of virtual learning. If CIS of NOVA is a safety net for at-risk students, Steffan is the safety net beneath the safety net, an extra layer of protection made necessary by the pandemic, which has caused some kids to fall behind.

Steffan describes his work as a site coordinator with two interesting verbs: unraveling and reaffirming. "I'm unraveling years of students' negative self and academic perception. Then I'm reaffirming their abilities." The school environment, he notes, can be focused on what students can't do. But Steffan focuses on what students can do: "That's what drives me in my job; I tell my kids all the time that I'm proud of them, that they're capable, that just because things are hard now doesn't mean they'll be hard forever."

APPENDIX 2:
HOW TO GET INVOLVED

The following list includes dozens of outstanding national youth-serving and education-support organizations at work in thousands of communities across America. They represent some of the many worthy groups with whom Communities In Schools is proud to partner.

THE AFTERSCHOOL ALLIANCE

The Afterschool Alliance is a nonprofit organization dedicated to raising awareness of the importance of after-school programs and advocating for quality, affordable programs for all children. It's supported by a group of public, private, and nonprofit organizations that share the Alliance's vision of ensuring that all children have access to quality after-school programs.

Website: www.afterschoolalliance.org

AMERICA'S PROMISE–THE ALLIANCE
FOR YOUTH

America's Promise–The Alliance for Youth grew out of the Presidents' Summit for America's Future in 1997 in Philadelphia, where Presidents Clinton, Bush, Carter, and Ford, with Nancy Reagan representing President Reagan, challenged America to make children and youth a national priority. Alliance partners—corporations, nonprofit service organizations, foundations, policy makers, advocacy organizations, and faith groups—work collaboratively to ensure that America's young people receive the Five Promises.

Website: www.americaspromise.org

AMERICORPS

Americorps is the federal agency that administers national service and volunteerism programs, including VISTA (Volunteers in Service to America), Learn and Serve America, the Foster Grandparent program, and the Retired and Senior Volunteer Program (RSVP). It also provides the Community Guide to Helping America's Youth, a web-based guide with up-to-date research on youth development and effective programs.

Website: www.americorps.gov

BIG BROTHERS BIG SISTERS

Big Brothers Big Sisters is the oldest and largest youth-mentoring organization in the United States, focused on developing positive relationships that have a direct and lasting impact on the lives of young people, ages 6 through 18, in communities across the country. National research has shown that positive relationships between youth and their Big Brothers and Big Sisters mentors have a direct and measurable impact on children's lives. Big Brothers Big Sisters currently operates in all 50 states and in 12 countries around the world.

Website: www.bbbs.org

BOYS AND GIRLS CLUBS OF AMERICA

The mission of Boys and Girls Clubs of America is to enable all young people, especially those who need us most, to reach their full potential as productive, caring, responsible citizens. With more than 4,700 clubs around the world, kids have access to a safe place to learn and grow; ongoing relationships with caring, adult professionals; life-enhancing programs and character development experiences; and hope and opportunity.

Website: www.bgca.org

BOY SCOUTS OF AMERICA

The purpose of the Boy Scouts of America is to provide an educational program for boys and young adults to build character, to train in the responsibilities of participating citizenship, and to develop personal fitness. More than 272 local scouting councils provide quality youth programs, including Cub Scouting, Boy Scouting, and Venturing.

Website: www.scouting.org

BUILDING EDUCATED LEADERS
FOR LIFE (BELL)

BELL is a community-based, nonprofit educational organization founded in 1992 by a group of Black students at Harvard Law School. Its mission is to enhance the academic performance and life opportunities of elementary school children living in low-income, urban communities. BELL's school-based programs are characterized by small-group tutoring and mentoring, curriculum-based instruction, rigorous evaluation of results, and strong training programs for staff.

Website: www.bellxcel.org/

CAMP FIRE USA

Founded in 1910, Camp Fire USA is one of the nation's leading not-for-profit youth-development organizations, currently serving nearly 175,000 children and youth annually. Programs include youth leadership, self-reliance, after-school groups, camping and environmental education, and child care. Camp Fire programs are delivered through 1,300 program sites across the nation.

Website: https://campfire.org/

THE CENTER FOR SOCIAL ORGANIZATION
OF SCHOOLS (CSOS)

CSOS is an educational research and development arm at Johns Hopkins University. The Center includes sociologists, psychologists, social psychologists, and educators who conduct programmatic research to improve the education system and provide technical assistance to schools. Among its signature projects are studies on the graduation gap, so-called dropout factories and the promoting power of high schools across the country, and the National Network of Partnership Schools.

Website: https://education.jhu.edu/csos/

CITIZEN SCHOOLS

Citizen Schools is a leading national education initiative that uniquely mobilizes thousands of adult volunteers to help improve student achievement by teaching skill-building apprenticeships after school. Programs blend real-world learning projects with rigorous academic- and leadership-development activities, preparing students in the middle grades for success in high school, college, the workforce, and civic life.

Website: www.citizenschools.org

CITY YEAR

City Year's mission is to build democracy through citizen service, civic leadership, and social entrepreneurship. Citizen service means citizens of all ages and backgrounds will unite to serve their community, nation, and world; civic leadership means every citizen will have the skills, values, and inspiration to be a leader for the common good; and social entrepreneurship means that one day human inventiveness and compassion will be unleashed systematically to solve the pressing social problems of the day.

Website: www.cityyear.org

COALITION FOR COMMUNITY SCHOOLS

The Coalition for Community Schools is an alliance of national, state, and local organizations in education K through 16, youth development, community planning and development, family support, health and human services, government, and philanthropy, as well as national, state, and local community school networks. The Coalition advocates for community schools as the vehicles for strengthening schools, families, and communities so that together they can improve student learning.

Website: www.communityschools.org

GIRL SCOUTS OF THE USA

Chartered by Congress in 1950, Girl Scouts is helping today's girls become tomorrow's leaders. Girl Scouts of the USA today numbers more than 100 local Girl Scout councils or offices.

Website: www.girlscouts.org

GIRLS INC.

Girls Incorporated is a national nonprofit youth organization dedicated to inspiring all girls to be strong, smart, and bold. With roots dating to 1864, Girls Inc. has provided vital educational programs to millions of American girls, particularly those in high-risk, underserved areas. Today, innovative programs help girls confront societal pressures and prepare them to lead successful, independent, and fulfilling lives.

Website: www.girlsinc.org

JOBS FOR AMERICA'S GRADUATES

Jobs for America's Graduates (JAG) is a school-to-career program implemented in 700 high schools, alternative schools, community colleges, and middle schools through 40 state affiliates across the country. JAG's mission is to keep young people in school through graduation and provide work-based learning experiences that will lead to career advancement opportunities or to enroll in a postsecondary institution that leads to a rewarding career.

Website: www.jag.org

JOBS FOR THE FUTURE

Jobs for the Future (JFF) believes that all young people should have a quality high school and postsecondary education, and that all adults should have the skills needed to hold jobs that pay enough to support a family. As a nonprofit research, consulting, and advocacy organization, JFF works to strengthen our society by creating educational and economic opportunity for those who need it most. Through partnerships with states and communities, national and local foundations, and other organizations, JFF accelerates opportunities for people to advance in education and careers through research, analysis, and policy development; practical, on-the-ground projects; and advocacy, communications, and peer learning.

Website: www.jff.org

KNOWLEDGE IS POWER PROGRAM (KIPP)

KIPP is a national network of free, open-enrollment, college-preparatory public schools in under-resourced communities throughout the United States. There are currently 255 locally run KIPP schools in 20 states and Washington, D.C., which are serving more than 112,000 students. KIPP schools have been widely recognized for putting underserved students on the path to college.

Website: www.kipp.org

MENTOR/NATIONAL MENTORING PARTNERSHIP

MENTOR/National Mentoring Partnership works to expand the world of quality mentoring. MENTOR believes that with the help and guidance of an adult mentor, each child can discover how to unlock and achieve his or her potential. Widely acknowledged as the nation's premier advocate and resource for the expansion of mentoring initiatives nationwide, MENTOR works with a strong network of state and local mentoring partnerships to leverage resources and provide the support and tools that mentoring organizations need to effectively serve young people in their communities.

Website: www.mentoring.org

NATIONAL 4-H COUNCIL

The mission of the National 4-H Council is to advance the 4-H youth development movement to build a world in which youth and adults learn, grow, and work together as catalysts for positive change. The National 4-H Council provides grants, establishes programs/initiatives, designs and publishes curriculum and reference materials, and creates linkages fostering innovation and shared learning to advance the 4-H youth development movement.

Website: https://4-h.org/

NATIONAL ALLIANCE FOR
PUBLIC CHARTER SCHOOLS

The National Alliance for Public Charter Schools develops sound, coherent policies that support high-quality public education options for families who need them the most. Key priorities include lifting arbitrary "caps" on charter growth, closing the finance gap between charters and other public schools, and updating the federal Charter Schools Program to spur a new era of charter achievement.

Website: www.publiccharters.org

THE NATIONAL ASSOCIATION OF CHARTER SCHOOL
AUTHORIZERS (NACSA)

NACSA is a professional organization of authorizers and other education leaders who work to achieve quality public charter schools. Fifteen years of chartering has resulted in thousands of quality charter schools. Authorizers protect the public interest as these entrepreneurial schools come into being. Authorizers include state and local boards of education, colleges and universities, special-purpose boards, municipal bodies, and nonprofits. These are the entities charged by law to approve, oversee, and evaluate the performance of public charter schools. NACSA developed principles and standards that define professional practice for quality authorizing across America.

Website: www.qualitycharters.org

NATIONAL COLLABORATION FOR YOUTH

The National Collaboration for Youth (NCY), a 30-year-old organization, is a coalition of 50 member organizations that have a significant interest in youth development. NCY members collectively serve more than 40 million young people, employ over 100,000 paid staff, utilize more than 6 million volunteers, and have a physical presence in virtually every community in America.

Website: www.collab4youth.org

NATIONAL DROPOUT PREVENTION CENTER/NETWORK

Since 1987, the National Dropout Prevention Center/Network (NDPC/N) has worked to improve opportunities for all young people to fully develop the academic, social, work, and healthy life skills needed to graduate from high school and lead productive lives. By promoting awareness of successful programs and policies related to dropout prevention, the work of the NDPC/N and its members has made an impact on education from the local to the national level.

Website: www.dropoutprevention.org

NATIONAL PARENT TEACHER ASSOCIATION

The mission of the Parent Teacher Association is to support and speak on behalf of children and youth in the schools, in the community, and before governmental bodies and other organizations that make decisions affecting children; to assist parents in developing the skills they need to raise and protect their children; and to encourage parent and public involvement in the public schools of this nation.

Website: www.pta.org

NEW LEADERS

New Leaders is a movement dedicated to promoting high levels of academic achievement for every child. It promotes high academic achievement by attracting, preparing, and supporting the next generation of outstanding education leaders for our nation's urban public schools.

Website: https://www.newleaders.org/

PEER FORWARD

Peer Forward strengthens schools' capacity to prepare all students for success after high school. Trained student influencers build college-going culture, while teachers and counselors use a managed curriculum and technology tools to help all students create postsecondary plans and apply to college.

Website: https://www.peerforward.org/

PUBLIC ALLIES

Since 1992, Public Allies has built a powerful model for identifying, training, and supporting talented and diverse young adults to lead positive community change. Young people ages 18 to 30 serve in full-time apprenticeships creating, improving, and expanding services at local nonprofit organizations, and they participate in a rigorous leadership development program that combines weekly training, coaching, team projects, and reflection.

Website: www.publicallies.org

TEACH FOR AMERICA

Teach For America (TFA) is the national corps of outstanding recent college graduates of all academic majors who commit two years to teach in urban and rural public schools and become leaders in the effort to expand educational opportunity. TFA's mission is to enlist our nation's most promising future leaders in the movement to eliminate educational inequality. TFA serves more than 50 communities, supports 6,192 current corps members, engages 55,700 alumni, and serves 383,000 students annually.

Website: www.teachforamerica.org

UNITED WAY

United Way is a national network of more than 1,800 locally governed organizations that work to create lasting positive changes in communities and people's lives. Building on more than a century of service as the nation's preeminent community-based fundraiser, United Way engages the community to identify the underlying causes of the most significant local issues, develops strategies and pulls together financial and human resources to address them, and measures the results.

Website: www.unitedway.org

YMCA

YMCAs are at the heart of community life across the country: 77 percent of the U.S. population is located within ten miles of a YMCA. The nation's 2,650 YMCAs work to meet the health and human-service needs of 11 million people in more than 10,000 communities in the United States, supported by 233,000 volunteers, who are central to the YMCA mission.

Website: www.ymca.org

YOUTHBUILD

YouthBuild champions today's opportunity youth who aspire to improve their lives and communities by building the skills and resources to reach their full potential. Through hundreds of YouthBuild programs in the United States and around the globe, these young people pursue their education, prepare for future careers, and grow into community leaders—building brighter futures for themselves and their neighborhoods.

Website: www.youthbuild.org

YOUTH SERVICE AMERICA (YSA)

YSA is a resource center that partners with thousands of organizations committed to increasing the quality and quantity of volunteer opportunities for young people ages 5 to 25 to serve locally, nationally, and globally. Founded in 1986, YSA's mission is to strengthen the effectiveness, sustainability, and scale of the youth-service and service-learning fields.

Website: www.ysa.org

YWCA

The YWCA, whose mission is to eliminate racism and empower women, is the oldest and largest multicultural women's organization in the world, comprising 120 countries, with 2 million members and participants in more than 200 local associations in the United States. It provides safe places for women and girls, builds strong women leaders, and advocates for women's rights and civil rights in Congress.

Website: www.ywca.org

APPENDIX 3: RESEARCH ON ASSET-BASED APPROACHES

The America's Promise Alliance, whose mission is to help deliver the "Five Promises" (based on the Five Basics of Communities In Schools) to children across the nation, is one of several organizations providing useful summaries of current research on asset-based approaches to improving outcomes for young people in school.

The group's website (**americaspromise.org**) describes findings from four research projects:

- The Search Institute's 2006 study of 40 developmental assets among youth in 2,000 U.S. cities
- University-based research (including the well-regarded Hawkins and Catalano work) on risk and resiliency among youth
- The National Academy of Sciences' 2002 report "Community Programs to Promote Youth Development"
- A meta-study in Child Trends' American Teens series that summarizes the results of more than 1,000 research studies

The research reveals a consistent positive correlation between developmental assets such as the Five Promises/Basics and success in school and in life—and a consistent negative correlation between lack of these assets and being at a clear disadvantage compared to better-equipped peers.

The Search Institute's study, for instance, finds that young people with at least 31 of 40 developmental assets "consistently engage in fewer risk behaviors and have more indicators of thriving (such as doing well in school, helping others, and overcoming adversity) than young people with fewer assets." The 40 assets include categories such as family support, other adult relationships, a caring school climate, service to others, safety, youth programs, and a host of social and psychological competencies.[1]

The American Teens series meta-study's emphasis on relationships as key to teens' well-being and its rejection of "silver bullet" solutions are both particularly congruent with the CIS approach to building assets. "Parent-child interactions and bonding greatly influence adolescents' choices and attitudes," the authors write. They also say:

> Peer relationships—including positive ties among teens—are important; and siblings, teachers, and mentors can provide additional support to young people. Significantly, research indicates that supportive relationships seem to trump lectures that simply tell teens "to do" or "not to do" something as a strategy to enhance adolescent development. Program developers and policy makers should view adolescents as whole people, not just as students, patients, or delinquents, and not expect a "silver bullet" solution to improve teens' lives.[2]

Based on its overview of this research, America's Promise is clear that:

> . . . unless they have a critical mass of key developmental resources in their lives—four or five Promises—children are far less likely to achieve academic success, avoid violence and become involved in their communities. Children who experience at least four of the five Promises are significantly more likely to be successful, as measured by four indicators: social competence, frequency of volunteering, avoiding violence, and earning mostly A's in school.[3]

Communities In Schools practitioners have repeatedly found that their own experiences with young people reinforce this research, and the CIS movement confidently offers an asset-based model—the Five Basics—as a vital tool to combat the dropout epidemic.

ENDNOTES

Introduction

1. Emily A. Shrider et al., *Income and Poverty in the United States: 2020* Current Population Reports, P60-273 (Washington, D.C.: U.S. Census Bureau, September 2021), https://www.census.gov/content/dam/Census/library/publications/2021/demo/p60-273.pdf.

2. Shrider et al., *Income and Poverty in the United States*.

3. Joel McFarland et al., *Trends in High School Dropout and Completion Rates in the United States: 2019* National Center for Education Statistics, 2020-117 (Washington, D.C.: U.S. Department of Education, January 2020), https://nces.ed.gov/pubs2020/2020117.pdf.

4. McFarland et al., *Trends in High School Dropout and Completion Rates in the United States*.

5. McFarland et al., *Trends in High School Dropout and Completion Rates in the United States*.

6. CIS National, *Data Book 2020-21* (Arlington, VA: Communities in Schools, 2022), https://www.communitiesinschools.org/articles/article/2020-2021-communities-schools-data-book/.
   In 2020–'21 school year, 81.7% of students case managed by CIS were eligible for free and reduced price lunch (FRPL). This percentage does not include students whose FRPL status was unknown.

7. Communities In Schools. (2022). 2020-2021 Communities In Schools Data Book. Retrieved from https://www.communitiesinschools.org/media/filer_public/bb/0d/bb0d66e5-e0ed-4cbe-8bd1-e1e195b7312b/cis_databook_2020-21_final.pdf

Chapter 2

1. Courtland Milloy, "What a Curfew Can't Accomplish," *The Washington Post*, July 26, 2006, https://www.washingtonpost.com/archive/local/2006/07/26/what-a-curfew-cant-accomplish/0c608837-834c-4ef4-8e8c-91601e2eac81/.

2. "Our Model," Communities In Schools of Los Angeles, accessed May 24, 2022, https://www.cislosangeles.org/our-model.html.

Chapter 3

1. Jean E. Rhodes, "School-Based Mentoring," MENTOR (website), accessed March 15, 2007, www.mentoring.org.

2. Eugene C. Roehlkepartain et al., *Relationships First: Creating Connections that Help Young People Thrive* (Minneapolis, MN: Search Institute, February 2017), https://page.search-institute.org/relationships-first-020217a.

3. Roehlkepartain et al., *Relationships First*.

4. National Center for Homeless Education. *Student Homelessness in America: School Years 2017-18 to 2019-20* (Browns Summit, NC: University of North Carolina at Greensboro, 2021), https://nche.ed.gov/wp-content/uploads/2021/12/Student-Homelessness-in-America-2021.pdf.

5. Afterschool Alliance. *Evaluations Backgrounder: A Summary of Formal Evaluations of Afterschool Programs' Impact on Academics, Behavior, Safety and Family Life* (Washington, D.C.: Afterschool Alliance, March 2015), http://afterschoolalliance.org/documents/Evaluation_Backgrounder.pdf.

6. Jean E. Rhodes, "The Critical Ingredient: Caring Youth-Staff Relationships in After-School Settings," *New Directions for Youth Development* 2004, no. 101 (March 30, 2004): 145–161, https://doi.org/10.1002/yd.75.

7. "Table A-4: Employment Status of the Civilian Population 25 Years and Over by Educational Attainment," Economic News Release, U.S. Bureau of Labor Statistics, accessed May 6, 2022, https://www.bls.gov/news.release/empsit.t04.htm.

Chapter 4

1. Jed Horne, *Breach of Faith: Hurricane Katrina and the Near Death of a Great American City* (New York, NY: Random House, 2008).

Chapter 5

1. Jim Collins, *Good to Great: Why Some Companies Make the Leap . . . and Others Don't* (New York, NY: HarperCollins, 2001).

Chapter 6

1. Communities In Schools National website, posted December 11, 2015, https://www.communitiesinschools.org /blog/2015/12/what-were-reading-this-week-12-11-15/.

2. Communities In Schools National website, posted December 11, 2015, https://www.communitiesinschools.org /blog/2015/12/what-were-reading-this-week-12-11-15/.

3. "Every Student Succeeds Act (ESSA)," U.S. Department of Education, accessed May 27, 2022, https://www.ed.gov /essa?src=rn.

4. Sean DeLancey, "Clark County School District: 10K Students Are Homeless, Aid Is Available to Help," *KTNV Las Vegas*, March 9, 2021, https://www.ktnv.com/news/clark-county -school-district-10k-students-homeless-aid-is-available-to-help.

5. "National School Lunch Program," Food Service Department, Clark County School District, accessed May 25, 2022, https://www.ccsd.net/departments/food-service /free-reduced-meal-program.

Chapter 8

1. David S. Broder, "Rosalynn Carter's Favorite Program," *The Washington Post*, July 10, 1977, https://www.washingtonpost .com/archive/opinions/1977/07/10/rosalynn-carters-favorite -program/079cfbcc-50f9-482b-9f04-eb496a88ea6d/.

2. Bill Drayton, *Leading Social Entrepreneurs Changing the World* (Ashoka Innovators for the Public, 2004).

3. "The Charitable Sector," Independent Sector, accessed May 25, 2022, https://independentsector.org/about /the-charitable-sector/#:~:text=Facts%20and%20 Figures%20about%20the%20Nonprofit%20 Sector&text=There%20are%201.6%20million%20 tax,banks%20and%20disaster%20relief%20organizations.

4. CIS National, *Data Book 2020-21* (Arlington, VA: Communities in Schools, 2022), https://www .communitiesinschools.org/articles/article /2020-2021-communities-schools-data-book/.

5. CIS National, *Data Book 2020-21*.

6. Melanie Hanson, "U.S. Public Education Spending Statistics," Education Data Initiative, updated March 15, 2022, https:// educationdata.org/public-education-spending-statistics.

7. Economic Modeling Specialists Inc., *The Economic Impact of Communities In Schools* (Moscow, ID: Economic Modeling Specialists Inc. [EMSI], May 2012), http://www.cisga.org /cisgawpress/wp-content/uploads/2012/05 /The-Economic-Impact-of-CIS_May2012.pdf.

8. Marie-Andrée Somers and Zeest Haider, *Using Integrated Student Supports to Keep Kids in School: A Quasi-Experimental Evaluation of Communities In Schools* (Washington, D.C.: MDRC, April 2017), https://www.mdrc.org/publication /using-integrated-student-supports-keep-kids-school.

9. Leigh Parise et al., *Two Years of Case Management: Final Findings from the Communities In Schools Random Assignment Evaluation* (Washington, D.C.: MDRC, April 2017), https:// www.mdrc.org/publication/two-years-case-management.

10. Cathy Hammond, Jay Smink, and Sam Drew, *Dropout Risk Factors and Exemplary Programs: A Technical Report* (Rexford, NY: National Dropout Prevention Center/Network [NDPC/N], May 2007), https://dropoutprevention.org/resources /major-research-reports/dropout-risk-factors-and-exemplary -programs-a-technical-report/.

Chapter 9

1. West Virginia Department of Education, *West Virginia's Voice, Final Report, May 2019* (Charleston, WV: West Virginia Department of Education, May 2019), https://wvde.us /wp-content/uploads/2019/05/Final-Report.pdf.

2. "Expanding Integrated Student Supports through a Licensed Partnership: Success in West Virginia," Communities In Schools, 2021.

3. "Number and Enrollment of Public Elementary and Secondary Schools, by School Level, Type, and Charter, Magnet, and Virtual Status: Selected Years 1990-91 through 2018-19," Table 216.20, Digest of Education Statistics, National Center for Education Statistics, updated September 2020, https://nces .ed.gov/programs/digest/d20/tables/dt20_216.20.asp.

4. Charter Schools USA (website), www.charterschoolsusa.com.

Appendix 3: Research on Asset-Based Approaches

1. Peter C. Scales et al., *Keeping America's Promises to Children and Youth* (Bethesda, MD: Child Trends, April 1, 2006), https://www.childtrends.org/publications /keeping-americas-promises-to-children-and-youth.

2. Kristin A. Moore and Jonathan F. Zaff, *Building a Better Teenager: A Summary of "What Works" in Adolescent Development* (Bethesda, MD: Child Trends, November 1, 2002).

3. America's Promise Alliance, *Every Child, Every Promise: Turning Failure into Action* (Washington, D.C.: America's Promise Alliance, January 2014), https://www.americaspromise .org/sites/default/files/d8/Every%20Child%20Every%20 Promise%20-%20Full%20Report.pdf.

ACKNOWLEDGMENTS

This book draws on the collective wisdom of so many individuals who have helped shape my life and set the course for the Communities In Schools movement. For this new edition of the book, four friends and colleagues deserve my special gratitude:

Rey Saldaña is guiding CIS into a new era, and I am incredibly thankful he is part of our story. His enthusiastic participation in the updating of *The Last Dropout*—writing a new foreword, joining me for the in-depth conversation that forms the afterword of this edition, and going over draft after draft for the highest possible quality—has made an enormous difference.

John Morris was for years the anonymous voice of Communities In Schools, and his exceptional gift for words is complemented by his strong faith and unwavering commitment to getting the story right. His light shines through every page in this book. Once again, John took the lead in writing and editing the new text.

Sarah Vogt managed the revision project from start to finish, and her wisdom born of years of committed work on the CIS front lines was critical to our approach this time out. She has been my constant and invaluable support.

Aimen Khan, senior specialist, research and evaluation, at CIS National gave us her time, expertise, integrity, and diligence as we strove to make the new edition as accurate and comprehensive as possible.

I extend my heartfelt appreciation to **Anya Harrington**, CIS National VP of Marketing & Communications, and her team, especially **Arina Stopa**, Senior Specialist Graphic Design, who helped design the cover for this new edition, perfectly capturing the spirit of hope that is the signature of all we do at CIS.

I also want to offer my sincere thanks to two other members of the CIS family: **Laura VanDeusen**, senior director, licensing, and **Jennifer Herrera**, senior policy specialist, both of whom shared their experiences and insights to make this book better.

My gratitude to those who played such a big role in the original 2007 edition is undiminished:

Sally DeLuca kept me focused and supported from the first word. Without her deep insights about, and passion for, our work with young people, and without her extraordinary editorial and management skills, this project would never have crossed the finish line.

Neil Shorthouse, my colleague and friend for 50 years, has shared my journey with me in more ways than I can possibly say. The writing of this book was no exception. Thank you, Neil—I couldn't have asked God for a better partner, or a smarter reader.

Dan Cardinali, whose wisdom, leadership, and commitment to children are reflected on so many pages of this book. His generation will write an exciting new chapter in the Communities In Schools story.

Dale Erquiaga kept CIS going and growing during his tenure as national president and chief executive officer and helped build great credibility for CIS in the education world, especially among chief state school officers.

ABOUT THE AUTHOR

Bill Milliken, founder and vice chairman of Communities In Schools, Inc., is one of the nation's foremost pioneers in the movement to give young people the help they need to graduate from high school and go on to rewarding lives.

Mr. Milliken's activism began in 1960 when he joined Young Life, an ecumenical youth organization. He helped initiate "Street Academies" for young people who had dropped out of school and wanted a chance to resume their education, as well as live-in programs for substance abusers and youth in need of shelter and support. His experiences led him to search for a comprehensive approach to helping young people. This search culminated in the 1970s with the development of a model program that repositioned existing community resources into schools—the Communities In Schools network, which Mr. Milliken led as president until May 2004.

Communities In Schools is the nation's leading community-based organization helping students achieve in school and prepare for life. Currently, the organization directly serves more than 1.6 million students and their families each year in more than 2,800 schools in 26 states and the District of Columbia. Mr. Milliken has served three U.S. presidents and has received numerous honors for his commitment to young people.

Most recently, he was the recipient of the Martin Luther King Jr. Legacy Award for National Service. Prior to that, he received the Visionary Ambassador's Award from Usher's New Look Foundation and the National Jefferson Award for Public Service, which is widely regarded as the "Nobel Prize" for outstanding community and public service.

Mr. Milliken is also the author of *So Long Sweet Jesus, Tough Love,* and *From the Rearview Mirror: Reflecting on Connecting the Dots.* He received an honorary degree of Doctor of Humane Letters in 2007 from Bard College.

Hay House Titles of Related Interest

YOU CAN HEAL YOUR LIFE, the movie,
starring Louise Hay & Friends
(available as an online streaming video)
www.hayhouse.com/louise-movie

THE SHIFT, the movie,
starring Dr. Wayne W. Dyer
(available as an online streaming video)
www.hayhouse.com/the-shift-movie

***

CONSCIOUS PARENTING: A Guide to Raising Resilient,
Wholehearted & Empowered Kids,
by Pedram Shojai, O.M.D., and Nick Polizzi

All of the above are available at your local bookstore,
or may be ordered by contacting Hay House (see next page).

***